Elizabeth Winder

Parachute Women

**MARIANNE FAITHFULL, MARSHA HUNT,
BIANCA JAGGER, ANITA PALLENBERG,
AND THE WOMEN BEHIND THE**

Rolling Stones

hachette
BOOKS

New York

Hachette Books
Hachette Book Group
1290 Avenue of the Americas
New York, NY 10104
HachetteBooks.com
Twitter.com/HachetteBooks
Instagram.com/HachetteBooks

First Edition: July 2023

Published by Hachette Books, an imprint of Perseus Books, LLC, a subsidiary
of Hachette Book Group, Inc. The Hachette Books name and logo is a
trademark of the Hachette Book Group.

The Hachette Speakers Bureau provides a wide range of authors for speaking
events. To find out more, go to www.hachettespeakersbureau.com or call
(866) 376-6591.

The publisher is not responsible for websites (or their content) that are not
owned by the publisher.

Print book interior design by Amy Quinn

Library of Congress Control Number: 2022952037

ISBNs: 9781580059589 (hardcover); 9781580059596 (ebook)

Printed in the United States of America

LSC-C

Printing 1, 2023

for Susanna

Contents

Contents

Introduction

There are three roles for women in the hypermasculine world of traditional rock culture. First are the long-suffering wives and girlfriends, inevitably pretty but undeniably weary from juggling children, scrounging up bail money, and serving crowds of twenty drunks beef bourguignon. After years of enduring endless absences and affairs, they are saluted for their stoicism, sometimes even praised as being "smarter than she looks." Then there are the groupies, content to bask in the glow of the male rocker's vigor. Some carve out fashionable lives from this—like professional groupie Pamela

Des Barres. This role, while not as sanctified as the live-in wives and girlfriends, poses no threat to the status quo.

And then there are the bad girls, the Yoko Onos and Courtney Loves, who are often more gutsy and visionary than their male partners. Thanks to the systemic misogyny of rock culture, their own contributions are diminished and belittled. At best they are viewed as unruly muses, but more often they are condemned as hangers-on, gold diggers, and power-crazed witches. Their drug use is demonized, their parenting skills criticized, all while their partner's behavior slips by without reproach. They are blamed for breaking up bands, inconvenient arrests, sometimes indirectly for murder. Because, in the so-called lawless world of rock and roll, women who break rules are punished.

Sixty years ago there were rockers but no Rock Stars—the concept simply hadn't been invented yet. The Stones, for now at least, were not much more than unbrushed Beatles dressed in playclothes. Mick Jagger still slouched like a teen onstage, Keith Richards and Brian Jones still wore pants bought by their mothers. And yet in the span of a few short years, they'd be the unassailable pirates that we know today—the world's first rock stars. And they got all their strut and glamour from four women—Marsha Hunt, Bianca Jagger, Marianne Faithfull, and Anita Pallenberg.

These women put the glimmer in the Glimmer Twins and taught a band of middle-class boys to be bad. They opened the doors to subterranean art and alternative lifestyles, turned them on to Russian literature, occult practices, LSD, and high society. The Rolling Stones may have risen to fame as rock's favorite outlaws but only under the tutelage of these remarkable women, whose attitudes, creativity, vision, and style were devoured, processed, spat out, and commodified by the relentlessly male music industry.

The Stones benefitted immensely from their cachet and were never so strong as when they were in their orbit. But Marianne, Anita, Marsha, and Bianca struggled to define themselves in the aggressively masculine world of rock—a world that they, inadvertently, had a crucial hand in creating.

They paid a steep price to be the consorts of rock gods. Caught in the vortex of the biggest rock band in the world, they struggled every day to maintain their identities. Music contracts dried up. Money ran out. Reputations were sullied. Marianne, who was at first used as a pawn-like foil thanks to her virginal image, was then slut shamed, then dragged through the press until she nearly took her own life. Bianca had fled her totalitarian state only to be trapped by a totalitarian husband. Anita's own behavior equaled Keith's— he was celebrated; she was mocked, demeaned, then shunned as an outcast. One way or another, the very culture that they helped create turned against them.

In liberal and progressive circles today, rock is the last bastion of acceptable sexism. The very concept of the rock star in all his ragged glory is male, and his subject—whether sluts, scolds, or somewhere in between—is women. Even in its gentler versions— Cat Stevens's mournful mansplaining in "Wild World," Tom Petty's Jesus-loving "good girls" pining after "bad boys" in "Free Fallin'"—the image of the rebel male is so locked in our collective psyche that we scarcely notice, much less question it. And the seed was planted by the Rolling Stones. Even the name of the band— ripped from a Muddy Waters song—suggests the idea of flight from domesticity—which inevitably means flight from women. Because women don't roll like stones, they sink like them.

It's time to start questioning this received wisdom and sexist dichotomy. Marsha, Bianca, Marianne, and Anita never wanted to domesticate the Stones—it was the other way around. Bianca never wanted to marry Mick, Marianne was polyamorous from the start. Marsha—steeped in the ethos of the liberated sixties—hoped to practice a new kind of coparenting, and her idea of happy marriage meant living in separate countries. And Anita was on a different planet. She slept with more fans than Mick did. She had Keith leaping up to carry her purse. She brought Brian to sex clubs dressed up as Françoise Hardy. She turned the cliché of long-suffering rock girlfriend on its head.

This story—set in the tumultuous years of the late sixties and early seventies—is about women who refused to define themselves as girlfriends. It's a story of lust and rivalries, friendships and betrayals, hope and degradation, and the birth of rock and roll. It's the story of women diminished by years, sometimes decades, of trauma and heartache, who are finally able to take their power back. It's about tabloids that condemn women as sluts and baby mamas, and hail men as virile marauders. It's about, as Marianne Faithfull once said, "the frustration and fury you feel, as a talented woman, of not being recognized, understood, people not getting you." It's about women of such potency that their sheer proximity turned a band of mama's boys into Luciferian demigods.

Our story begins, as so many do, in 1965 when a girl met a boy . . .

One

The Phoenix

What does Mick Jagger mean to you? He makes me think of Anita Pallenberg.

Kim Gordon

September 14, 1965, Munich, Circus Krone Bau. You could tell she was different from the other Stones groupies, in her beige fur jacket, skintight sweater, and Ossie Clark mini. She looked nothing like Carnaby Street's trendy dolly birds with their knee socks and baby-doll dresses, their saucer stares of white liner, gobs of mascara, and strips of Glorene. Everything about her suggested experience, from her hard-to-place accent to the gladiator sandals she'd had handmade in Rome. She was overtly sensual—sexual even—but exuded an almost masculine energy. Even Mick was intimidated by this German/

Italian actress, who pounced backstage with the stealth of a cat. Was she just another fangirl or Jack the Ripper in disguise?

She hovered in the door of the dressing room, her gaze sharp, her smile cocky, revealing flashes of fang-like teeth. She dug around her pockets for a vial of amyl nitrate. "Vant to smoke a joint?" Mick and Keith eyed her suspiciously. They'd never done drugs before—the only coke they had was mixed with rum. She glanced at Brian. "Yeah, let's smoke a joint," he said, eyes filled with tears. "Come back to the hotel." They returned to his room to smoke and talk for hours, and he spent the night weeping in her arms.

Anita followed the Stones to Berlin the next day. Tours were strictly girlfriend-free zones, and here Brian was flaunting his be-witching new lover. He was breaking all his rules, and he'd only known her a day.

Compared to Anita, the Stones were grubby adolescents, awk-ward and hopelessly naive. London wasn't quite swinging yet, and British rock was barely emerging from its gawky teen phase. Anita was "cosmopolitan beyond anyone's imagination" and catnip to young rockers who craved the aura of experience. It was clear she'd lived many lives—skipping school with the street kids and artists in Rome, grave digging, beach drinking, boyfriends with Vespas, Café Rosati with Federico Fellini—"all that Dolce Vita stuff." She'd lived in Warhol's Manhattan as a Factory girl; she'd danced on tables at Regine's in diaphanous gowns. Whatever you'd experienced, she'd already done it a thousand times.

Mick stared at her with lustful awe, Keith admired her from a distance. "The first time I saw Anita my obvious reaction was, 'What the fuck is a chick like that doing with Brian?'"

It wasn't that they were intimidated by her model status. Mick and Keith were both dating models—English ingenue types with no runs in their stockings and long-lashed doe-eyed stares. But Anita was a different breed entirely. She'd been one of Catherine Harlé's models in Paris—a champagne-popping modeling agent known for rebellious It Girls with rock and roll connections. Half eighteenth-century salon, half Warholian Factory, Harlé's agency in Place des Vosges didn't churn out your typical mid-century models. Harlé's girls included Snowqueen of Texas Deborah Dixon, hippie icon Talitha Getty, Dalí muse Amanda Lear, and Teutonic rock goddess Nico. They stormed down Rue de Turenne like granny-booted gladiators, with men like Bob Dylan, Jim Morrison, and Brian Jones trailing helplessly in their wake.

These girls were miles apart from the dolly birds and English roses across the channel. The Twiggys, Patties, Chrissies, and Jeanies, so popular in London, remained in the shadow of their male counterparts. They earned their own money, lived in their own flats, and enjoyed more freedoms than their mothers had done. But they didn't cleave from the roles society molded for them, nor did they challenge their male peers.

Harlé's models didn't just challenge society—they laughed in its face. No milk baths or 10 p.m. bedtimes for them. "They behaved like men," wrote Parisian journalist Fabrice Gaignault. "They were so important for the culture of the time. They were a little frightening for the Parisian male, because Parisian men were bourgeoisie, and they were nothing like that. They were free, stronger than men." Pop singer Jacques Dutronc even wrote a song about them, "those who know how to speak to the models of Catherine Harlé."

These were women who made a living out of terrorizing men, and Anita was at their helm. She partied harder, drank more, danced more, smoked more than any of the men around her. "We were out every night," recalled Deborah Dixon. "Of course, we were smoking dope—they were wild days—but we were having a lot of fun. In those days, especially in London, the girls were all wishy-washy—we were completely the opposite. Anita was different. She set up sort of an aggressive look. A look that said she was not just going to be a doll."

Nor would she submit to the macho celebrity photographers. She stopped their bravado dead in its tracks, ripping off her lash strips, smudging black liner with her thumb, bitching about the hot stage lights and the thick cold cream assistants used to clean her face. She sometimes blew off gigs entirely, instead made her name on the dance floors of Maxim's, Regine's, and Chez Castel (always slipping in the side door for free). She wore undereye circles like a badge of honor and sneered at models who "went to bed at nine, wearing eye masks."

Brian prided himself on being the only Stone brave enough to take Anita on. (He was, at this point, "the only Stone who inhaled.") "They were still schoolboys," Anita said of Mick and Keith. "Brian was acting on it faster than anyone else—he knew his stuff very well." But Brian—the band's self-proclaimed leader—was also the Stones' most vulnerable member. Mick and Keith had bullied him for years, and Anita walked into this fractured dynamic.

Of all the sexist cultural myths floating around, women as gossips might be the worst. Mick was the emperor of gossip and bitchery—setting the tone for childish power struggles from the band's very inception. Three years in and they were still at it—classic playground lunch-table snubbery—with Brian as the target. "Mick and I were incredibly cruel to Brian," Keith wrote years later. "I used to do this vicious impression of Brian. It was all funny, but incredibly cruel, and people just used to roll up laughing. It was a period that was really bitter, very nasty—not for Mick and I particularly, but for Brian."

Emotions embarrassed the repressed English Mick and Keith. Anita was attracted to Brian's emotional intelligence. His delicate looks appealed to her too, the way he straddled masculine and feminine. Sharp cheekbones, Pan-like movements that were more fey than androgynous. "Sexually I like girls as well as men," Anita explained, "and Brian seemed to combine both sexes for me at the same time." Despite his insecurities, Brian was remarkably comfortable with his sexual identity. Mick and Keith were still trapped in mid-century gender norms and fifties homophobia.

At a time when women were expected to be earth angels, Anita was sexually brash—propositioning John Phillips of the Mamas and the Papas (it was really an excuse to hitch a ride to Tangier), sending Jeff Beck notes in the middle of the night. She was nonchalantly bisexual. (Anita: "Everyone does it in Italian summers.")

Men of course were allowed their peccadillos—especially rock stars with all their proverbial fans and groupies. But for the Stones in '65 this was mostly male bluster. Mick and Keith had barely slept with anyone. Only Brian was sexually experienced. "Brian was so far ahead of them you wouldn't believe it," Anita recalled to David Dalton. "He had chicks. All the chicks. And he used to fuck everybody else's chick. I mean, he knew it, he really had it down and they didn't. Here are Mick and Keith up onstage trying to learn how to be sex objects, and Brian already had a string of illegitimate children! Except for Brian all the Stones at that time were really suburban squares."

Brian was the real deal. Mick kept a bottle of Scotch rattling in the back of his car, but it was really just for show. By the time he met Anita, Brian was consuming two bottles a day. In fact, he usually stunk of brandy—he'd read somewhere that jazz musicians used it as a food substitute.

Alcohol exacerbated Brian's fragile disposition—leading to tantrums, meltdowns, car crashes, and crying jags. But that didn't bother Anita. She liked Brian's mercurial nature—moody was better than boring in her book. He'd quickly shake off the doom and snap back to his jaunty self. In those days his curiosity was stronger than his self-destructive impulse.

They both shared a natural curiosity and innate receptiveness—qualities that formed the backbone of their relationship. "He had a wonderful curiosity," remembered Anita. "Curious about new things, new places. He wanted to know everything that was going on, wanted to meet new people, new ideas, learn the new dances; the other Stones were more like frightened. Brian was much more ready to go to strange places to meet people he didn't know. Not like Keith, who in those days sort of sneered at anybody who tried to get too close to him."

For now, Keith and Mick regarded her with suspicion. ("You could see them exchanging looks like *Who's this weird bird?*") Years later they would realize that Anita was the magic ingredient, the secret to their success.

She grew him, the way women do grow one.

Prince Stanislas Klossowski

Thanks to Anita, Brian soon found himself half of the sixties' hottest, most dangerous couple. He'd always been known as the "edgiest Stone," but Anita pushed boundaries even further—S&M,

sex clubs, dildos, hot wax, sadomasochistic games. One house-guest caught Anita creeping into the bedroom with a giant whip. Through the wall he could hear her whipping Brian.

They were mad, bad, and dangerous to know, tearing around London in Brian's black Rolls-Royce—license plate DD[Devils Disciple]666, making the rounds at clubs like the Ad Lib, the Speakeasy, and the Scotch of St. James. Their antics were bound-less, especially at parties, where they were known for spiking drinks with LSD. She revived Brian's boldness and vitality, and a large part of that was her unabashed sexuality. At a time when most women were still in hairspray and girdles, she'd be pantsless in riding boots, rumpled hair, and a black rugby shirt, sipping liq-uid mescaline at a party. Even rocker Pete Townshend was blown away by Anita when he ran into her in Paris on the arm of Brian Jones: "They were so sexually stimulated, they could hardly leave the room before starting to shag." He was in awe of the pair, who seemed to be "living on a higher plane of decadence" than anyone he'd ever met.

Much to the chagrin of Brian's bandmates, Anita dipped in and out of the American tour in the fall of 1965. Her presence em-boldened Brian's obnoxious behavior, as displayed in their speed-boat stunt at Miami's beachfront Fontainebleau hotel. Anita raced around like a maniac, cackling as she terrorized the others by slamming her boat into theirs. Brian went a step further, driv-ing his boat out to sea until he ran out of gas. One thing was for certain—there'd be no smooth sailing with Anita on board.

By the end of the American tour, the worldwide press had started to follow their romance. *Bravo* magazine featured a two-page spread, with Brian declaring, "Anita is the only girl for me."

Rave magazine followed with its own exposé, "A Story About a Stone—a Love Story." In Paris they were the talk of the town—and all anyone talked about at Françoise Hardy's engagement party. Rumors swept through Europe that the two would soon be married, and by Christmas *Disc Weekly* posed the provocative headline "Brian Jones Wedding?" *New Musical Express* suspected that "the wedding is definitely on, and Bob Dylan will be the best man."

Reporters met them at Heathrow post–American tour, demanding answers about their supposed engagement. Brian could not resist tantalizing the press: "Anita is the first girl I've met that I've been serious about . . . [W]e're very fond of each other. Obviously, it's more than a casual acquaintance." Anita's response was typically cryptic: "It will be very soon . . . otherwise it won't be at all."

Brian was downplaying the relationship. He'd spent most of 1965 debating going solo. While Mick and Keith rose to power as the songwriting duo, Brian slowly lost control of his own band. It was more than just pride—the music they were making ceased to mean much to him. He detached himself, numbing out with booze between blasé recording sessions. He'd started to collapse on tours, sometimes requiring hospitalization. He didn't give a damn—about himself or the Stones.

All that changed when he met Anita. With her by his side, he felt competent, confident, and strong enough to take on Mick and Keith. Quitting the band was now the furthest thing from his mind.

At the time she first started to hang out with those guys. She opened up a whole world to them. She was the most attractive girl any of them had ever been around, and she had a genuine feeling for books and poetry, and the guts to get involved with things.

Donald Cammell

By early 1966, Anita and Brian were officially living together in his flat on Elm Park Lane. Brian was the first Stone to discover Chelsea, which was rapidly becoming London's fashion mecca. Mod shifts and minis had lined the streets of the neighborhood since Mary Quant opened her shop years before. But a new look was emerging in the shops of Kings Road. Something elegant and deconstructed and totally unique.

"I wasn't into Mary Quant," Anita explained years later. "She was too middle-of-the-road, and that mod, op-art thing wasn't really for me. And Biba was too big. I wasn't so into that very English look. In Italy we always had salsa, the mamba, all those Latin dances, which gave me a different feel for things, so my style was fedoras, belts, little twenties jackets, lace that I'd collected. If I wore miniskirts, I'd have them made by Granny's."

Granny Takes a Trip was a tiny boutique at the end of Kings Road. Purple walls hung with art nouveau posters and drawings by Aubrey Beardsley, green-tasseled lampshades, gilt lustre glass, Victorian sunshades made of fringed black silk—even an old-fashioned phonograph. Granny's resembled what a "not too expensive Victorian brothel may have looked," and it quickly became Anita's second home. "Everyone knew everyone. We'd try on clothes and smoke a joint in the back."

Anita's influences rubbed off on Brian, who was by far the most sartorially inclined Stone. Men's fashions were changing—vivid velvets, pointy boots, and gender-fluid styles. The "Peacock revolution" had begun. Under Anita's influence, Brian styled himself in Edwardian ruffles, William Morris prints, and Oscar Wilde frills. His flourishes were noticed all over London—the strands of pearls and cobalt beads, pink suede button-ups trimmed in hand-made lace, Anita's silk scarves tied round his knees and wrists, and plumed cavalier hats à la the Three Musketeers. With his hair dyed the color of Anita's, they blurred the line between masculine and feminine. Two lithe blond devils.

At identical heights and weights with matching flaxen page-boys, it was easy for the couple to swap clothes. They spent hours in front of the mirror trading jewelry, scarves, and velveteen trousers. After one acid trip Anita dressed him as Parisian pop chanteuse Françoise Hardy—a longtime obsession of Brian's. Anita merrily brushed out his blond fringe, lined his lashes with kohl, zipped him up in a line skirt and Vivier boots. A black-and-white-striped pullover and vinyl trench completed the outfit. They spent the evening in a strange kind of role reversal, with Anita pretending that she was Brian seducing Françoise as impersonated by Brian.

"When Brian turned up in Anita's outfits," wrote Marianne Faithfull, "fashion changed. It was the beginning of glam rock, David Bowie and Alice Cooper." In today's parlance, she was an influencer, a stylist, a cultural maven. Not only was she transforming Brian, she was about to transform the Rolling Stones.

Cross-dressing and gender-bending were virtually unthinkable in midsixties mainstream society. Libertine rumors of bisexuality trailed Anita and Brian like a glamorous mist. The London scene was rapidly changing—Mick and Keith were in danger of being left behind. Until now it had been dominated by late-fifties rockers—all grotty leather jackets and beer-soaked pub brawls.

But a new aesthetic was emerging. Suddenly it was hip to read poetry, talk about cosmology, occult lit, and conceptual art.

With her Continental background and keen social instincts, mixing crowds came naturally to Anita. She'd befriended Lord Harlech's children years ago in Italy, and through them groups of other aristocratic hipsters. Thanks to Anita, the Stones were soon socializing with Robert Fraser, Sir Mark Palmer, Christopher Gibbs, and Tara Browne. It was the first time in history that aristocrats of that caliber so blatantly sought out the company of rock musicians in such large numbers, and the Stones benefitted immensely from Anita's cachet.

"How Anita came to be with Brian," wrote Marianne Faithfull, "is really the story of how the Stones became the Stones. She almost single-handedly engineered a cultural revolution in London by bringing together the Stones and the *jeunesse dorée*. . . . The Stones and these hip aristos were a perfect match for each other. A union of the two later seemed inevitable. But no one had the foggiest idea how to go about it. Except for our Anita."

She pushed Brian into fraternizing with flamboyant Eton art dealers—something the Beatles had already dabbled in but initially disinterested Mick and Keith. One of those art dealers was Robert Fraser, London's enfant terrible, who by the end of the year was enmeshed in the Stones' inner circle. Anita and Robert were two Pied Pipers of the wild Chelsea art scene. Parties at "Groovy Bob's" always began with glittering bowls of drugs and everyone helping themselves. With plenty of hash and lively art banter, these evenings were more like salons than see-and-be-seen parties. Mick and Keith would eventually join in. Anita loved these parties from the beginning.

The crowd at Robert's found Anita equally fascinating. Art dealer Chrissie Gibbs found her "highly intelligent and extremely well read." After art school Anita had lived with Italian painter Mario Schifano, dabbled in the anarchist Living Theatre, and was equally comfortable with German Romanticism and Andy Warhol. Her intellectual pedigree saved her from labels like "girlfriend" or "arm candy," and she led as many conversations as she listened to.

Rockers, artists, and experimental trendsetters now socialized with rich young aristocrats—shattering the barriers of England's highly stratified class system. In April 1966, Guinness heir Tara Browne celebrated his twenty-first birthday at the family estate in Ireland's Wicklow Mountains. Caravelle jets were hired to transport Tara's two hundred guests to Dublin—Paul McCartney, Mick and his girlfriend Chrissie Shrimpton, Christopher Gibbs, Paul Getty and his girlfriend Talitha Pol. Limousines were waiting to whisk them over to Luggala. Anita and Brian—who had already dosed themselves with liquid LSD on the flight over—shared a ride with photographer Michael Cooper, Paul and Talitha, Bill Willis, and Tara's wife, Nicky.

Giggling, excited, and high, they crossed the craggy mountains. The air was chilly, they were close to the estate. They pulled over for Brian to pee. Everyone jumped out of the car. That was when they saw the dead goat. Michael Cooper captured the happy troupe in snapshots, playing leapfrog, clowning around the cliffs, cavorting in the brisk April air.

Once ensconced in Luggala, Anita and Nicky somehow decided that Mick was the devil and managed to lock him into a courtyard behind the house. They raced through the woods, leaping over briar, crouching behind trees, speaking paranoid code on walkie-talkies (someone had given as a birthday gift for Tara), watching Mick struggle to free himself from the pen. Just one more of Anita's wild scenes.

All to the magical backdrop of the Lovin' Spoonful playing their "good-time music." It *was* a good time, a great time, a moment in history—and it wouldn't last.

The blink-and-you'll-miss-it pace of the sixties was much slower to change when it came to women. Anita had the self-possession of a cat, that same steely defiance and obstinate will, but most women—especially the girlfriends of rock stars—didn't share her audacity. "You could see that she could do exactly what she wanted," recalled model Pattie Boyd. "She was actually a bit scary. . . . I've never met a young girl with such incredible confidence."

Rock girlfriends were deluged with stalking, death threats, and hatred—a rabid jealousy addressed in *Pop* magazine's "don't hate Jane Asher" letter. It was common for fans to wait outside their idol's homes—an occurrence that frightened Mick's girlfriend Chrissie Shrimpton. But Anita saw them for what they were— harmless teenyboppers eager to please and easy to manipulate. When lovestruck Stones fans camped outside her house, Anita invited them in, served them tea, and let them make Brian's bed.

Anita was well aware of how she differed from the other Stones girlfriends, with her pan-European cosmopolitan, high-art Fellini background: "The others all seemed to have a chick on the side, with a toupee, false eyelashes, and all that. You know what I mean, and foam for the fanny and stuff for not getting pregnant and all that shit. Mick's girlfriend Chrissy Shrimpton was a secretary type—nine to five, Miss Proper, hairdressers on Thursdays. The girl Keith had: very normal, very plain, no challenge. Charlie Watts had a kind of drab wife he kept in the background—you know background women with personalities like elevator music."

Chrissie—model and younger sister of Jean—was part of the "old" (but still quite current) look and scene—miniskirts, double-decker lash glue, hair falls and white boots, makeup columns in *Fabulous* and *Tiger Beat*. And though she modeled Ossie Clark and appeared in fashion pages, she'd never be part of a celebrity couple like Anita and Brian. Those two were the very first rock star couple—a concept that hadn't even existed yet. Yes, fans knew about Jane Asher and Pattie Boyd, but these women simply lacked the drama and otherworldliness of Anita.

Only Anita had those qualities, and for the moment, she was shining her light on Brian. That made Mick seethe. He was always paranoid about falling behind and not being hip. About being the last one to the scene, which he often was—jumping on the psychedelia bandwagon a year too late, trying acid long after the others. The way Brian was worshipped by hot California bands stoked Mick's insecurity further. He had a fraught relationship with his middle-class background, and Chrissie's parents were farmers from Buckinghamshire. In other words, Chrissie was as milk-fed as Mick himself, and he hated her for it.

If Mick was self-conscious about being middle class, he was still inextricably drawn to its trappings. When he bought his first home—a fifth-floor flat on an Edwardian mansion block of the grand, bourgeois Marylebone Road—it only underlined his alienation from the current Brian/Anita/Keith alliance in wild bohemian Chelsea. When Keith's girlfriend left him for Jimi Hendrix in the fall of 1966, Anita and Brian took him under their wing. Now everyone was having fun without Mick, and Anita was the ringleader. He'd bullied Brian to tears, but like most bullies, Mick hated being on the outs himself.

He envied Anita's obvious power—the way high society (Mick's ultimate goal) and bohemians alike seemed to court her. Then there was her influence over Brian and now Keith. He lashed out at her with dismissive insults and mockery. "Mick really tried to put me down, but there was no way some crude, lippy guy was going to do a number on me. I found that if you stand up to Mick, he crumbles. I was always able to squelch him."

Mick couldn't control Anita, but he could control Chrissie. His Harley House was intended to be their newlywed home. But after moving in, Mick coolly announced that he no longer wanted to marry her—he just wanted to live with her. Chrissie was devastated but accepted her fate. She was now completely dependent on his success and his bank account.

Banished from her family, Chrissie languished alone in Harley House for weeks while Mick toured with the Stones in the summer of '66. He'd telephone her at every chance, send telegrams and copious letters. Yet more often than not his calls and telegrams were ways of taking charge of her, even thousands of miles away. He was "very controlling, very paternalistic, very caretaking. I used to go to the Scotch of St. James club every night when he was on tour. He arranged for a car to be sent for me at three in the morning and I'd be taken home. And then he'd ring me as soon as I got in to make sure I was there." Chrissie routinely mistook controlling for caring.

Anita—a dazzling presence on the tours of '66—loved the slapdash spontaneity of pre-corporate gigs. "It was like that then, not organized. None of those passes or any of that shit." Even the trashed hotel suites left her unfazed.

She expertly navigated airports, speaking fluent French, Italian, and German, hoop earrings swishing, hobo bags dangling from her arms. Anita and Brian were photographed constantly, which triggered Mick's competitive insecurity. In what would become a familiar pattern, Mick lashed out at the women in his life—and this time Chrissie took the brunt of it. He returned from the American tour distant and aloof, dropping her hand when fangirls drove by, even cutting her off from her Harrods account. At parties he blatantly flirted with other women and, worse, publicly insulted her. Chrissie knew it was the beginning of the end.

"I knew the reason why he was getting fed up with me; it was because I wasn't cool. He was taking acid by that time, and I was always scared to try it. It was also when Anita Pallenberg had just come on the scene and those orgies started happening over at Brian's. . . . Now Mick wanted to sleep with everyone. . . . I remember him calling me 'uncool' and it being the most terrible insult."

The irony was, Mick was the "uncool" one. He himself had been wary of acid—dropping it for the first time at Tara Browne's party because everyone was there and everyone was doing it. And he ended up making a big scene, escaping at night over the grounds of Luggala, thinking that he was a small brown crow. While there may not have been "orgies happening over at Brian's," there was certainly an air of sexual permissiveness— largely thanks to Anita, which is exactly why Mick kept Chrissie far away from her. Despite his meager on-tour dalliances, Mick was possessive of Chrissie and banned all possible friendships with men. "When I was first with Mick, I wasn't allowed to look at anyone else or even be friends with girls he considered 'tarts.'" But Mick's need to be hip overruled his sexual jealousy, and in these rapidly changing times, a "tart" like Anita was exactly who he needed.

Chrissie would soon be "out of time." Mick, who throughout his life chose women more cultivated than he, was on the prowl again.

Lucky for him, another woman would enter the strange ménage at Anita and Brian's, one who shared Anita's vanguard iconoclasm, lettered and erudite with a dash of sweet naivete. A woman who would tutor him, spark new passions, and vitalize his image as Anita had for Brian. What he didn't reckon for is that she would be an artist in her own right.

Two

The Songbird

In those days I really didn't know I had a story of my own. I was just part of their story...

Marianne Faithfull

arianne met the Stones at a Decca party for Adrienne Posta in March 1964—a time when she was, admittedly, "very pretentious about pop music." Instead of poring over copies of *Jackie* and swooning over Cliff Richard like a normal seventeen-year-old, she worshipped Paul Valéry, Marcel Proust, and obscure cabaret artists of the Weimar Republic. That was Marianne—not just precocious but from another dimension, in her own rarified world.

Whatever her louche, esoteric world was, it certainly wasn't this—an industry launch swarming with slick, sleazy managers and would-be pop chanteuses in baby-doll frocks, gobs of mascara, and trendy falls, desperate for a single or a contract with Decca. Braless under her boyfriend's blue button-up, her blonde hair loosely tangled, she clung to the arm of her new man, John Dunbar, a gallery and bookshop owner who sold rare books and art to Paul McCartney. All four Beatles were there, and so were the rambunctious Stones, pranking around like "spotty school-boys." They were nothing to her Cambridge-educated, bespecta-cled John, whose tailored pants and artfully disheveled waves put Keith's ill-fitting leather jackets to shame. Mick was in the midst of a flaming row with Chrissie, who was sobbing her way toward a modish meltdown, tear-drenched lash strips dangling halfway off her lids. Nearly everyone at the party was drunk—at least half were there for the free booze alone. They barreled around shov-ing each other, slurring too loudly and hovering too close, their faces sweat-slick and pinked from cheap beer. Desperate for a lit-tle space of her own, Marianne wove her way through the crowd and perched atop a space heater. "My God," she thought. "What awful people."

One man, however, did intrigue her. Andrew Oldham, the Stones' flamboyant manager—with his silky ties, campy drawl, and neon-green eyeliner. The feeling was mutual. He marched right over with his characteristic pomp and announced, "I'm in-terested in you—you have a contemporary face. You are today."

Marianne didn't know what to make of him, "beaky and bird-like," lurching toward her one second, then whirling around to address her boyfriend, as if she couldn't hear or speak.

"Who is she? Can she act? What's 'er name?"

"I can make you a star," he blabbered, his pancake makeup be-ginning to melt, "and that's just for starters, baby." The fawn-ing was flattering, but this seemed more like the ravings of a self-satisfied drunk. Marianne dismissed his blather, and John drove her back to her mother's house in Reading. One week later the telegram arrived—and an attached Decca contract. Thanks to Marianne's youth, a work permit had to be signed by her mother—Baroness Eva Erisso. Eva eventually signed the permit, on the condition that Marianne would be chaperoned on tour.

Andrew's version was crude: "I saw an angel with big tits and I signed her." But his boasting vulgarity belied real possibilities. Like all modern iconoclasts, Marianne broke the molds of her current zeitgeist. She was of her time yet far beyond it. Though still a teenager, she was as far removed from the gum-snapping youth-quakers as Lady Guinevere herself. There was something misty and regal about her, like she'd been wandering the forests of Brocéliande. Andrew knew how well she'd translate onstage—standing stock-still the way the nuns taught her. So he locked Mick and Keith in his kitchen overnight, with instructions to write Marianne a song—a song with doves and high convent walls, laden with chaste longing.

Fiction wasn't far from fact. Marianne had spent the last several years behind convent walls. Her time at the convent was much like Emma Bovary's Ursuline education or Anne Boleyn's years in France. The nuns taught her everything—singing, piano, classical dance. Her talented music teacher coaxed out a husky mezzo-soprano wise beyond her years. She joined an amateur theater group and dreamed of playing Ophelia, Cordelia, and Desdemona at the Royal Court. Marianne planned to be *known*, but a pop princess career was the last thing on her mind. She'd be an artist of some kind—she'd go to Cambridge, or the Royal Academy of Music to continue classical singing. She idolized the young Vanessa Redgrave, who once came to talk to Marianne's theater group. Perhaps Marianne would also play Rosalind, or Imogen in *Cymbeline*, or even sing *Tosca* in Covent Garden. Awake long in the night in her convent room, she bent over her workbook, filling page after page of potential stage names, pen names, fantasy names. In time she would realize her real name was her own.

Mick and Keith's assignment was cool and clear pop. Though they barely knew her, the song evoked Marianne herself—wistful, sweet, and vaguely tubercular. It was gorgeous, haunting. "That a song of such grace and sensitivity was recorded by two twenty-one-year-olds was astonishing."

"They mixed it then and there, and that was it." It was recorded in thirty minutes. Marianne recalls being strangely let down after the session, eerily aware that she was nothing but a pretty product to them, a gorgeous means to advance their own creative paths. It's not that they were rude, but there was something crass about the way they ignored her, like boorish schoolboys turned into equally boorish rockers. "Nobody paid attention to me. It was like I didn't exist, they were so excited. . . . After the session Mick and Keith gave me a lift in their car to the station. Mick tried to get me to sit on his lap. . . . What a cheeky little yob, I thought to myself. . . . I wasn't a person to them; I was a commodity that they had created. That's what Andrew liked doing, and he was very good at it. I was a hunk of matter to be used and discarded."

The recording session stood out like a bad omen. But the song, "As Tears Go By," with its melancholy sweetness and French jukebox flair, was a sleeper hit, shooting up the charts that autumn and launching Marianne's singing career. Before long she'd left the convent, abandoned her O levels for record contracts and *Ready Steady Go!* She fit easily into the songbird cliché—a popular representation of early womanhood characterized by heavy makeup and songs of subtle desperation. It was the first song Jagger and Richards wrote together.

But Marianne, as Andrew anticipated, put her own unique spin on the look. Lulu wore Mary Janes and knee socks—as did half the dolly birds who flocked the Carnaby Street shops—but on Marianne you actually believed it. It was like she'd been wearing them all day, daydreaming in a classroom, elbows propped on a book. Not a hasty costume change backstage at *Top of the Pops*. Petula Clark wore nightgown dresses too, but only Marianne could make them look authentic, standing at the microphone like some grave Flemish angel. She wore bell-shaped frocks like everyone else, but in sensual textures with unexpected trimmings, a layered confection of sheer lace. On Marianne, the flute-shaped flutter sleeves suggested something else—a christening gown, a baby's bonnet, or a sixteenth-century courtesan.

Like most British pop acts in the mid-1960s, it was Marianne's contractual duty to join national bus tours. They were a charming mix of Merseybeats, Europop, and American doo-wop, hitting various locations throughout the UK. She first toured with the Hollies and Freddie and the Dreamers, as a means to her own flat, her own grin money, her own bank account. But was this really freedom, cramming herself on a bus, eating cheap food, and enduring smarmy come-ons? In a sea of uniformity and fluff, Marianne was an intellectual misfit, lugging around copies of Tolstoy and the complete works of Shakespeare. She threw up backstage before each performance. One hotel room after the other, no sleep, no food, "flirting with drugs with a copy of Jane Austen on my knee."

She dealt with the trials of touring by treating the whole thing as a sociological study. The Kinks were moody and gothic, with resentful family dynamics. Roy Orbison was "large and strange and mournful looking, like a prodigal mole in Tony Lama cowboy boots."

Though young and naive in some ways, Marianne knew from the start this image was forced on her by corporate men. From the very beginning, starting with Decca's press release for her first hit single: "MARIANNE FAITHFULL is the little seventeen-year-old blonde . . . who still attends a convent in Reading . . . daughter of the Baroness Erisso. . . . She is lissome and lovely with long blonde hair, a shy smile and a liking for people who are long-haired and socially conscious."

Convent school, implied virginity, aristocratic lineage, and blonde blonde blonde, the themes had been stacked against her from the very beginning, thrown down like a gauntlet. She longed to escape, like the sparrows and wrens in her mournful pop ballads. "There's a part of me that always wants to fly off, to escape. That's what drew me to 'This Little Bird.' The words are from Tennessee Williams's *Orpheus Descending*. It's that famous speech about the bird who sleeps on the wind and touches the ground only when it dies."

The photo shoots, the makeup columns, the requisite inquiries about boyfriends and family, all those expectations of how a female pop star "should" behave abounded. On top of all this there was bossy Andrew, who would call before interviews with specific instructions, down to what to wear. ("Wear the white suit, but lose the boots. No hat, try a scarf. Ciao.") This piqued Marianne's contrarian nature, so she began to play little games with reporters.

"I don't give a fig whether I'm a success as a singer. In the pop business, talent doesn't count."

"Andrew's different. He's sincere. Well, he says he is, so let's pretend he is."

Or: "I believe in living on several different planes at once. It's terribly important, don't you think?"

After an interview with *Record Mirror* on a bench in Kensington Gardens, she'd run breathlessly after the bewildered journalist, waving two volumes of *Big Ben* by A. P. Herbert. "You simply *must* try this," she'd purr in lusty mezzo-soprano, her eyes widening behind bug-eyed horn rims, clutching a worn-out copy of *Bitter Lemons* to her chest.

"I gave them not only the acerbic, aphoristic Marianne but the dotty daughter of the Baronessa as well. . . . This projected an eerie fusion of haughty aristocrat and folky bohemian child-woman. It was a tantalizing ready-made fantasy. Unfortunately, it wasn't me."

Andrew prepped journalists with frilly bite-sized images. Some were accurate—"Marianne digs Marlon Brando, Woodbine cigarettes, poetry, going to the ballet, and wearing long evening dresses." But most interviews began with references to St Joseph's school, tales of singing folk ditties for pocket change in local coffee bars, and most importantly, "Mummy," the mysterious Baroness who hovered over her like a duenna. Her music was described as girly-folk, commercial in a good way. Marianne herself was "shy, wistful, waif-like," a "self-styled angel blonde." Close-ups of her snuggled in bed with blankets and teddy bears, one shoulder glowing bare, but cheeks flushed like a child just roused from her nap. Their articles were littered throughout with nods to Andrew, or "Loogy" as they called him on the beat scene. And always, inevitably, the Rolling Stones.

"Would You Let Your Sister Date a Rolling Stone?" That was rapidly becoming the Stones trademark—schoolboy anti-charisma incited by Andrew. He delighted to feed the press copy like this: "They look like boys any self-respecting mum would lock in the bathroom. But the Rolling Stones—five tough, young London-based music makers with door-stop mouths, palled cheeks and unkempt hair—are not worried what mums think." Andrew cultivated their image as marauding sexual nomads. Mick and Keith might not have known it yet, but Brian did. Underneath the pissing outside, gum-under-the-desk hooligan antics was something much darker—rebel male youth preying on bourgeois girls.

Marianne was the perfect foil for Andrew's young ruffians, her Continental refinement and angelic features throwing their vulgarity into high relief. The Stones, of course, were cast as corrupting pirates. But little did Andrew know, Marianne would be the one corrupting the Stones.

By 1965 she grew weary of Oldham and his speedy mod prattle. (She preferred a little old fat man as her manager, preferably bald with corkscrew glasses.) She wanted to distance herself from Andrew and the Rolling Stones. Andrew was, after all, *their* manager. "I didn't want to be seen as just an adjunct to the Stones. I didn't like the fact that the press was already printing that I was their girlfriend or their this or their that. Whereas I'd barely spoken two words to any of them."

The Stones were too juvenile for Marianne. Out of all the current rock-pop sensations, she liked Bob Dylan the best, with his methedrine Beat rhythms, Spanish boots, and druggy shades. The way he made the simplest statements sound almost biblical ("And the rain came down for two days straight").

But Mick was circling her like a hawk, getting closer and closer to his blonde prey. He'd bump into Marianne at parties and vie for her attention in his own sophomoric way. At one industry event for *Ready Steady Go!*, Mick was especially lust-struck, as well as intoxicated.

"It's been altogether too long, Marianne, darling!" Mick was sashaying toward her, brandishing a champagne flute like a courtier.

"Has it?" Marianne replied, with all the ice she could muster, hoping to shut him down on the spot. Egged on by her repulsion, Mick smirked, raised his glass as if he were making a toast, then tipped the entire thing down the neckline of her scoop-neck dress. She fled and slipped into an unlocked studio, and found Keith playing a piano alone in the dark. "Very moody and intense and completely silent. He didn't speak at all in those days. I stood there for a long time in the shadows listening to him play."

Despite Mick's clumsy attempts at wooing, Marianne was occupied with other relationships. She still had John and was now entering an experimental new phase, with many participants she met touring. First there was Jeremy Clyde from Britpop duo Chad and Jeremy, who'd explained "the code of casual sex" over toast and marmalade. Then there was Gene Pitney ("dark glasses, cheap fake emotion, pompous, self-satisfied. But oh, what a good fuck he was!"). Shortly after that Marianne met Sadia, "small, dark, short hair. Exquisite, like a little figurine in an Indian temple. . . . She gave me a Tuinal and seduced me." That amour was cut short when Baroness Eva walked in on them, rolling around Marianne's childhood bedroom.

The fun stopped in April 1965 when Marianne discovered she was pregnant. In an era when "slut," "frigid," and "good girl" were flung around like weapons, pregnancy was the ultimate scarlet letter. Love was rarely "free" for women, and in 1965 attitudes toward sex and gender were still very much in flux. This rattled Marianne's sense of self. Was this her punishment for sinning? Had she slept with too many people? Here she was, eighteen, pregnant, still living in her mother's home. You didn't just call up a doctor back then—it was all whispered names, unlisted numbers, or worst of all, back-alley abortions. So when John proposed on Wigan Pier, Marianne accepted.

That May she married John Dunbar in Cambridge. They spent the morning before the wedding wandering through fields of wildflowers. John picked blossoms from honey-scented hawthorn trees. He presented the bouquet to Marianne—white petals on stems spiked with black thorns. "It was all so beautiful and enchanted. But as it turned out, it was the wrong kind of magic."

The couple honeymooned in Paris—but they never saw Montmartre, or the roses of Places des Vosges, or the sailboats in Jardin du Luxembourg. The Beat poets were in town, and John invited them to crash the honeymoon. Soon Allen Ginsberg, Gregory Corso, and Lawrence Ferlinghetti were knocking at their door at the Hotel de Lausanne, bearing jugs of abominably cheap rosé. They made themselves at home—shooting up, throwing up, and raving about everything from Rimbaud's haircut to young boys in Tangier. Needless to say, hardly a magical springtime in Paris. Instead of candlelit dinners at Le Grand Véfour, there was Lawrence Ferlinghetti eating baguettes in their bed. Instead of evenings at the opera or Club Saint Germain, Allen kept them up all night ranting about Julius and Ethel Rosenberg. Instead of breakfasting on croissants at Café de Flore, Gregory Corso mixed up his morning Brompton cocktail—half morphine, half cocaine, followed by an eight-hour nap on the floor.

Marianne had always admired the Beats—especially Allen Ginsberg (you could have a normal conversation, "the way you would, say, in a faculty lounge"). But when they followed them back to London and made themselves at home in their new flat, Marianne's attitude changed. Especially after birthing Nicholas in November. She'd wake at dawn to an ice-cold flat, step over a gauntlet of bodies and needles, and slip into the kitchen to warm the baby's milk bottle, careful to dodge bloodied needles in the drainboard. Despite turning their place into a junkie's paradise, John "forbade" Marianne to roll a single joint. Instead, she was reduced to keeping heroin jacks away from the baby. This was worse than life at the convent, worse than living with her mother. The hypocritical chauvinism of "progressive" men, the ones who rant about egalitarian utopia while expecting their girlfriends to cook a fry-up so they may attend the important business of making art, doing drugs, and saving the world. "I had been badly miscast," Marianne remembered bitterly, "as mother angel girlfriend wife and Blessed Virgin Mary." She'd joined the convent to escape the Baroness, signed with Decca to escape the nuns, and married John to break free from the hamster wheel of touring. Now she felt more caged than ever.

By the spring of 1966, Marianne started to venture out on her own. It was the ideal moment for youthful gallivanting—that heady spring of 1966, when Swinging London started swinging. The boutiques of Kings Road and Carnaby beckoned—pop art murals painted on the storefronts, shop girls wearing rubber skirts and paper paisley dresses. At Hung on You, models changed in the windows, stripping down to their bras and knickers on Cale Street. Marianne spent and spent and spent—suede boots, sequined bolero jackets, velvet mini dresses patterned in green and purple butterflies. John hated all this, which only encouraged her more. She loved piling on her glad rags, doing her makeup in their shared bathroom mirror while John glared angrily behind her. But what could he do? She paid for the flat, the groceries, the nanny. All around her was London's expanding sense of freedom, and Marianne was finally taking flight.

Still oblivious to Mick's intentions, Marianne was drifting closer to his orbit. Ironically, it was John who pushed her his way—she'd met Robert Fraser at the Indica Gallery. Through Robert she met Anita and Brian, who by now had moved from Chelsea to 1 Courtfield Road in Kensington. Flanked by Harrods and the mod boutiques of Walton Street, it was the epicenter of London's rockstar version of landed gentry. Marianne loved to visit. She'd fight her way through peddlers selling knockoff Lucite bracelets and self-styled troubadours strumming hurdy-gurdies. Brian would open the door and invite her in with a gallant little bow. He always seemed to be in the midst of some earnest conversation—talking theory or philosophy in his whispery little voice. She always loved that about Brian, the way he'd light up in animation whenever you brought up a topic he loved—Ingmar Bergman movies, train models, Hermann Hesse, or William Blake.

And then there was Anita. Bewitching Anita. She held court for hours on a magazine-strewn mattress, surrounded by dirty teacups, falling-down posters, and Moroccan tambourines. "Always at the center," wrote Marianne Faithfull, "the wicked Anita, like a phoenix on her nest of flames. . . . Dazzling, beautiful, hypnotic and unsettling."

With her knowledge of art and esoteric literature, Marianne felt at ease immediately, and Anita and Brian officially adopted her. She loved every detail of her adoptive home—the piles of records, newspapers, strings of ghungroo bells, the scarves tossed carelessly on lamps, the glockenspiel you'd trip over on your way to the bathroom (with *The Psychology of Insanity* laid helpfully on the toilet). Even the "grotesque little stuffed goat" perched on Brian's amp made her smile.

The best part was Brian's minstrel gallery. You'd climb a rope ladder, open a trapdoor, and there it was, an exquisite little loft of carved wood filled with lutes, antique train sets, and trunks of beaded belts, lace jackets, vintage uniforms, and textiles. Anita and Brian could play dress-up for days, transforming themselves into ruffled duchesses and pink-caped archdukes or bauble-laden Druids communing with old gods. Confines of time, place, and gender melted away with these magical creatures in matching flaxen pageboys.

Here at Courtfield Road Marianne could smoke to her heart's content. In fact, the women were often more stoned than the men—or at least held their drugs and liquor better. Anita sure did, rolling joint after joint with nimble nonchalance. (Marianne could watch her do this for hours.) They'd stumble back to Chelsea for pasta at Alvaro's—only Anita would be lucid enough to carry a conversation—usually something about lace-up sandals or Florentine art, and often in Italian.

Marianne did all this with no thoughts of Mick Jagger. He never crossed her mind. It was never Mick, or his fame, or even the raucous glamour of the music that drew her to the Stones' inner circle. It was always Anita.

Sometimes Anita and Marianne would go to Olympic Studios to watch the Stones record *Between the Buttons*. Studio lackeys would chauffeur them to 117 Church Road, often stopping along the way to pick up Michael Cooper or Robert Fraser.

One of the great mysteries of life is why people flock far and wide to watch men fiddle with guitars. Recording sessions, Marianne quickly learned, were "stunningly boring." During breaks she'd escape to the attic with Mick—old rooms stacked with amps and musty old papers, the perfect spot to smoke a joint and talk. But the bulk of her time was spent with Anita, feeling vaguely ornamental while they gossiped with Robert, dropped acid with Tara Browne, or rummaged in their bags for Tuinals and Mandrax.

They were working on "Ruby Tuesday"—a song Keith had written for his ex-girlfriend Linda. Brian added Elizabethan trills on the harpsichord but hunched over as if he were already haunted, like he knew that this gorgeous collaboration with Keith would be his last.

It was odd watching them—a band known for sexist lyrics about bitchy models and bored housewives—now laboring over this touching tribute to a woman who could not be tied down. "Ruby Tuesday" was more than a fresh take on courtly love. Woven through the ballad's lyrics were real revelations underneath their bravado. Were these rockers starting to understand the complexities of womanhood? There was Brian, decked out in Anita's regalia and sinking under the weight of it; there was Mick, setting his cap for a woman far more experienced than he. With time she'd see the underbelly of the idyllic lie.

Three

Traps and Troubadours

A woman, to live with a rock star, must find her ways of independence.

Anita Pallenberg

I n July 1966, Anita and Brian were photographed for a special double-page feature for *Vogue*. The title, "Girls Dress Men to Suit Themselves," celebrated the couple's gender-bending dynamic, as did this accompanying copy: "When a girl with strong ideas chooses clothes for a man with equally strong ideas and both of them are happy with the result, it's pretty good (if not downright miraculous)."

In a fresh take on gender roles, Brian stood straight like an old-school Saks model, while Anita struck a playful pose. She ducked and cavorted in a belted mini with wide stripes of magenta and mustard. Caught mid-laugh, she seemed relaxed, as if she were enjoying herself with friends or shopping or passing a joint at Granny's. "Brian Jones, a Rolling Stone," ran the text, "in a double-breasted black suit, striped red and white, chosen by Anita Pallenberg. Bright pink shirt, scarlet handkerchief and tie. All bought in New York. Black and white shoes found in Carnaby Street." Until now, the world of high fashion had snubbed or ridiculed the Stones. Thanks to Anita, Brian finally made it to the hallowed annals of *Vogue*.

But all was not well with the stylish couple. At first there was something childlike in their fights—he'd rip up her Aleister Crowley books, she'd set fire to his Scalextric train set. Now nursery squabbles were escalating into physical violence. Anita would throw drinks at women who chatted Brian up ("I don't want you talking to this slag").

At times these nights ended in bloodshed. Brian's friend Ronni Money told A. E. Hotchner about her first encounter with Anita. "I was at the Scotch of St. James on one of those nights when everybody in London seemed to be there. I was at a table talking to Jimi Hendrix and Eric Burdon when I caught a glimpse of Brian on the other side of the room. We hadn't seen each other for a couple of months. He spotted me, shouted my name, and came dashing over—hugs, kisses, all that—then he introduced me to Anita Pallenberg."

Instead of greeting Ronni with a friendly hello, Anita lashed out at Brian. "So who is this one," she snarled with all her Teutonic rancor. "Another one of your one-nighters? I thought I'd met them all by now." Ronni took the comment in stride. But Brian whirled around and punched Anita in the face. "You can't talk to Ronni like that, you bitch!" Anita's nose was gushing blood—waiters swarmed around her with napkins—some blotting her dress to avoid permanent stains.

Underneath his womanizing bravado Brian was quite fragile, plagued by addictions and a desperate need for approval. Already he was showing flares of insecurity, sulking over the band, convinced that Mick and Keith were conspiring against him. Or he'd mope for days because of the bags under his eyes, agonizing over whether to see a plastic surgeon. "He was a tortured personality," remembered Anita, "insecure as hell."

The band's self-appointed Lothario found himself dominated by his unflappable girlfriend. Unlike starstruck groupies who felt honored to be chosen by the Stones as consorts, Anita was nonchalant, like she was doing them a favor, like she deserved their worship and adulation. She simply commanded it, as if it were her birthright. It was Anita who was the star, it was Anita everyone came to see in Brian's flat on Courtfield Road—not Brian, not Keith, and not even Mick.

As Brian descended into paranoid insecurity, his fights with Anita began to escalate. It was not unusual to see her covered in bruises, and though she was technically stronger than he, she began to worry that Brian might kill her. Friends would find Anita with black eyes, blue bruises blooming over her face and arms. "I'd leave him, against his wishes, to take on modeling jobs for a few days, and when I'd return he'd come at me with a fury, beat me mercilessly. He was short but very strong, and his assaults were terrible—for days afterwards, I'd have lumps and bruises all over me. In his tantrums he would throw things at me, whatever he could pick up—lamps, clocks, chairs, a plate of food—then when the storm inside him died down he'd feel guilty and beg me to forgive him."

When Brian's abuse landed her in a local clinic, Anita turned to mystical means of revenge. "I was sitting there, in tears, getting my wounds treated, feeling terrible. I decided to make a wax figure of Brian and poke him with a needle. I mounded some candle wax into an effigy and closed my eyes and jabbed the needle into the wax figure. It pierced the stomach."

The next day she found Brian doubled over in stomach pains, the floor littered with green bottles of Milk of Magnesia. It was days before he recovered, and the spell left him even more wan and pale. Brian was cracking like Goya's dark demons hanging on his wall. But Anita was unflappable. "Her toughness was a predominant trait of her personality," wrote Marianne, "the way she just didn't give a damn about anything."

Of course, some of that could be attributed to all the drugs they took—uppers, downers, acid, Mandrax, and hash—a cornucopia of chemicals was consumed almost daily. Narcotics weakened Brian's fragile ego. As her boyfriend declined, Anita grew only shinier and more vigorous. The drugs worked for her—for years—until they didn't.

Marianne never could work out whether Anita was really a witch or a sorceress. Could she put a hex on her boyfriend while harnessing the power of a midheaven moon? But when she looked at you, your thoughts were "beautiful wickedness," and her Queen of Cats smile covered secrets like shrapnel—secrets so dark they could swallow you whole. Anita was dark—despite the blonde hair and alpine nose. That smile—that incredible smile—was like nothing Marianne had ever seen—at least not on a human. "The best way I can describe Anita is that she was like a snake to a bird, and she could transfix you and hold you in place until she wanted to make her move."

In the last week of August, Anita and Brian flew to Tangier and decamped at the boho-glam El Minzah. The fighting began almost immediately, over everything from restaurant menus to the price of a taxi. Brian was beating Anita within days. While lashing out one night, he flung a fist at her face and missed, smacking the metal window frame instead. Brian spent the rest of the holiday in Tangier's Clinique California, all the while telling friends he'd broke his wrist mountain climbing. Anita shrugged it off: "He always hurt himself . . . if he tried to hurt me, he always wound up hurting himself."

Besides, now she could drift through the city in peace. She wandered the souks of the inner Medina and spent hours combing through long duster coats, silk scarves, and raw wool woven mantles in marigolds and burnished reds. She rummaged through beaded djellabas and shimmering metals, white cotton kaftans embroidered in lacy Berber tattoos. Back in London, she blended these textures with her own signature pieces. As always, Anita made it fresh—brass bracelets jangling on her wrists, a tunic sliced at the hip and worn as a blouse, a miniskirt sewn from an ikat tapestry. Effortless, outré, and irreplaceable.

By now, Brian depended heavily on Anita and resented her all the more for it. Frequently sick and drinking more than ever, he was fading as fast as Anita rose. Her star power was noticed everywhere, eventually catching the eye of German director Volker Schlöndorff, who offered her the lead in *Mord und Totschlag*.

Time and time again men are drawn to rebel women, then are furious when they defy their expectations. Now Brian was livid with Anita for not accepting her "proper role." She competed with him rather than complementing him, and she refused to stop working as an actress and model. "Brian didn't like the fact that I was working. So when I came home with this big fat script, he tore it in half. Jealousy."

Anita began filming in Munich that fall. She brought her signature irrepressible joy to the set, that same impish grin, as if a day's shoot brought the same pleasures as smoking hash all day at Granny's or an acid-laced picnic on Primrose Hill. She relished her time away from Brian, immersing herself in the film, Munich, and even the occasional love affair.

Soon Brian was angling for a visit. He arrived in early November, with a scheme to upstage Anita in an upcoming photoshoot for *Stern* magazine.

On the morning of the shoot, Brian took Anita to the costume house Heiler KG and bought an SS officer's uniform, replete with livery and silverware. He met *Stern*'s photographer in full Nazi regalia, with Anita in sober black—schoolgirl or nun? For once, she paled next to Brian, submissively posed with her head in his lap. It speaks volumes that for Brian to outshine Anita he needed a swastika round his arm and jackboots on his feet, crushing the skull of a porcelain doll.

Of course *Stern* rejected the feature, leaving sleazy pop rags to scramble for the pics. *Sunday People* ran the photos, along with this descriptive text: "A doll lies fallen at their feet, near an ornament showing another swastika. These are the clothes Jones and his girlfriend, German actress Anita Pallenberg, both born in the war year of 1942, chose to wear for a publicity photograph in Munich."

The headline: "She Has a Heart of Stone."

While nominally living as Brian's girlfriend, Anita began to disengage herself emotionally. It simply wasn't worth it anymore. "I think Brian was a terrible person. And I put up with a lot. I was fascinated by his talent, but all the side effects weren't worth it."

She wasn't interested in Keith at first—skinny and painfully shy, crouched over his guitar and averting his gaze. He had none of Brian's fallen-angel hipness. Side by side they looked like a peacock and a toad. "Keith," wrote a friend, "with his cheeky face and chunky leather coats, looked at first like a jobbish apprentice."

Yet in his own quiet way, Keith was more comfortable with Anita's total self-possession, and his natural reticence made him more than happy to take a back seat. He loved watching her hypnotize a room full of people. He loved that she could talk circles around anyone, including him: "She knew everything and could say it in five languages. . . . She scared the pants off me."

He could barely believe that Brian had snagged Anita, how he flourished in her dazzling proximity. "I think that Keith was looking at Brian with Anita on his arm," observed London boutique owner Michael Rainey, "and realized he had a lot of self-confidence." Still, Keith kept his distance and had no intention of stealing "Brian's old lady."

The Stones at their core were deeply English. Emotion was embarrassing—even to themselves. Only the eternally perceptive Marianne sensed Keith's feelings. She seemed to know quite possibly before Keith even did that he was in love with Anita. Who wouldn't be?

By the fall of 1966, Marianne had become a regular at Courtfield Road. Brian or Keith would drive round to pick her up, and they'd all have dinner at the Golden Egg or Aberdeen's. Then it was back to Brian's for a night of dropping acid and lolling around on the floor. Every once in a while, Mick would drop by, usually with the air of a proprietor or landlord. Even at twenty-three, Mick had "an absolute horror of bohemian living," grimacing at the sink full of dishes and cigarettes stubbed on the floor. "He'd come by sort of to inspect everything, see that all was going along well with the Firm, smoke a joint and split."

Marianne didn't really get to know Mick until Brian and Keith invited her to a show at Colston Hall in Bristol. She drove there alone in her new Mustang, then Keith and Brian ushered her backstage. Ike and Tina Turner were on the bill, and outside the dressing room Tina was teaching Mick the sideways pony. Ikettes giggled in the background. "Mick could dance," she remembered, "but compared to Tina he was, well, spastic."

Brian and Keith snickered in a corner, but Mick was intent on learning the steps. Eventually he threw up his hands in despair. "Does this mean I won't be black in the next life?" (Tina: "Are you sure you want to be?")

She'd never really taken him seriously before. In fact, they all laughed behind his back: sniffing around Courtfield Road like a disapproving schoolmarm, too timid to drop acid or smoke more than half a joint. But here, ignoring Keith's and Brian's immature guffaws, paying rapt attention to Tina, Mick seemed lucid, humble far beyond his hoodlum image.

After the show Marianne joined Keith and Brian at the Shipt Hotel, where they all settled into Mick's room. Someone had brought a fresh copy of *Repulsion*, and they flopped on bed and floor, passing around joints, watching Deneuve in smoky silence. Tina's dancers were there, as well as the usual roadies and groupies, and Marianne noticed the requisite silent negotiations of pairing off. The last three standing were Mick, Marianne, and one final girl. ("She was one of the Ikettes and really sat it out.") When the movie ended the girl gave up, leaving Mick and Marianne alone.

It was nearly dawn, so Marianne suggested a walk. ("I found that moment where you're about to have sex so difficult, always have.") Together they roamed the grounds of the Shipt, where the damp grass and hedgerow mist prompted her to grill Mick on his knowledge of King Arthur, her way of "ascertaining whether he was all right or just a jerk."

"Do you remember the name of Arthur's sword?"

"Come forth from the stone, Excalibur!" (He'd practiced often in his childhood home of Dartford, using a wooden sword and a cardboard box.)

"Have you ever been to Stonehenge? How do you think they did it?"

"Druidic Department of Works, Merlin, wasn't it?"

Did he know anything about the Holy Grail?

"The Holy Grail . . . let's see . . . Joseph of Arinthea. Isn't he the one that lost the damn thing?"

What was the name of that knight that Guinevere deserted King Arthur for?

"Sir Lancelot du Lac, wasn't it? Am I going to pass my A levels, Marianne?"

By now the sun had risen, and they were soaked to the ankles in dew. Mick led Marianne back to his room, knelt at her feet to unlace her boots, which he put by the heater to dry. Marianne couldn't be more impressed by Lancelot himself. "I was completely moved by his kindness. And then we made love."

Two days later Marianne left with Nicholas for Positano. A pile of letters waited for her, including one from John, begging her to come back, which she tossed out the window. Much more exciting was the stack of letters from Mick, which she read and reread at length on the balcony. She'd packed the Stones compilation *Big Hits* (*High Tide and Green Grass*), and Mick always seemed to call when she put on the opening track. "It was only then, while I was there, that I got an inkling of his persona."

Unlike the too-cool-for-emoting John, Mick was affectionate, interesting, funny, and very attentive. He asked about Nicholas, whether she was sleeping well, did she have enough nausea pills. He was wooing her, troubadour-style.

Still, she remained ambivalent. It wasn't as if she were pining after Mick, waiting to be swept off her feet. This was a girl who a mere days before in Oxford Circus had spontaneously invited a model she barely knew to join her in Positano, then proceeded to sleep with her new friend's boyfriend because "there was a full moon and it was beautiful." (In those days that was her idea of extenuating circumstances.)

Unlike Chrissie Shrimpton, Marianne didn't long for traditional family life. She was in fact still married, she did have a child, and she found it lacking. But she did begin to wonder what it might be like to have a man who took care of her for a change. The pop star grind was becoming unbearable—she hated the monotony of touring, she even hated her latest record. For years she'd dreamed of acting in Royal Court—but she needed to make more money. John was too busy tripping on acid and putting methedrine in his coffee to take care of her. "Either John had to make a lot of money, or I had to find someone else. Makes it sound very cold, doesn't it?"

Marianne left Nicholas behind with the nanny, ruminating on Mick as she drove up the Amalfi Coast in her Mustang. She went straight to the Mayfair after arriving back in London—she simply couldn't face her lonely, empty flat. But it wasn't Mick she called after checking in. She dialed the number for Courtfield Road, hoping to hear Anita's sultry alto.

Anita was out, but Brian was there, along with Keith and Tara Browne, who were all delighted to hear from her. They immediately piled in Brian's Fiat and drove to the Mayfair to collect her. On the way back to Brian's they passed around tabs of acid.

Marianne observed her three friends flopping around the flat, their gold-flecked cravats gleaming against the jewel tones and burnished velvets of Brian's pillows. That was her last thought before the acid took hold—how resplendent they looked in their gear from Hung on You, Granny's, and Chelsea Antiques. Their silky finery began to dissolve into glittering molecules. ("It was very good acid. Brian had got it from Robert who had got it from the CIA.")

But this was more than the visual haze of good LSD. She saw "soul genealogies," past lives unfolding like "tiny mercurial operas." It was as if her friends' true selves were emerging—their very "spirit selves."

Tara Browne was "pure courtier," a dandy in amethyst cuff links and blond curls, enveloped in menthol smoke from his Salems. Marianne knew he was sad, with his wife off in Marbella gallivanting with "hunky Spanish guys." She knew he liked her. She also knew he was very rich, with five titles, two castles, and a Shelby Cobra painted in psychedelic splendor. But this left Marianne cold. Tara may have been heir to the great Guinness fortune, but the Stones were the real aristocracy here, and everyone knew it.

Brian was, unsurprisingly, Pan, "an urbane Satyr in crushed velvet, horned, goat-legged. A voluptuous, overripe god gone to seed." But in Marianne's altered state he wasn't quite Pan himself, more like an eighteenth-century nobleman dressed as a faun, frolicking around the gardens of Versailles. (Marianne: "One really gets to know one's friends in such detail on acid.") This ersatz Pan played his pipes—inhaler in hand—against a Boucher mountain backdrop, chasing gauzy nymphs, unaware of the encroaching doom, the guillotine's blade hovering over his head, a drumbeat's brutal staccato faint but ever closer.

Suddenly all that giggly acid euphoria sharpened into something sexual. "I thought they wanted to be with me because I was such fun and one of them," she wrote, remembering her disappointment. "Of course they were all wondering when and if they were going to have sex with me. That's the way things go."

Brian, despite being the most hesitant and stoned, wobbled over to Marianne's cushion. Marianne loved Brian but was never drawn to him sexually; now here he was leaning over her like some "weary, asthmatic god." Yet she followed him up the pull-down ladder, into his cushion-piled "minstrel gallery." Marianne dealt as she always did, by retreating into her rich and varied imagination. She tried to imagine herself in a scene from an Elizabethan play where the lovers slip behind a painted cloth bower. But this wasn't some Shakespearean frolic—Brian was pathetically wasted—which only aroused Marianne's feelings of pity. "It was like Pan out of breath, reaching for his inhaler."

Marianne quickly realized she'd rather be alone. Being felt up by rock stars was yesterday's news, and conked-out Brian was diluting her trip. Craving her own subversive cocoon, she crept out unnoticed onto the dark streets of Soho, winding down to her flat in Lennox Gardens.

Still in her travel clothes (she hadn't changed since Italy), she lay down on her bed. The posey-patterned wallpaper suddenly sprang to life, cabbage roses pirouetted in pink on the wall. A breeze blew in from her open window, rustling her heavy purple curtains. Moonbeams shone through the plummy wool.

This was more like it! She knew there was more to acid than letting Brian Jones grab her breasts.

The phone rang. It was Keith, sounding shaken and uncharacteristically lost. "Where did you go, Marianne? We looked everywhere for you."

He was upset that she'd "disconnected" from the crowd. ("You can't just abandon ship like that!") You just didn't go off and shatter the "vibe," which in those days was sacred. Marianne should have known better. She grabbed her bag and called a cab straight away.

But there were reasons for her urgency beyond acid etiquette. Marianne was secretly in love with Keith. For months she'd been watching him at Courtfield Road, fiddling around on the jaw harp, hotboxing with Brian, smiling wordlessly when they hit the right chords at the studio. To her Keith was "perfection," yet she never considered herself edgy enough for him.

She somehow saw the rebel seed in Keith that would one day come to fruition. Keith was still exceptionally shy—he'd barely been with any women, Linda was his first, and even then he had to be pushed by Andrew into pursuing her. (Andrew: "It's better for publicity, man, you need a model girlfriend.") Onstage he bobbed Beatle-like, low-key and cheery, with none of the raw sexuality Mick was starting to cultivate. But to Marianne Keith was Byron, a doomed Romantic hero.

When she got to Courtfield Road, Keith, her proto-punk Lord Byron, dark and dazzling, was waiting at the door to pay her cab fare:

"Brian's passed out and Tara's gone home. Let's go back to your hotel."

It was the best night of Marianne's life.

The next morning, Keith was pulling on his boots when he dropped the bomb: Mick was "smitten" with Marianne, he "really had it bad."

"I knew in my heart of hearts that Keith was already in love with Anita. And I could just feel that whatever he wanted, I wasn't it. I was too English and too conventional for him. The signals I was picking up were accurate; he was already a man obsessed."

A few hours after Keith sauntered off, Mick called. His boyish enthusiasm was infectious. ("Great! You're back! Let's do something!") Especially after Keith's affable brush-off. Even better, Mick wanted to go shopping.

Soon they were strolling arm in arm through Harrods, where Mick bought Nicholas a shiny new tricycle. The implicit intimacy of holiday shopping drew them closer, with its twinkling lights and fluffy window displays. Suddenly they were browsing the toy department with the warmth and ease of an established couple.

But Mick was already part of an established couple—he had yet to break up with the depressed Chrissie Shrimpton. In fact, Chrissie was at Harley House this very moment, packing suitcases full of bikinis and Bain de Soleil. She and Mick had booked a holiday in Jamaica—a holiday she hoped would bring them close and heal the hurt of months before. It wasn't until she called Mick's office that afternoon that she discovered the flights had been canceled.

While Mick and Marianne lunched at the trendy San Lorenzo and strolled through the Christmas-lit Bond Street arcades, Chrissie was in shock, freshly abandoned at Harley House, alone with six kittens, a Yorkie, and three white songbirds chirping in their gilded cage. She took an overdose of sleeping pills. "I really wanted to die. I thought my life was over."

Chrissie awoke in a private Hampstead clinic. Her feet were mysteriously damp, nurses hovered over her, calling her by a different name. (Mick couldn't risk a scandal like this in the press.) "Where am I?" she weakly asked her psychiatrist. "What's happening?" He wordlessly jabbed a needle in her arm, and she was out cold again.

Once lucid, Chrissie sent a telegram to Mick, begging him to bring Dora, her little Yorkie. Mick arrived wrapped in a new black fur coat, holding the dog, and asked to speak to Chrissie's mother. He acknowledged that Chrissie had been "losing her spark" and astonishingly admitted that he was the cause.

Mick was correct. He had enforced curfews, vetoed friendships, and turned her on to his Harrods account. Where was the rebel girl he'd met three years ago, the convent school dropout who dressed like a beatnik, got drunk at the Crawdaddy, and crowd-surfed across the dance floor to kiss him on a dare?

Even worse, Mick had cut Chrissie off from her family. When Chrissie abandoned her bedsit and moved into Harley House, her parents cut off all contact. She'd done this under the assumption of marriage, but soon Mick claimed that he'd never said such a thing, and he didn't believe in such "bourgeois institutions." Friendless, financially dependent, and separated from her family, Mick had gaslit the once-vibrant Chrissie until she truly was under his thumb.

Thirty months later, Mick would find himself in another hospital on another continent, consoling another distraught mother whose daughter had attempted suicide. Was there a shred of shame under his English politesse or at least a sense of culpability?

Four

Butterflies

There were a lot of things I could have done at nineteen that would have been more healthy than becoming Mick Jagger's inamorata.

Marianne Faithfull

In January Marianne flew to Italy for the San Remo song festival. Mick bombarded her with phone calls, but Marianne remained ambivalent. She had Nicholas with her, and between festival obligations and her jet-setting friend group, she had very little time to muse about Mick. But a few days in, and seemingly out of nowhere, that familiar restless anxiety took hold, and she was struck by a sudden desire to see him. One phone call was all it took, and Mick was on a plane the next day. Marianne—along with Nicholas and his nanny—met him at the Cannes airport, which already swarmed with anticipating press. Mick, ten steps ahead in eluding the press, had already hired a tiny boat, with one captain and one mate, where the little party spent a week at sea. Two nights in there was a terrible storm: "Mick was wonderful. We all got into the same bunk, Mick and Nicholas and I, and held each other. I think that is where I really fell in love with him."

The two were inseparable in San Remo, snuggled up together at Whiskey a Go Go in crushed velvet and Victorian frills, Marianne slipping into various Hellenistic nightgowns and pants suits for her onstage appearances. She sang "C'e Chi Spera" in near-perfect Italian but lost in her first round.

Marianne didn't care—she was floating on Mick's urbane attentiveness. She'd never been with a man like this before—the way he managed everything with such effortless gallantry. Like when she smoked too much hash and went mute at a nightclub, he simply snagged some Stenamina tablets from the local deejay. Mick took care of her in those immediate moments, moments that mean everything when you're nineteen.

For the first time, the press acknowledged Marianne and Mick as a couple. It was an irresistible story—young love, the rebel wins the angel, against the chic backdrop of Continental pop.

The paparazzi trailed them throughout San Remo, caught them lunching at seaside trattorias or strolling hand in hand down the cobblestone streets. Both wore gauzy garments in whites and creams—palazzo pants, tunics, sandals, and espadrilles. (Did Mick—with his keen sense of image—match her on purpose?) In the bleached-out landscape clad in head-to-toe white, they projected some beatific innocence, something almost holy. Youthful divinity meets the world of rock.

Like many philanderers, Mick was also a serial monogamist and preferred the comfort of living with women. Cautiously, Marianne moved into Harley House. The ghost of Chrissie

Shrimpton hung heavy in the air—stray straight strands of chestnut hair, strips of Glorene lashes still sticky with glue, little square bottles of Givenchy L'Interdit with the lingering scent of fizzy orange and powdered makeup. A Victorian birdcage with a brass bird that sang, a rocking horse from Harrods named Petunia. It was eerily childlike yet shot through with the pain of Chrissie's shattered dreams.

This was a girl Mick had courted, chased after, now languishing in disgrace like an exiled mistress. Everything she'd represented became a lifestyle he now mocked, turned into cruel fodder for songs like "Yesterday's Papers" and "19th Nervous Breakdown."

For now, Marianne told herself she was different. She wasn't needy and high-maintenance, wearing two pounds of false hair and makeup in the bath. She didn't make jealous scenes at parties or scream in the streets while stumbling out of the Scotch. Her mother didn't care if she was "living in sin," she wore men's shirts to dinner, and never blow-dried her hair. She didn't demand bourgeois trappings like marriage. She was cool, she was sophisticated, she was in love.

"I forgot the first two cardinal rules of relationships: they are never accidental and they always follow a pattern. . . . It would only be a matter of time before my experience became material for songs in the same way as Chrissie's had."

February 1967. "Ruby Tuesday" had just been released. The Stones' popularity was snowballing, and the band spent the weekend dropping acid at Keith's country house. Keith tumbled around the lawn in his Afghan coat while a scarf-swaddled Mick tossed rocks in a stream. Marianne was in the bath when the cops burst in. Startled by the commotion and shouting below, she hastily grabbed the nearest piece of "clothing"—which happened to be a fur skin rug.

At first it seemed like one big joke—she giggled with Keith while the cops stormed around gathering cigarette butts and incense, labeling it "evidence." But it soon became obvious this joke would have consequences. Despite the goofy innocence of the trip, she was the only woman in a roomful of men, naked under an enormous fur rug.

The shocked constable saw her as some sort of sacrificial virgin unicorn, a child-woman corrupted by thugs. Mick and Keith were quickly whisked away by the police for glamorously rumpled mug shots. The seedy rattle of it all made the two men legendary, propelling the dangerous Stones mythology. But Marianne—who made headlines as "the girl in the fur rug," or simply "Miss X"—may as well have been branded with a scarlet *A*.

The public liked seeing Mick and Keith strike poses in handcuffs, strutting down the steps of Old Bailey or quietly conferring with their lawyers. But they didn't want to see Marianne this way. Marianne had been photographed wearing peacoats and nuzzling kittens, petting a Dalmatian in a fresh meadow, or lounging in a booth at the Salisbury, wearing white cable-knit knee socks. "Mick and Keith came out of it with an enhanced bad-boy varnish. I came out of it diminished, demeaned, trampled in the mud."

The headlines continued for weeks and weeks: NAKED GIRL AT STONES PARTY. SCANTILY CLAD WOMAN AT DRUG PARTY. STORY OF A GIRL IN A FUR SKIN RUG. Just when she thought it couldn't get worse, the vulgar Mars bar rumor emerged. "I was the lowest of the low. The slut. Miss X."

Marianne wasn't aware of it yet, but her own degradation would have an inverse relationship to the status of the Stones. The idea that they'd ruined this sweet English rose, this aristocratic blonde songbird fresh out of the convent, dragged her through the mud and stuck a Mars bar up her fanny had only made them more sexual, raw, and dangerous.

"The press behaved disgustingly towards her," said Chris O'Dell. "They are an absolute disgrace to humanity. Sex, drugs and rock 'n' roll became an icon, and Marianne became sacrificial to this end. She was a symbol for the general moral degeneracy." After the press came the inevitable hate mail: "The sooner you leave this island with your long blond hair floating in the sea, it will be a cleaner place."

"I was young and impressionable," Marianne wrote years later. "I must have believed those hate letters I got."

It would be decades before Marianne could defend herself. By then, she'd have six albums, a long-conquered drug addiction, and six Grammy awards. But for now, she was confused, barely twenty, and Mick Jagger's girlfriend. The real hurt was still more than a year away.

Five

The Wilder Shores of Love

Anita said she'd been to the Wilder Shores of Love. Not sure I have!

Marianne Faithfull

Keith, in a rare moment of assertiveness, insisted that Anita and Brian travel with him. Everyone else in the band and its entourage was flying to Tangier—but the Courtfield Road Trio would travel the way they did everything else—romantic, risky, expensive, and utterly complicated.

Besides, Keith was eager to test out Blue Lena—his new Bentley Continental, freshly upholstered with smooth leather seats and tricked out with a hi-fi system and 8-track. The back was piled with fur rugs, red silk Moroccan cushions, stacks of blues records, and Italian porn magazines. He even had a driver ready (despite owning the car for a year, Keith still hadn't passed his driving test).

Tom Keylock was just the type of brute the Stones delighted in hiring—ex-military, protective in a sinister, thuggish way. Keylock took Blue Lena over on the Channel ferry while the trio flew to Paris. The plan was to speed through France and Spain, take the ferry to Tangier, where they'd connect with Mick and Marianne, then follow the hippie trail west to Marrakech. Anita's old friend Deborah Dixon tagged along. She'd just split with Donald, and what better distraction than a road trip through Europe bound for Morocco? Deborah got a lot more than she bargained for.

The madness began their first morning in Paris, when Keylock tried to pay the bill at the Hotel George V. He handed the clerk Keith's Diners Club card, which was refused. Brian and Keith were nowhere to be seen. There was only Anita, who claimed not to have any cash. Flustered, he pulled out Keith's wallet and forged a check. This was spotted at once by the manager, who picked up the phone to call the police. Then Keith and Brian came barreling through the lobby with Anita's luggage, feathers and fedoras flying. They jumped in the car, which was waiting on the street, and escaped down the Champs Élysées.

Keylock later suspected this was a stunt—orchestrated by Anita. How else could Keith and Brian have timed their hasty exit? And everyone knew she was loaded with cash, rolls of francs and pounds and lira clanging around in her bags. But Anita thrived in chaos—a mad dash through Europe on a felony charge wasn't enough—she had to risk a run-in with the French police as well. Never miss an opportunity to make a scene, especially one involving forgery, the *gendarmes*, and noisy escapes from five-star hotels. "She used to do people's brains in," remembered Keylock, shuddering at the ordeal.

Despite his irritation, Keylock kept his post at the wheel of Blue Lena. Keith rode shotgun and manned the tape deck, while Deborah, Anita, and Brian snuggled up in the back. With the city behind them, they dug into their drugs. Pills, powders, and hash were shared in abundance, bottles of brandy passed between them. Everything seemed like some exquisite romp, like stars in their own film of merry bandits. Even Brian was back to his charismatic self, relieved to have fled the pressures of London. The bonhomie continued well into the evening when they checked into a roadside pension. It was nearly booked, only the attic space was left. Somehow even that matched the mood of the moment, and they spent the night frolicking the poky halls, giggling like children.

The next morning they piled back in the car, eager for another day of hijinks. But somewhere between the Loire's slopes and valleys, Brian began to crack. Demerols, Seconals, liquid mescaline, and speed had thrown him into a sleep-deprived state of constant chemical flux. A deep cough rattled through his chest, exacerbated by cigarettes and hash. His asthma flared up, his pallor worsened, and his feeble state ignited insecurities. Between slogs at the bottle and puffs on his inhaler, he tore into Anita, railing at her disloyalty, how she'd jilted him for her acting career, she was a bitch, a slag, a liar. Half bleary-eyed Saturn, half Little Lord Fauntleroy, Brian stewed in the back seat, wrapped in blankets like an invalid king, taking long slugs from his bottle of Jack.

The others sat mute while Brian sulked and raged, a ticking time bomb as Blue Lena hurtled toward the Pyrenees. Keith's eyes were locked on Anita in the rearview mirror. "I was still playing it very cool not to push it. I figured if anything was going to happen, Brian was gonna be the one who was going to blow it. He was becoming increasingly vicious."

They were approaching Cordes-sur-Ciel, a walled medieval city on a hilltop, when Brian began to lose his mind. He'd been ranting at Anita all day and now, in the midst of an asthmatic rage, spotted an ambulance. "Follow it," he demanded, and Keylock gave chase, careening through the cobblestones. They briefly checked into the local hospital, where some quick tests revealed blood in his lungs. He was diagnosed with pneumonia and transferred to a larger medical center near Toulouse.

No one recognized him in the Hospital d'Abil. In fact, he'd been confused for a girl. ("Je presente une fille," the paramedic explained to the night nurse, thrown off by the creamy silk suit and pale bangs.) Someone injected Brian with Cedilanide, and the exhausted party checked into a nearby hotel.

Tomorrow would be Brian's twenty-fifth birthday. Would he recover enough to join them? Would their Moroccan idyll stop short in Toulouse, trading Bedouin tents for starchy French clinics? What would this mean for that unspoken, woozy ménage and Anita's slow destined slide toward Keith?

The next morning they checked on Brian—he was sitting up in bed, drinking café au lait. The nurses coddled and petted him, snuck him extra biscuits for his birthday. "Go on without me," he waved breezily, before pulling Deborah aside: "Do NOT leave Keith alone with Anita."

One man down, Blue Lena hit the road again, this time with Deborah in front and Keith in the back. As they passed over the Pyrenees, a sweet sense of relief suffused the caravan. By the time they crossed the sunny Spanish border, giddy levity took over once again, buzzing warmly in the orange-scented air.

It was long past dusk when they reached Barcelona and hit up a flamenco guitar club in the Ramblas. They left the club around three and immediately found themselves surrounded by a mob. Keith had adorned Blue Lena with the Vatican flag—this set off a group of local hooligans, who were pelting his beloved Bentley with rocks. (Keith: "Maybe they were anti-rich, anti-us, maybe it was because I was flying the Pope's flag that day.") The cops didn't take kindly to blasphemous hippies, and soon enough Keith found himself in another courtroom, then a cell block, along with the rest of the crowd. Exhausted and desperate to flee the situation, Keith confessed to vandalizing his own car.

At this point Deborah bade the dwindling group goodbye. Hospitals and jail time had dampened her spirits, and even she couldn't keep up with such rowdy company. All night, every night scuttling through the corridors, snorting coke and guzzling cava, banging on her door, demanding she join the revelry. The sexual tension had gone from innocent to oppressive.

And then there were three—just the soon-to-be lovers in furs and Keylock at the wheel, tearing south through Catalonia. Between his innate shyness and his loyalty to Brian, Keith would never make the first move. So Anita did, with a back seat blow job on the outskirts of Valencia.

Keith was shocked. Of course he had a thing for Anita—who didn't? But he'd never dream of stealing Brian's girl, and besides, he assumed he'd been designated for Deborah. His mind spun as they hurtled through the orange groves: "I still remember the smell of the orange trees in Valencia. When you get laid with Anita Pallenberg for the first time, you remember things."

That night, he told Keylock to book one room for them both.

They drove south in silence, toward the foothills of Andalusia, through fields of poppies and broom flower, the air heady with almond and cherry blossoms. "Suddenly we're together. You don't talk a lot when that shit hits you. Without even saying things, you have the feeling, the great sense of relief that something has been resolved."

They stopped at the seaport town of Algeciras, their next suite booked under Count and Countess Ziegenpuss. Then they hopped on a ferry bound for Morocco. Alone now (save for Keylock) they felt less like a newly formed jet-setting couple and more like a half-stunned Bonnie and Clyde. They left their royal titles behind as they sailed into the city of Tangier, the old walled Medina rising like a fortress from a confetti of pastel rooftops. A thick stack of telegrams was waiting for Anita. "Must leave here as soon as possible for Tangier; assuming no complications. Very unlikely. Please book flights, first class, Toulouse/Paris/Tangier early next week and mail tickets immediately. Also notify others of arrival and ask them to wait for me. Will recuperate fully in sun. Love Brian."

They spent three days in Tangier's El Minzah hotel, reeling between passion, confusion, and guilt. The others were already en route to Morocco. What would happen if Mick—or God forbid Robert—caught them creeping in and out of each other's suites? Besides, for all Anita's rabble-rousing, she always stopped short of breaking up the band. Keith agreed, Anita must fly to Toulouse to collect her sickly boyfriend and put these last three delirious nights behind her.

"From the moment I arrived in Toulouse," Anita recalled, "Brian treated me horribly. Disapproving of everything about me, using abusive language, obviously sensing that something might be going on between Keith and me but not discussing it." Brian still needed one last night of treatment. So she flew with him back to London, where he checked into a clinic. The next day it was time to fly back to Tangier.

Desperate to avoid flying alone with Brian, Anita called Marianne, who agreed to join her. The two stayed up all night, dropping acid and packing. Marianne opened up her shapely little train case and threw in the essentials. Oscar Wilde's *Salome*, seashells, one single sari, and a book of illustrated fairy tales by Edmund Dulac. ("It was the suitcase of someone on acid—more a collage than a suitcase.")

By the time the three arrived at the airport, Marianne and Anita were in a raucous mood, giggling through customs, flashing acid smiles for the paparazzi, and striding through Heathrow as if it were their own personal runway. Marianne wore a velveteen jacket and pants with Anita's fedora perched jauntily on her head. In her signature boa slung round her neck, knee-high boots, and a belted leather mini, Anita was still fresh and dazzling after no sleep, two tabs of acid, and three flights in twelve hours. A white camellia looped through her belt like a clip-on by Chanel.

Frivolity aside, Marianne was startled by Brian's anemic appearance. His eye bags had sunken into deep violet grooves, his skin had that ashen tint of affliction. But he looked otherwise incredible in his Savile Row suit and kept pace with their jovial tone, joining in the laughter over a table of tea, their passports carelessly strewn amongst the cups, books, and cigarettes.

Time to board. Once seated, Marianne and Anita shared their acid with Brian, who chattered about their Gibraltar layover. He'd finally finished the *Degree of Murder* soundtrack and was determined to play it for the Barbary apes.

Mid–acid trip at six in the morning, the three took a taxi to the Rock of Gibraltar. They approached the monkeys solemnly, bowing ("we honor you monkeys")—after all, they were on their turf. Brian turned on his tape recorder, and after a few bars the monkeys threw up a collective shriek and scattered.

Only Brian would relegate a music critique to a group of tailless monkeys or interpret their antics as some terrible rejection. He'd been creatively blocked for months, battling self-doubt and censure. He collapsed in tears, screaming at the monkeys and begging them to come back. Triggered by the monkeys, the acid, and crippling self-doubt, he dissolved into madness. "The monkeys don't like my music! Fuck the monkeys! Fuck the monkeys!"

Anita froze, mute and shell-shocked. A group of tourists inched away in terror. Marianne tried vainly to comfort Brian, but there was no way of stopping his outburst. "I knew right then it was going to be a fatal week . . ."

Brian had already snapped—and they still had their connecting flight to Tangier. This was clearly an emergency. Marianne always found a way to touch Brian's vulnerable brain and suggested they read aloud Oscar Wilde's play *Salome*. Brian would read the part of Herod, Marianne Salome, and Anita Herodias. It worked.

Still, something concerned Marianne. Throughout the entire trip—the airports, the taxis, the lunatic scene with the Barbary apes—Anita had been jabbing at Brian or whispering to her these cutting asides. "Don't you think Brian looks very pale and so dull, and not very alive? He's very bloodless, wouldn't you say?"

Of course Marianne liked Brian's look—his sickly pallor reminded her of Keats. But even she had to admit Brian was wilting next to Anita, who glittered beside him. "I had never seen anybody so gleaming and alive and vibrating," she remembered.

Wrapped in her own splendor, Anita seemed cruelly indifferent to her pitiful boyfriend.

Then it dawned on Marianne: Anita was going to leave Brian.

Keith was waiting for the trio back in Tangier, along with Mick, Robert Fraser, Brion Gysin, and Christopher Gibbs, who had recently arrived. Anita vanished into the depths of El Minzah's lobby, spotted William S. Burroughs, the already-legendary author of *Naked Lunch*, and cornered him for hours. Marianne stumbled off alone and wandered into a souk, wearing only her sari and stoned out of her mind. She followed a teapot-carrying man into an underground shop where she smoked more hash and danced. By the time the others found her, she was whirling to the beats of Moroccan music, with Achmed—the beaming shopkeeper—clapping along. The sari slipped off and the dance continued (she was Salome after all), to the delight of Achmed and the annoyance of Mick, who stormed out.

That jolted Marianne back to reality. She grabbed Brian and fled back to El Minzah, where they huddled in the hallway on straw mats, still in the depths of their acid trip. Keith lingered behind in Achmed's shop, settling in like a local and smoking hash from sebsi pipes. Swaddled in his favorite sheepskin coat, staring darkly out on the sun setting over the city. Twenty-four and bright-eyed yet somehow looking like an old Berber shepherd in the dimming blue light.

They spent the next day winding through a maze of hash-heavy streets, past spice stalls, woven baskets of dried leaves and flowers, carts of figs and oranges, and women shelling peas. Marianne slinked around in a floaty paisley frock, hiding from the sun in Anita's straw hat. (Everyone pilfered from Anita's travel wardrobe—Keith was festooned in her Victorian mourning pins, Brian wore her scarves as cravats, Mick strolled around in her floppy fedora.) Anita and Keith avoided each other, which of course aroused suspicion. Brian's "paranoia meter" had already blown through the roof, with him accusing random strangers of espionage and disrobing in the streets. They'd have to hustle him into doorways, stuff him back in his suits. Even the musical vendor's flutes left him cold. He bought a bendir and slumped in a café, kicking together his dirty Chuck Taylors.

The next morning Anita spotted the notorious British criminals the Kray twins on the beach. They took it as a sign to move on to Marrakech.

They settled in the Es Saadi Hotel, on the top floor overlooking the pool. Brian punched Anita the minute after checking into their room. "I looked a pretty sight when we all went out to dinner that night. All through dinner, Brian kept staring at Keith, but everyone was having too good a time drinking, smoking dope, and eating couscous to pay any attention to him."

Anita gulped down Seconals and crashed in her room. Brian dropped acid with Robert by the pool. Robert crouched on the ledge like a gargoyle wearing a black felt hat, staring into the water. Brion Gysin floated around, observing Keith and Anita. "I saw something I can only call mythological. At the deep end Anita is swinging on a canvas seat. Keith is in the pool, dunking up and down in the water, looming at her. When I go to pass between them, I see that I can't. I can't make it. I can't make it. There is something there, a barrier, I can see it. What I see looks like a glass rod, revolving rapidly. Between Keith's eyes and Anita's eyes, it shoots back and forth at the speed of light. As bad as a laser beam."

That evening Cecil Beaton met them as planned. He found a heavy-lidded Brian in his silky white suit sprawled out like a pimp on a cushion in the lobby. Next to him was Anita, whom he found vaguely repulsive ("dirty white face, dirty blackened eyes, dirty canary drops of hair, and barbaric jewelry").

Beaton was, however, besotted with Mick, whom he sat next to later that night when he joined the crew for dinner at a traditional Berber restaurant. Two pale peas in their fussy little pod, Mick and Beaton chatted about British journalism, Indian bhangra, Hungarian folk music, the restaurant's blue tiles and red leather banquettes. Mick encouraged Cecil to eat the chicken Moroccan-style with his fingers, expounded on his love of Marrakech, how he preferred its authenticity to the seedy tourist trap Tangier. Even the belly dancers were more "real"—so "rustic, heavy, lumpy," shaking to the music's thrum and moan. "What marvelous authority she has," Mick observed coolly, a cigarette clasped between his pointed fingers. "She follows through."

Marianne sat mute, watching the dancers. Mick was distracted with Beaton discussing Giacometti doorways. There's a particular kind of demoralizing hell when your lover rebuffs you on vacation. Even in their sumptuous Marrakech digs, Mick wasn't much of a lover. "I often thought that it might have been a help if Mick and I had tied on a good drunk together, maybe if we had loosened up that way, we might have stood a chance of talking and of getting ourselves on track. But that was the sixties, and we just didn't drink. I suppose the prevalent belief was that to take LSD or smoke hash was a pure sort of organic thing and that alcohol was going into the straight world of our parents, and since that was what older people did to get off, we absolutely rejected it."

Without the easy aphrodisiacs of cocktails and champagne, Marianne resorted to more drastic measures. While wrapping up dinner, Marianne snuck off to find a dancer backstage. She had her eye on a girl named Yasmin, whom she found and discreetly paid backstage.

"I did it to turn Mick on," Marianne recalled years later, "and it did. I enjoyed playing the role of the adventurous one, the one who would do things Mick wanted to do but didn't dare." Yasmin had little interest in Mick: "As usually happens in these situations, the man ends up watching the girls from the other side of the bed. Mick rolled a joint and watched as Yasmin and I carried on." What followed was hardly *une nuit d'amour* but a languid, somewhat tepid *ménage à trois*.

Cecil photographed them the next day. Brian wore last night's suit, clutching his 8-track like a teddy bear. Mick pranced and preened by the pool, his girl-rugged features bleached out by the light. Cecil managed to get some shots of Anita, perched on a chimney in a cotton print dress and pussy-bow tie.

No interest in posing for photoshoots, Marianne sulked in the shade with Keith, smoking and drinking warm Coke from a bottle. Photographer and friend Michael Cooper managed to snap a photo—Keith scowling and gulping down Coke, Marianne smoking, looking adrift, draped in Anita's feather boa, which by now had wilted with the heat. Happier in the fairy-tale world of Dulac, she leafed through her picture book. Only Mick seemed grounded and confident, posing pastily by the pool, lapping up attention from the adoring Cecil.

This early into their relationship, Marianne was already sensing Mick's essential coldness. He was giving of flowers and hobby horses and chatty art banter, but not of himself. These past few days she'd been slipping, yet she couldn't confide in him. "The last person in the world I could discuss anything with was Mick. We never talked about anything really personal, about anything that really mattered to us. I tried on some occasions, but it didn't work. In a way he resented it, as if it were an intrusion into a private part of him he didn't want to share with me."

Her feelings hit a peak during an afternoon ramble in the Atlas Mountains. She deeply regretted this trip. Dehydrated, on acid *again*, no food, and no sleep. It was hot, and she hadn't packed any real clothes. She fretted over Brian's delicate health and the prickly tension of the emerging love triangle. She even felt uneasy around Christopher and Robert—if anything they were more *her* friends, but unlike Mick, the constant entourage cramped her need for space.

Here she was in the Atlas Mountains at sunset, wandering through Paradise Valley—a spot so known for its beauty people flocked worldwide for its restorative healing. Those fashionable Kings Road hippies—didn't they come here for these tangerine skies? All that beauty, and in the company of her lover and friends, yet all she could feel was loneliness. What on earth was wrong with her? Marianne began to cry, choking back her sobs, having to seem cool and with it and down for anything, the brutal loneliness of Cool. Mick, uncomfortable, shuffled away, pretending not to notice. Christopher Gibbs tried to comfort her. "Christopher was very concerned and wanted to know what the matter was, and I couldn't talk. There wasn't anything to tell him. It was just all those emotions exploding in the midst of that beautiful terrain."

A thunderstorm broke the tension and hurried them back to the hotel. Now Anita had to face what she'd been avoiding all day—Brian's condition. They'd left him in his suite, passed out in a stupor of downers. But he woke up. "Brian started drinking, getting himself into a state," recalled Tom Keylock. "Next thing anyone knew was that he'd picked up a pair of dodgy Berber whores, tattooed all over."

By the time Anita arrived, the sordid display was in its final act. She walked in on Brian with the two women, in basket-woven body tattoos, hennaed hair, and multiple piercings. Unabashed, Brian commanded she join them. Anita was humiliated. This wasn't sexual freedom or experimentation, this was abuse. She refused, turned her back, and went for the door. Brian lashed out, punching Anita in the face, throwing lamps, and overturning a tray of sandwiches. Once Brian started flinging bread and cold cuts, she ran to Keith's room in tears.

"I can't watch Brian do this shit to you anymore. I'm taking you back to London."

Keith spent the next morning lying by the pool. His bond with Brian was fierce and tight. It had always been him and Brian—ever since their grotty little flat on Edith Grove—eating stale bread while listening to Muddy Waters, sleeping in the same filthy bed for warmth. Keith was never one to step into other's affairs. But he already loved Anita. And he knew she wouldn't have come to him unless she was terrified. He made up his mind and plotted their escape from Marrakech.

That night, Keith appointed Brion Gysin with the task of distracting Brian. They'd taxi to Marrakech's Square of the Dead to watch acrobats and record music. "As soon as Brian left, Keith and I packed up and went off together," Anita explained. "I was terrified but exhilarated to be freeing myself from Brian's tyranny. At the same time, there was the good side of Brian that still intrigued me, the way he was when he wasn't being paranoid. But I was more than ready to give that up, especially since I was now almost in love with Keith."

When Brian finally returned to the Es Saadi, he was alone. Mick and Marianne had already flown back, so had Robert Fraser and Christopher Gibbs. "They've all left me," Brian cried pathetically, then turned frantic. Gysin alone was left to console Brian, "like a tiny celluloid Kewpie doll, banked all around by a choir of identical little girl dolls looking just like him, chanting his hymns."

The trip started out as a carefree escape, but it changed their lives forever—as well as the career of the Rolling Stones. Michael Cooper caught this pivotal moment on camera: Anita in a Tangier café flanked by her two amours—Brian in ruffles and Keith in a tee, both scowling and looking away from the camera, as if they were physically unable to look truth in the eye. Only Anita looks directly at the camera, unflappable in her pink boa and suede. It will be the last picture of the three ever taken together.

Only a fool would call Anita Pallenberg a muse. She was a force of nature, and rapidly becoming the central axis of the Stones. "At the rock n roll round table occupied by the Stones," wrote Robert Greenfield, "Anita is key. Whoever possesses her has the power. But as time will prove, no one can keep her for long. For in the end, she belongs only to herself."

Six

Children of the Moon

Who manages Keith Richards? Probably Anita Pallenberg.

Interview in *Melody Maker*, 1973

On returning to London, Anita jumped between various hotels, occasionally spending the night at Keith's in St John's Wood. Still reeling from the breakup, she moved out of Courtfield Road, weeping as she threw her things in bags—blonding bleach, waistcoats from Granny's, sashes and trinkets from their Moroccan exploits. Keith hung on by her side, a steadying rock, stacks of Brian's records shoved under his arms.

No one had ever seen Keith like this—protective, decisive, a knight defending his lady. His cool exterior melted for Anita. Within days he'd already introduced her to his mother. "We live like gypsies," Keith boasted when Doris came to his flat for tea. But there was no time to revel in that first flush of love. The Stones were due to start that year's European tour, which meant Keith must face the heartbroken Brian.

Despite finding Harley House full of sad ghosts, Marianne enjoyed those first months with Mick—the halcyon days before she zonked out on pills while he climbed the social register. They spent hours in bed engulfed by her books—Rimbaud, Eliphas Levi, and Aleister Crowley—and he'd listen raptly to her ramblings on Symbolism, Zoroastrianism, or *The Secret of the Golden Flower*.

Those were the days when everything happened in bed—and most of it wasn't sex. That was how you entertained—guests would pile into your pillows, smoke hash or drop acid, then bask in the rosy glow of your scarf-draped lamps. You might roll over a pen, a tin of Tiger Balm, or a dusty-soled slipper in tattered pink satin. Velveteen frock coats would be spread over the coverlet, along with Marianne's fairy books with those lavish Victorian watercolors—goblins, selkies, and undines, mossy glens where ancient trees guided lost maidens. It was almost as if the drugs were an excuse for unbridled whimsy—lute strumming, dream analyzing, all while leafing through picture books by Rackham and Dulac.

Marianne didn't mind the constant stream of company. Even if she didn't have Mick's full attention, she had his utter devotion. Besides, these weren't the sycophants of later years, seedy hangers-on lured by proximity to fame. People were interested in talking about the past back then; you might find yourself discussing baroque furniture, the Tang dynasty, or Victorian mourning rituals. After a few bottles of wine, the records would come out, and Mick would be shuffling about to Motown, dancing his R&B vaudeville act, shimmying right up in your face ("listen to this one man, knock your socks off"), always Smokey Robinson ("ya gotta hear this track. . . . Please girls, a little reverence for the Godfather of Soul . . .").

This was before hard drugs hit the scene—just acid, grass, and the occasional speed leaper. Mick at his heart was secretly straight—half a joint and one drink was enough for him. Marianne had to push him to let loose and drop acid. What they both loved most was the ritual of it—the pillows would come out, then the records—Ravi Shankar, Otis Redding, *Blonde on Blonde*, obscure Indian ragas.

Marianne loved watching Mick dance. Between flashes of movement, she'd glimpse the real Mick, that pale self he took such pains to hide from the world.

It was always magical times like these when the Small Faces would barge in with their guitars. The spell broke, and the dancing stopped because someone had "dropped by to jam, man."

That spring Marianne landed the part of Irina in *Three Sisters*. Eighteen pounds a week, versus two hundred and fifty per pop concert. But this is what she always wanted—Chekov, dusty Edwardian costumes, the Old Vic.

To Marianne's astonishment, Mick attended every performance of *Three Sisters*' two-month run. He hadn't taken her acting ambitions seriously at first. If anything, he encouraged it as a hobby, something to keep her busy while he recorded or toured. Yet here he was, making the nightly pilgrimage to Sloane Square, slipping in through the side door, filling her dressing room with orange trees and bottles of Shalimar Eau de Toilette. There was some-thing combative about his sudden interest, the way he'd started reading Shakespeare and Ibsen at Harley House. Was this envy disguised as interest?

Marianne's success made Mick deeply uncomfortable. "I think it touched off something seriously competitive in him and for the first time planted in him the notion that he might want to be an actor as well as a rock performer. Not only was he jealous of the success of my performance, but the fact that I was being acclaimed critically for my acting ability was very upsetting to him, because he had firmly cast me in the role of being his pretty girlfriend who stayed in the house and didn't assert herself. The last thing he wanted was for me to become someone in my own right."

Marianne wasn't Chrissie—he couldn't curate her phone book or "forbid" her male friends. He couldn't get away with that any-more anyway—social norms were changing so fast. But Mick could try to outshine Marianne. Within months, he'd become an actor himself.

May 1967. Against a lineup of Vanessa Redgrave, Jean Shrimp-ton, and Monica Vitti, Anita was hardly the film festival's most popular actress. She was, however, the indisputable Cool Girl of Cannes. While starlets shivered in bikinis for publicity shoots, Anita played on the beach with two leashed setters, bundled in her high-necked poet blouse and twilly scarf. She never preened for the press, though they followed her everywhere—having her hair washed in posh salons, parading down the promenade in trench coat and boots, or trying on chain-mail bibs in local bou-tiques. Officially Anita was there for work, to promote *Mord und Totschlag* and pose for the paparazzi. But she frolicked through

Cannes with her usual insouciance, munching green apples while chain-smoking through interviews, carelessly answering questions, mouth full of fruit and nicotine.

You'd never guess the turmoil brewing under all that nonchalance. In a desperate bid to win her back, Brian had followed Anita to Cannes. As he'd done the soundtrack for *Mord und Totschlag*, they planned to attend the premiere as a couple. But Keith refused to leave her side and flew to the Riviera himself.

They spent the day of her premiere on the Carlton's private beach. In slim trousers and jangle belt, Anita leapt about ordering Aperol spritzers, lighting cigarettes, and hamming it up for the paparazzi. Keith, more smitten than ever, followed her like a page boy, carrying her purse, visually scanning the sand and plastic tables for wallets and trinkets, anything Anita might have left behind. Already he wore her signature skull rings, just as Brian had.

For the sake of the film and both their careers, Anita and Brian put on a unified front, accompanied by mutual friend Stash Klossowski, merrily oblivious and dressed like a troubadour. They stood side by side on the red-carpeted steps of the Palais, flooded by flashbulbs of competing paparazzi. Brian's stock and jabot flounces among the buttoned-up dinner suits, Anita's high-necked nightdress trimmed in broderie anglaise. Covered head to toe in shapeless white, yet somehow more provocative than the shortest minis. She giggled, ruffling the feathers on Stash's pageboy cap. *Mord und Totschlag*—and Anita—were that night's headliner. The pair were given a standing ovation—Anita for her acting, Brian for his soundtrack—and they processed down the stairs toward the VIP seating like two flamboyant monarchs.

The revelry moved to a late-night trattoria—a glittering cavalcade down La Croisette. Andy Warhol was there, so were poet/

photographer Gerard Malanga and French singer Amanda Lear. Surrounded by friends and admirers, Anita laughed, drank pastis, and danced on red-checked tablecloths between plates of Bolognese. It was a wild time. Brian slouched miserably in a booth by Stash. By morning he'd fled the Riviera for Paris.

Anita and Keith were now free to sun themselves on the beach or promenade arm in arm. Keith emerged in his full plumage, embracing his role as Anita's official consort. That evening they made their first public appearance together at the *Privilege* premiere. Decked in skull rings, an India scarf—already borrowing her clothes—Keith walked with a newfound swagger in his step, a proud jauntiness so unlike the shy boy hunching around the grotty Crawdaddy Club. He'd never been public with a girlfriend before—certainly not one as glam as Anita. He'd dealt with crowds and cameras on tour, but the shiny jet set was as foreign as Mars. Yet here he was in Cannes, navigating red carpets and mics like a pro.

Each night, Anita and Keith strutted their way through premieres, in frilly necks and matching fedoras. They walked the Croisette hand in hand, weaving past parasols of hot pink and marigold. It was astonishing how effortlessly he slipped into the role of protective sidekick boyfriend, popping by the *tabac* for cigarettes and newspapers, hailing cabs, or kissing in the sumptuous lobby of the Carlton. The reserved, surly Keith was emboldened to confirm their romance publicly. Not only did he admit to the affair; he was quick to clarify that Anita and Brian had "long been over," and the switch-up had caused no tension within the band. "Brian is kaputt," reported British pop mag *Fabulous*, "and Anita's going out with—hold your breath!—fellow Stone Keith Richards." True to form, the fanzine referred to Pallenberg as "lucky old Anita," jumping from one "dishy Stone" to the next, provoking envy in readers with giddy reports of the couple sunning themselves in glamorous Cannes. Yes, Keith and Anita were officially "going steady," while she and Brian were now "just good friends." These breathless accounts were for teen pop fans, written in the parlance of swooning Beatlemaniacs.

French *Elle* devoted a two-page spread to the couple in its May issue. Keith, more like a backdrop in a plain black sweatshirt, peers furtively from his girlfriend's shoulder. Anita shone in her signature kohl eyes, feathers, and wide-brimmed hat. Her eyes dreamily unfocused, indifferent to the photoshoot, focused on her next adventure.

Far too cool for bougie schedules, they had no particular plans other than dozing off under the Moroccan sun. (A paradox, *Elle* noted, given the couple's habit of cloistering themselves in hotel rooms by day and partying in clubs till dawn.) Keith awaited his June 22 drug sentence, while Anita looked forward to hearing from Alfred Hitchcock, who was eyeing her for his next film. Instead of focusing on her status as a Stones girlfriend or even her career as actress or model, *Elle* painted her as a globe-trotting vagabond, a lover of rock music, desert islands, big cities, and plumed jewelry. What does Anita love most? Her freedom. The title of the piece: "Il faut vivre à tout prix"—"We must live at all costs."

Unlike Brian, whose life resembled one tortured Byronic orgy, Mick was conventional at his core—Swiss bank accounts and Sunday crosswords, with a lust for the upper class. Even that bottle of whiskey stashed in the back of his Ford Zephyr was just for show. Before 1967 the books on his nightstand were only James Bond novels.

All that changed when he met Marianne: "I taught him to open up to a whole new world—theater, dance, pictures, furniture, fabrics, architecture—a whole new world." Nearly every night they were out on the town: club-hopping, gallery openings, the ballet and theater. It was the peak of the London fashion parade, the hipster version of Restoration England. The couple rarely missed a chance to step out in their frippery—toques and top hats, mandarin jackets with braided frog closures, velveteen trousers and cropped paisley boleros, metallic pumps, glittery stockings in pinks and blues.

Mick had never been to the ballet before, so Marianne took him to several performances of *Paradise Lost*. Naturally Mick fell in love with Nureyev, whose stark flamboyant features resembled his own. His sexually charged style inspired Mick's stage antics, and the ballet's shocking finale—Nureyev leaping into a lipstick-red mouth—would appear repeatedly on later Stones tours. Ultimately the red lips became the band's cheeky logo.

When the crush of paparazzi became too overwhelming, they stayed in and paged through books together—Hölderlin, William Blake's *Songs of Innocence*. "With me, he wasn't the repulsive chauvinist that he later became. About women and their place and all that stuff. In the early time, when it was still good, I really felt that we were partners, that we shared feelings and reactions." Mick hung on Marianne's every word—she even got him interested in the history of lace.

Through her Mick met poets and artists in the flesh. When Allen Ginsberg came to town that summer, she immediately invited him to Harley House—Marianne hadn't seen him in ages. Ginsberg perched at the foot of the bed, Marianne and Mick naked under the infamous fur coverlet.

It was times like these Marianne could see Mick's boundaries break before her eyes. Here he was, the loutish playboy chatting naked with a poet seventeen years his senior about the Marquis de Sade, Vietnam, and *Le Mystère des Cathédrales*. He even considered setting Blake's "The Grey Monk" to music. (Ginsberg, who felt a personal calling to turn the rock scene on to early Romantic poetry, would later himself set all of *Songs of Innocence and of Experience* to music.)

"Who could speak more eloquently of our condition than Blake?"

"My thought exactly, Allen," Mick would say, winking cheekily at Marianne.

Heiress Panna Grady threw a party for Ginsberg that summer. Mick and Marianne attended, along with the underground literary scene—objectivist poet Charles Olson and writers like Bill Burroughs, R. P. Blackmur, and Patrick Kavanaugh. Mick huddled up in an alcove with Allen, humoring him and calling him Krishna, festooning himself in giant Shivaite beads.

In an odd way, Mick was his best self around poets. That hard rock ego cracked like a shell around the hidden, the haunted, the esoteric. In these moments Mick seemed his least masculine and mercenary.

That summer all rockers were dreamy and ridiculous. But those balmy nights on Primrose Hill, dropping Owsley acid and tracking ley lines, looking for Blake's "spiritual sun," they really did feel protected and blessed. A coddled dauphin and dauphine, heralding a new era of peace.

For Marianne, it was a season of unfettered adolescence. After a childhood blighted by war and her late teens wrapped up in motherhood and fame, she could finally relax into tender curiosity. And though their playthings were designer clothes, cars, and elegant houses, this period was marked by an innocence rarely associated with the Rolling Stones.

Marianne's happiest memory of that idyllic summer: a day with Mick and Keith touring Castlemartin—one of those Irish rococo homes that resembles a jewelry box or the inside of a seashell. After a ramble round the castle grounds, they found Pinkeen Stream—one of those fairy-tale brooks with mossy banks dotted with pink bog rosemary and bright buttercups. They spent hours there, shaded by laurels, drifting in and out of sleep, lounging about in their glad rags like the merry teen aristocrats who roamed the grounds before them.

Just as the sun was setting, Marianne looked up: "I saw Keith in the middle of the stream with his shoes off, poking about in the stones, looking like an old Gypsy man, in one of his manifestations—as a poacher. And Mick lying there looking as he always did in those days, like a multicolored, medieval boy."

Seven
The Black Queen

Shall I see you tonight, sister, bathed in magic grease?

Marianne Faithfull, "Witches' Song"

ummer 1967. Keith joined Anita in Rome where she was filming *Barbarella*. Writer Terry Southern had convinced director Roger Vadim to cast Anita as Great Tyrant, the Black Queen of Sobo—mostly spell casting, knife play, and lesbian fight scenes.

Anita was thrilled to be back in her old stomping ground, where she'd spent hours at Café Rosati sipping coffee with Fellini. Keith had never spent any real time in Europe before and for the second time that summer found himself following Anita's lead. He held her bags while she fiddled with bottles in jewel-like perfumeries and patiently waited while she tried on mules in boxlike boutiques, negotiating prices in perfect Italian. The paparazzi trailed them constantly—snapped them shopping, leaping into taxies, huddled together over an English newspaper. Anita was nonchalant, while Keith hadn't acquired his coolness yet and couldn't resist flipping the paps the bird.

Each day Anita reported to the Cinecittà, Italy's "Hollywood on the Tiber" and the largest production studio in Europe. Outside the Cinecittà, Rome swung between *dolce vita* glam and explosive avant-garde. Alongside Via Tagliamento's many trendy nightclubs was the legendary Piper, an experimental disco designed by radical Italian architects. The sprawling multimedia venue merged pop art, tech, and music, with multilevel dance platforms and work by Warhol, Rauschenberg, and Anita's ex-boyfriend Mario Schifano. Overhead projectors flashed wildly fractured images, while the Who, the Byrds, and Jimi Hendrix took turns on the stage. Thanks to Anita, they were always ushered straight to a little table crammed with whiskies (Keith), Campari (Anita), metal ice pitchers, and perpetually overflowing Cinzano ashtrays. He'd reach for her hand under the rickety table, while Talitha Getty and Rudolf Nureyev whirled to the beats around them. This sort of conceptual chic was utterly new to Keith, miles away in spirit from the grubby Crawdaddy.

At night she'd hook up with the Living Theatre crowd—an anarchist acting troupe that courted controversy, nudity, and fireworks. Theater directors Judith Malina and Julian Beck were old friends from her New York years; so was Donyale Luna, a supermodel turned actress and fellow provocateur. Like Anita, Donyale loved drugs; hated bras, shoes, and labels; and had been one of Warhol's Factory girls. She was known for crawling pantherlike down catwalks and claimed to any journalist she was "from the Moon, darling!"

The Living Theatre was "hardcore" even for Keith, who watched their nightly street demos in transfixed admiration. The spectral Julian Beck would be brandishing a shovel, while the sinuous Donyale undulated in the streetlights. Others cried out to abolish money and prisons, stripped off their clothes, goading the audience to do the same. At least half of these night shows ended in arrests for indecency, but these actors were activists, and a night in the slammer was part of the show.

Anita went straight from the Cinecittà to these gatherings, rarely bothering to change out of her Black Queen costume. She simply slipped into the mayhem as is, frolicking in her cutout catsuit and wig. One night she was hauled in by the Roman police, who, much to her delight, mistook her for a transvestite. At the station the starstruck *polizia* gawked and fawned and almost seemed willing to let her go. But by now she'd swallowed a whole cube of hash. "I am not Anita," she said haughtily. "I am the Black Queen. You cannot arrest the Black Queen." They locked her into a cell full of trans prostitutes. She let them try on her horned wig and regaled them with stories of Andy Warhol's parties.

Marianne and Mick soon flew down to join them. That summer Marianne was "blissfully happy." Rome was an escape from the Redlands trauma, and Mick was doting on her like a madman. Her divorce from John Dunbar hadn't even been finalized, but Mick was already talking about marriage and children. Prince Stash came along too.

They all lived together in the Villa Medici, with its winding staircases and Renaissance gardens. Terry Southern was a frequent guest, as were Paul and Talitha Getty, who, according to Keith, always had the best hash. They'd wake up at noon, stumble down the Spanish Steps for lunch, then spend the rest of the day lazing around the villa or exploring the lemon-scented gardens.

Anita often spent days in her costume, stomping around the villa in black leather and horns. (Even when she wasn't in costume, her own wardrobe was just the casual version of the Black Queen.) Terry in particular adored Anita's antics and loved to egg her on: "Ah, by my troth," he'd tease, "here comes the Black Queen!" Anita, fully immersed in the role, hardly needed any encouragement. "Darling," she'd purr over breakfast, "sometimes vhen I am at Cinecittà, I really do believe I am the Black Queen." Five hours, a few drinks and a joint later, "But you know vhat? I really am the Black Queen," then in another five hours, "I AM THE QUEEN OF ALL I SURVEY!"

This was Anita at her very best. While she was indulging in hash and the stray line or two of coke, this was not the behavior of a drug-addled woman. She was living her role, basking in the Roman air, the formidable Cinecittà. Marianne understood the need for that level of immersion, especially for someone as intense as Anita, the simple relief of taking a break from being so relentlessly you all the time. Besides, Anita was right—she really *was* the Black Queen ruling over her floating city, suspended in her own heady atmosphere, wrapped in her dream chamber in the deep heart of Sobo, tapping into her subject's hidden thoughts.

Anita, according to Marianne, was "like a wolf, like a cat that got the cream. If you were a man, it must have been very powerful." It certainly was for Marlon Brando, who was zipping around Rome that summer on his motorcycle and kidnapped Anita one evening. When an all-night poetry reading failed to win her over, he tried to seduce Keith and Anita together. (Keith: "Later, pal.")

One day the two couples were strolling around Rome when a swarm of kids suddenly recognized Mick and Keith. The four broke out into a run, Marianne stumbled over the cobblestones in her T-strap heels, Anita was so terrorized she almost had a heart attack.

They reached a dead end with a tiny alley on the right. At the top of the hill was the villa. Stash was waiting, holding open the massive Renaissance door. It clanged shut behind them, and they raced up the marble baroque staircase to the sounds of beating teen fists.

They all dropped acid that night and walked the Medici gardens till dawn. The full moon lit up the Orangerie, bergamot scent of citrus trees. "We all became someone else, we all became characters out of the past." At one point Anita and Marianne saw the ghost of a courtier slinking through the halls, in boots and a frock shirt, whispering, *Nessuno puo trovare l'uscita*: NO ONE CAN FIND THE EXIT.

Within months, things would take a sharp turn for both women. But here in the garden of the Villa Medici, the air was thick with frangipani and lemons, and Anita's Cheshire smile seemed to promise everything in the world.

Eight

Blonde Leather

I felt the silken cord tightening...

Marianne Faithfull

A fter the success of *The Three Sisters*, Marianne hoped to move her acting career on-screen. Back in 1965 she rejected the girlfriend role in *Catch Us If You Can*, a *Hard Day's Night*–style band promotional featuring the Dave Clark Five. She'd sensed that the "too poppy" role would date her, and she was right.

Marianne's screen debut came when she effectively played herself in Jean-Luc Godard's *Made in U.S.A.*, a chic detective film about a private inspector (Anna Karina), searching for her lover's murderer in Atlantic City. Billed as "the girl in the café," she sang a melancholy version of "As Tears Go By." Next, she played Josie in Michael Winner's *I'll Never Forget What's 'Isname*, a fluffy piece of existentialism typical of the sixties, about a disillusioned ad man searching for "meaning" in a giddy blur of miniskirts, mistresses, and Alfa Romeos. Marianne spent most of her screen time nude in a bubble bath, arms and legs just barely concealing her breasts while Winner directed from the toilet seat. The film did bring one distinction, making her the first woman in British cinema to say "fuck" on-screen.

But in the summer of 1967, she found a project that truly appealed to her, a biopic of the journalist Anke-Eve Goldmann, the first woman to cross Europe on a motorcycle—in a one-piece leather racing suit she designed herself. *The Girl on a Motorcycle* would film that fall, and Marianne was delighted to be cast as the lead.

Her enthusiasm is visible in press dinner photos. She glows in her bright blue boa and floaty pastel minidress, wedged between Mick and her costar, the Continental heartthrob Alain Delon. Mick, perhaps displeased to be bumped out of the spotlight, sat in sullen silence, one skinny leg crossed over the other, revealing deliberately mismatched pink and blue socks, while Delon flirted heavily with Marianne. She smiled and chatted with reporters, pausing to pet the little Yorkie who slept on the table. When asked about the film's required nude scenes, Marianne brushed the issue aside. "It's just an additional hazard, really."

Director Jack Cardiff was less interested in Anke's unique story than introducing Delon to the English-speaking market. This wouldn't be a film about a bold and curious woman; this would be another apotheosis of male domination, at the expense of a "slut" on the verge of a breakdown. And who better for the role than

"Miss X" herself—the "girl in the fur skin rug"—the blonde ex–convent girl with a Mars bar up her fanny?

Marianne was about to be used as a pawn.

With Marianne's lead confirmed and Mick's appeal behind them, the pair were ready to celebrate. When Desmond Guinness invited them to Leixlip Castle in County Kildare, Mick jumped at the chance to hobnob with celebrities and chartered another plane to Ireland, this time with Chrissie Gibbs in tow. True to form, they dropped acid the morning of their arrival, just in time for their tour of Castletown House. Marianne in full leather gear, prepping for her *The Girl on a Motorcycle* role, Mick in a cloak with a scarf round his head, looking like a Celtic chieftain.

Marianne and Mick ran around the Leixlip grounds, frolicking with wolfhounds and snapping off branches of sweet chestnut trees. They carried them into the castle with childlike irreverence, stuffing them into the chinoiserie vases that lined the stately parlor.

Their merry mood continued into the evening when Desmond brought them to the handover ball at Kilkenny Castle. Mick arrived in his chieftain cloak and purple velvet trousers, Marianne still sported her zip-up leather catsuit, along with a fringed piano shawl and flowered milkmaid hat. Swaying among the starchy guests, all taffeta and tiaras, they stumbled past Chippendale chairs and bumped into Guinness portraits and original van Dycks. "It was like people from Mars landing among them on this great day," said Christopher Gibbs. The bolder ones inquired (with studied politesse) how they were connected to the family. Marianne and Mick, always at their closest when behaving like children, giggled, heads bent over plates of cake, out of their minds on LSD.

"This very old lady latched on to us: Lady Freda Valentine. She had rotten teeth and one of those hats which has pheasant feathers sticking off it in every direction, getting in people's eyes. We were tripping strongly. The effects had reached their full throttle. Desmond was, of course, in great disgrace for having brought all these raffish disreputables who had nothing to do with the event."

"We had a lot more Irish jaunts," remembered Chrissie Gibbs, "driving about Ireland, staying in fishing hotels on the west coast. It is a quiet, never-never land. In the remote parts of Ireland they did not know who Marianne was." Guinness later took them to meet the Smithwicks, a wealthy family who owned Ireland's oldest operating brewery. "The family were very kind of Irish and Catholic and uptightish," said Gibbs. "And I have this vivid memory of Marianne taking a picture of his Holiness the Pope that was propping something up. She put it on her knee and rolled up an enormous joint in the drawing room. The family did not notice but Mick and I did."

They flew back to Heathrow on August 14, and the airport's cool reception brought them back to reality. Resentment over their drug scandal simmered among the public, and several taxi drivers refused to give them lifts home. The mockery of Marianne had continued after the trial. *Private Eye* dubbed her "Marijuana Faithfull."

They'd been spending lots of time with the Beatles that summer—especially George and Pattie. Marianne loved weekends at their Weybridge home—a cozy little bungalow painted "sparkly psychedelic ice cream colors." They'd sit on cushions in the sunflower garden while Pattie cooked up some delicious vegetarian dish and George served joints and fragrant teas. All visitors were given cans of spray paint and encouraged to add to the bright graffitied house. "Mick and Marianne were here."

In the last week of August, Mick and Marianne joined them for a Transcendental Meditation indoctrination workshop in Bangor, North Wales, led by the maharishi himself. They met George and Pattie at the Paddington train station, along with the rest of the Beatles, Pattie's sister, and a somewhat annoyed Cynthia Lennon, who hoped the workshop might lead John away from drugs (it didn't). Press photographers swarmed around them while the maharishi beamed, assuming the paparazzi were there for him. Cynthia's annoyance turned to tears when John ran ahead and left her behind with their luggage, causing her to miss the train. She ultimately caught up with the group that evening, but the incident cemented in her mind. "John was on the train," she wrote later, "speeding into the future, and I was left behind." Within a year, Marianne would feel the same way.

The dormitory rooms and regulation bunk beds were as humble as the little seaside town of Bangor. They prowled the streets that evening in search of late-night dining, and the only joint open was a little Chinese restaurant. When the bill arrived, they couldn't pay—no one had any cash. The Beatles and the Stones were like the royal family—they didn't have money, they didn't use money. Luckily, George had stashed a twenty-pound note in his sandal (he saved the day, aside from the fact that his foot was on the table).

The introductory lecture was held the next morning. "It was an incongruous mix," remembered Cynthia Lennon. "The Maharishi's regular devotees joined by the psychedelically clad pop-star élite, all sitting cross-legged on the bare wooden floor. Marianne, next to me, whispered that she'd just started her period and did

I have anything with me? Fortunately I did. I liked her: she was sweet and seemed too fragile for the world of drugs and rock."

There's one poignant snapshot from this weekend in Bangor—five young women seated side by side, supposedly listening to the maharishi's lecture. At first glance it's hard to tell one from the other—all fair, all sedate, all rock wives or girlfriends. There is the beautifully bored Jane Asher and beside her an inscrutable Cynthia Lennon. Marianne looks positively Pre-Raphaelite, her crochet shawl and parted lips straight out of Waterhouse. Only Pattie appears to be truly engaged—this wasn't her first meditation workshop.

In the end, the maharishi didn't do much besides giggling a lot and handing out flowers. Marianne was unimpressed. "He reminded me of the sort of guru who might appear in a Beatles movie."

A phone call arrived their last day after breakfast—Brian Epstein had committed suicide.

Marianne was already suspicious of the maharishi because of rumors of fraud, sexual harassment, and a tendency to set off fireworks. But his mercenary reaction to the Beatles' loss horrified her.

"'There was a death in the family. There are many families, there is one family. Brian Epstein has moved on. He doesn't need you anymore and you don't need him. He was like a father to you but now he is gone, and I am your father. I'll look after you all now.' I was appalled."

The vulnerable Beatles would follow their guru to India, but the fine-china-loving Mick had little use for the maharishi's teachings—particularly the nonmaterialism. He stuck to his own version of spirituality—the occasional nap in a teepee he constructed in Olympic Studios. Marianne dabbled in meditation, which she explained to René Pieyns on Belgium's *Tienerklanken* television program.

"It's absurdly natural," she explained, wearing a fur coat and aviator glasses. "It's the same process which makes people want to go out to meet people and dance and be happy. . . . People have forgotten how powerful they are. . . . [T]hey're too conditioned, they've been given so much propaganda over the past two hundred years that they've forgotten the dignity of being human."

London's Summer of Love was too much for Anita, who would rather be looking for UFOs on Highdown Hill than flashing peace signs for a televised lovefest. She was rapidly losing interest in the scene, and as much as she loved acid, she wanted experience, not spectacle. Years later, she still shuddered at the memory of that commercialized, kaleidoscopic summer. "All that psychedelic stuff in England then, honestly, it was disgusting. The maharishi was a dyke from Yorkshire."

Keith thought the maharishi was "full of shit" and followed Anita to Venice for the September film festival. The paparazzi trailed them through the city's maze of canals, and their photos show Keith shadowing her happily, now wearing eyeliner, top hats, and a few stray bangles. Even in chic Venice Anita cut a striking figure, holding court on the terrace of the Lido in a lace blouse and mini, her tanned legs stretched out comfortably in the sun.

By fall, Anita was ready to begin her next film with Terry Southern, the druggie sex romp *Candy*. Once again, Keith followed Anita to Rome for filming. Left to his own devices, Keith would wander the city streets, sometimes getting drunk or high with Anita's foppish friends. He'd later describe this as his "grand tour," but he grew increasingly restless strolling past the fountains and dilapidated villas. He laughed about feeling like a Roman pimp ("send the woman to work, and hang about"), but the joke masked his unease with the position he'd landed in.

This was a role reversal Keith wasn't prepared for. In fact, months before he'd offered Anita £20,000 to decline *Barbarella* and *Candy*. It always seemed to be Anita's moment. Would he end up like Brian, trailing her around in a drugged stupor and collapsing in hospitals in Toulouse?

Shooting for *The Girl on a Motorcycle* also began in autumn, with production locations in Zurich, Heidelberg, and Provence. From day one, Marianne knew that she wouldn't get through filming without copious amounts of hash. Her body was fetishized through the entire film—the slow unzipping of her black leather catsuit, the circus ringmaster lover whipping her clothes to shreds. "I can't wait to get my hands on that," Delon leers, eyeing her character from afar in a bookshop. The bold, formidable Anke was degraded into a comically eroticized woman desperate for the attentions of an abusive man. The entire story was shown through the lens of the male lead, not the point of view of the courageous woman with a passion for journalism. In a simpering act of patronizing misogyny, it's Delon who introduces her to her first Harley-Davidson. Even the bike itself is anthropomorphized, with lingering shots of her straddling the seat, not to mention the cringe-inducing lines—"take me to him, my black pimp." It was all too typical of late sixties sex-kitsch, down to its sickeningly predictable finale, where a kirsch-drunk Marianne crashes into a truck, smashing headfirst through the windshield.

On top of everything else, she was subjected to Delon's smarmy advances, which he continued despite her daily rebuffs. She was stoned on hash for the duration of the shoot, which comes through on-screen in her heavy-lidded gaze. She'd come to regret that numbed-out look, which only made her appear more porny and pliable. Instead of the lead in an art house film, she'd been cast as a pitiful nymphomaniac in superficial smut.

Mick called each night and sent roses every day. He visited the set for a week in Heidelberg, and they walked together through the town, Marianne in a circle skirt and angora sweater, her blonde hair fastened with a black grosgrain bow. Mick wore a dappled frock coat, hand-painted in watercolors by his older brother Chris.

Photographs of the weekend reveal a frolicsome sensuality as they bounced around their suite like a pair of teenage runaways. Mick serenaded Marianne from the bed. Marianne threw blankets, scarves, and dresses around the room. In Heidelberg they weren't the rock princelet and his consort, just rambunctious young lovers reveling in the pleasures of being away from home.

Mick was unaware that she'd started an affair with the American photographer Tony Kent. She'd stopped by his studio for a photoshoot in Paris, where they smoked a couple joints and talked about magic. The smitten Tony then followed her to Heidelberg, where they became lovers during breaks in her rigorous shooting schedule. This whimsical amour was Marianne's idea of "heaven"—and she basked in the glow of their clandestine intimacy: "My relationship with Mick was completely public so I loved my extramarital affairs." They were private—hers and hers alone.

At the end of the shaky year of 1967, Mick and Marianne took their first long trip together and brought Nicholas. First they flew to Barbados. Mick was interested in buying one of those huge old Jacobean mansions. Resorts and rickety mini-planes weren't Marianne's style. She'd brought a bootleg of Dylan's *Basement Tapes*, which she played incessantly, driving Mick crazy with the "too much of nothing" and "the waters of oblivion."

Two weeks later they flew to Rio de Janeiro, where the heat kept them trapped inside their hotel suite, emerging only at night for caviar and champagne. By the pool they befriended American photographer Adger A. Cowans. When he spoke of a "wild place" on the coast north of Rio, they jumped at the chance for an authentic experience.

Their first night in Bahia, they smoked hash and explored. Mick had grown out a shaggy beard for the first time ever and swanned around in white flowy pants. Marianne, in a flower-print Ossie Clark jumpsuit, slung two-year-old Nicholas on her hip, and he played with her lengthening flaxen hair. They wandered into a nearby village, lured by the steady hammer of bongo drums, down narrow streets strung with twinkling lights. They stumbled upon a Candomblé ceremony outside a Portuguese cathedral, lit with brightly colored bulbs, pinks and greens and reds flashing in the night. The crowd erupted in inexplicable anger, but the night proved fruitful for Mick, and the bongo beat found its way into "Sympathy for the Devil."

They settled in a hut by the sea, on the edge of a tropical forest. No beds or cots, just hammocks and romance. Cowans captured these flashes of love in his pictures—eating street-side cotton candy in the back seat of a cab, bathing Nicholas together in tender domesticity. They talked late into the night about politics and art, and Cowans joined the lively conversation. "The energy was high," Cowans remembers. "We all connected on another level—about life and poetry and music. . . . Nobody knew Mick was in Brazil. He wasn't a star there, so we were just cool."

Marianne enjoyed this respite from fame but knew it was fleeting. In her bag she'd stashed a copy of William Burroughs's novel *Naked Lunch*. Was she planning ahead, her heroin-laced escape route? She would not be a high-end junkie like Talitha Getty with "little lines on expensive mirrored tables"; her path would be real oblivion, dirty and ugly in a bombed-out Soho alley, a place where no one could find her.

But for now she was happy. Mick was more communicative than he'd been in months. He was at his best in these hidden, private moments that had nothing to do with being a Rolling Stone, teaching Nicholas to read by the light of the moon, his arm wrapped around him with heartbreaking gentleness.

Near the end of their stay, another festival came along, a women's-only rite for the goddess of the ocean. This time Marianne was invited to participate. Mick found two dozen roses from a local hothouse, which she carried to the beach just before sunset. She tore off the red petals and tossed them into the water, as the chants of the women drifted over the sea.

Nine
My Gypsy Faerie Queen

In a more gracious age, Anita would have been called a witch.

Christopher Gibbs

Anita and Keith closed out 1967 where they began it— Morocco. They rented a house in Marrakech with an overgrown garden full of peacocks and datura flowers tangled up with weeds. When the rain came down, they built fires inside, warding off the cold with hot mint tea and majoun made from hash, spices, and apricot jam.

For Anita, the bulk of 1968 would be lived away from London, as it would for Keith. Long tired of the swinging scene—which had peaked for the couple in 1966—they decamped to Keith's beloved Redlands, his country house in West Sussex. After last year's havoc of police and paparazzi, Keith constructed a massive wall and moat. By dark he could be seen digging furiously with a shovel—a knight protecting his lady.

There they resided, lord and lady of the manor, ensconced by West Wittering's woodlands and wheat fields. The old Tudor hunting lodge with thatched roof and cross timbers looked just as it did when it hosted Henry VIII, with slatted fences, kitchen gardens, and Elizabethan topiaries. Anita filled the inside with rich tapestried rugs and stacked floor-to-ceiling bookshelves with copies of *The Golden Bough*, *The White Goddess*, and *The Tibetan Book of the Dead*.

Like proper country gentry, they surrounded themselves with a menagerie of animals—pheasants, the rat families that nested in the moat's swampy hedgerow, and Keith's beloved dogs—a docile old Labrador named Yorkie; the Great Dane Winston; Bernie, another Lab; and a lively terrier named Ratbag. Later they'd adopt a Scottish deerhound called Syph (Keith: "He looks like he has syphilis"), who flushed out birds and rabbits they served to dinner guests.

As always, Anita reveled in entertaining—Robert Fraser, Stash Klossowski, and Michael Cooper visited frequently. But their guests ranged from visiting musicians to Living Theatre nomads and even Marianne's ex, John Dunbar. They'd canoe round the rat-infested moat, play with the dogs, or try their hand at Keith's latest hobby, archery. (No one was very good, so the arrows would land in the moat, where Keith paddled around fishing them out for hours.) Afternoons they'd spend fishing in the rushes, wading through the lower meadows knee-deep in tussock grass, Anita in leather fringe and Daniel Boone boots, bucket of bait dangling from a stick flung over her shoulder, which Keith steadied with his hands as he marched on behind her. They'd often walk the two miles to West Wittering beach, past silver dunes and craggy lagoons, puppyish harbor seals, and brent geese on holiday from Siberia.

Geographically, West Wittering was tailor-made for Anita's burgeoning interest in megalithic history. Like many other late-sixties hipsters, she read deep in the texts of John Michell, who wrote of England's ley lines, stone circles, and their connection to UFOs. The rich history of the South Downs was the perfect playground for prehistoric fantasies, with Saint Roche's plague chapel, the Long Man of Wilmington, and the nearby Trundle Hill—an Iron Age hillfort you could climb at dusk to spot flying saucers and twinkling fairy huts.

That March, Anita hosted Tony Foutz and Sam Shepard while they wrote the screenplay of an experimental film. Gradually, the themes revolved more and more around Anita's obsessions—UFOs, esoteric rituals, desert wanderings, and magic. The more time they spent in Anita's sparkling wake, the more they absorbed her potent energy, and the script shimmered with her Mad Hatter riddles and deft turns of phrase. Eventually, they wrote Anita into the story as an extraterrestrial ninja assassin clad in buskins and beads.

"She was great," recalls Tony today. "She could have stood on her own as an actress because she had the charisma, she had a bit of wildness in her, she had a real presence on camera and a real nonchalance too. She had this natural joie de vivre intensity—real intensity, not manic, but an intensity of spirit. . . . She had a very unique quality and a smile that would have stopped a Trojan horse."

Anita was as comfortable in vinyl as she was in gypsy rags and as believable in a spaceship as she was in a stone circle. Like so many trendsetters, she was less interested in the present than she was the future and the past. "I have a quality that I can look very deep into things," she explained to A. E. Hotchner in her late forties. "I mean I can see through things and see what is beyond them. That is because I have a very old soul from another time that entered my body and lives in me."

Under Anita's influence, the Stones embarked on a journey into Celtic history. Her friend Sir Mark Palmer dropped his posh London lifestyle to wander the West Country in a gypsy painted caravan, and Anita began to join his jaunts to Tintagel, Avebury, and Dozmary Pool.

Planning these adventures was half the fun. First you got the acid (easy enough), then someone had to get the van, and then you mapped out the itinerary. Glastonbury, the Devil's Footprints, and the White Horse on the Downs were all popular destinations, and Anita was always up for an outing that involved Iron Age monuments and possible UFOs. "You'd be in your satin miniskirt out in the middle of nowhere," she mused years later.

One Stonehenge expedition was immortalized in photos by Michael Cooper. After a raucous Byrds concert at Covent Garden's Middle Earth, Mick, Marianne, Anita and Keith, Michael Cooper, and Chrissie Gibbs squeezed into Blue Lena and took off at two in the morning for a megalith trip. In an effort to approach Stonehenge with appropriate reverence, they parked in Wilsford and walked the long track east toward the prehistoric monument, as the sun rose slowly over the Salisbury Plain.

You could touch the stones back then, lean against them, even climb them. Anita, wrapped in marmalade fur and her widest fedora, gestured at the sarsens and trilithons, chunky rings flashing on her fingers. Mick and Keith looked like hip young cathbads, stalking the rocks in embroidered cloaks.

Marianne huddled between the stones like some gorgeous ancient owl, bundled in scarves and a Moroccan black caftan, her pale face veiled by ebony lace. "Michael Cooper took a very spooky picture of me that day. . . . The strange thing about this photo is it's of something that hadn't happened to me yet. There I am as the shady lady I wound up as. That was what was coming. The card had appeared in the deck. And I went right with it. To go to the bottom of the ocean and not drown."

While Keith and Anita busied themselves at Redlands, Mick bought a townhouse on Cheyne Walk in Kensington, with original Queen Anne dark-paneled rooms and balustrades and three original fireplaces. Marianne loved that it had "wonderful wobbly floors and a crooked staircase." She painted the walls varying shades of pistachios, pinks, and pastel blues. London townhouse meets Tiepolo fantasy sky.

Decorating Cheyne Walk was a real thrill, and her elegant whimsy matched the original tone of the house. Marianne would never dream of wall-to-wall carpeting—an assortment of oriental rugs would do. She adored antique shopping—in fact, that was one of her greatest shared pleasures with Mick. They bought lavish chandeliers and an original Louis Quinze bath. Mick was still granting her every whim in those days. The antiques, carpets, and velvets provided a theatrical backdrop, and they played like children, ducking in and out of floor-length festoon curtains.

The only piece she disliked was the gigantic king-size bed. "What in god's name is that," she said when Mick brought home the monstrosity. Why not a lovely old four-poster? Besides, weren't king-size beds for "fat American couples"? For Marianne, it wasn't just ugly ("a bloody battleship"), it was ominous—the sort of bed in fairy tales that leads to gruesome ends. "It might be said that it was this bed that began the decline of the drug-drenched Duchy of Chelsea."

Nicholas came to live with them, and Mick was every bit the devoted stepfather. He was still talking to Marianne about marriage, and though she declined, his confidence in their relationship was warmly reassuring. The first two months of 1968 blew by in a brief but happy flutter of domesticity. They'd go on book-buying binges at Watkins on Charing Cross Road, then spend the weekend in bed swathed in newspapers, magazines, copies of Baudelaire's *Les fleurs du mal* or Ray Bradbury's *The Illustrated Man*. "Marianne, take a look at this," Mick would call out. "It'll knock yer socks off!" Perhaps this is what she'd been missing with John Dunbar—the books, the quiet weekends, and space for mutual dreams. In a way, their life together seemed blessed.

Cheyne Walk was a space of creativity for Mick, who after a year of turmoil turned back to songwriting. Marianne wasn't just his girlfriend, she was his creative partner. "One of the things Mick liked about me was the way we discussed his ideas for songs. . . . I was more educated than he was. I was very good with words. And when Mick was working on the words for a song, he'd go over them with me."

When Marianne lent him her copy of *The Master and Margarita*, Mick latched on to the book's apocalyptic themes—Satan, revolution, the meaning of good and evil—and harnessed them into his hit single "Sympathy for the Devil." Mick's attraction to Bulgakov's novel had nothing to do with Satanism—he was simply drawn to the devil's charisma. ("Mick as the disciple of Satan?! A devotee of satin, perhaps!") But hungry Stones fans ate the imagery right up. "Sympathy for the Devil" matched the darkness of 1968, and Mick became their Lucifer.

"I think that Mick did some of his best work, really, in the period we were together," Marianne observed years later. In 1968 she still enjoyed collaborating with Mick, working on his songs, showing him books and discussing new ways of thinking, going over lyrics like they were poems. His songs seemed so much more important than her pop songs—songs she didn't even write. "It made me feel that I was doing something very creative, in a way. It's a funny thing, that. I think women can slip into that. Living through a man. Letting somebody use them and not thinking that it's at all strange."

At the time she didn't question getting credit for her work. Royalties? What about her own creative path? Was it languishing? Years later she read about Zelda Fitzgerald. The wildness, the ballet slippers, the awful death by fire. Undervalued, unrecognized, then locked in an asylum. There was something familiar about this kind of feminine tragedy, something that resonated deeply within her.

"I identified with Zelda," she explained to A. E. Hotchner. "Now I think it's very odd that I put myself at his disposal like that. . . . They use the life around them for their subject matter. And if you're living with someone who writes, your life will be used. They're going to feed off you. I eventually hated that, but at first I liked it, I enjoyed it. . . . I accepted my role, although I was very jealous as well. But I tried not to show it—in the sixties it was very important to be cool. If you died in the attempt, you could at least have it on your gravestone: 'She Kept Her Cool.'"

With their social life still humming, Mick and Marianne spent far more time in London than the Stargroves, the country manor in West Sussex Mick had recently purchased. They went to the Hatchet Club, the Mangrove, and the Baghdad House on Fulham Road, where you could smoke hash in curtained booths, eat tagine, and listen to chromatic maqam music. Out on the party circuit they met and bonded with another hip young couple—James Fox (actor and son of Marianne's agent) and his girlfriend Andee Cohen—an "unrepentant bohemian."

Marianne loved Andee at once—her obsessions with the Tang dynasty and the court of Louis I, the "profound, preposterous" observations she'd blurt out randomly at dinner. James and Mick held each other in mutual fascination. "Mick always had a thing for upper-class folk, especially when he suspected they might enjoy a guided tour of rock slumming."

James and Andee started dropping by Cheyne Walk to smoke hash, discuss Carlos Castaneda, and drink Mick's expensive Bordeaux. The night might end with a platonic pileup in Mick's gargantuan bed. However innocent, these shenanigans always left James Fox somewhat flustered, which only encouraged Mick's affable teasing: "'Ello, James, you're late for the orgy again. What's your excuse this time?"

Mick loved throwing James off-kilter. Sometimes Mick would pull Andee into a broom closet. "Excuse us," he'd say, winking at James, "we have some very private business we urgently need to attend to." It was all light and fun. Mick's androgyny gave him an edge—he was somehow less threatening than a rugby-playing brute. And when there was a ménage à trois, Marianne was the instigator, pulling Andee onto the bed while the men sat and watched. Aided by acid, the women imagined themselves as "two odalisques in a Beaux Arts painting of harem girls." As usual, Marianne was motivated by art, not eroticism.

Marianne was amused by Mick's flirting with women—and men for that matter. Not that she minded, it was just part of Mick's very English way. They were rarely alone in 1968—always at receptions or launch parties or industry events, surrounded by a throng of admirers, all beautiful, dazzling, scintillating, all in love with Mick. "Living with Mick I learned early on to disregard myself as a sexual entity. He was the sex object. To everybody!" Not that she wanted to be objectified, and the "angel with big tits" days were hopefully well behind her. But this was a different kind of fame, something more akin to worship. Mick wasn't forced into boxes or judged. He wasn't denied power. Now she felt erased. "To feel all that charge and to know it mustn't come from you is a funny thing for a woman."

Robert was out of prison and throwing parties again. She'd been comfortable last year in his intimate milieu, but now the scene had exploded. Now everything was about status and celebrity. Unlike Mick, she was never impressed by star power or pedigree. She didn't need a nod from Tony Curtis to enjoy a chat with Bill Burroughs—she'd known the Beats personally for years. Besides, "it was very cool not to say much," Marianne reflected years later. She used to love going to Robert's—for the lively conversations on esoteric subjects and experimental art, but now no one seemed to say anything at all.

Marianne felt stifled by the shifting social tenor. The echelons they moved in rose higher and higher, but all this surface lightness was unbearable. Even their own parties at Cheyne Walk were changing. Their guests more and more illustrious, much to Mick's delight, and now included prize-winning writers, producers, and even politicians. But the vibe had changed from collective, open experiencing to showing off by reticence. On one occasion Harold Pinter stood up to bop around to a record he liked, prompting Mia Farrow to hush him—"it wasn't cool to dance at Mick's."

Most disturbing was Mick's essential detachment. All of this might have been bearable had she and Mick had those moments of connection, but his evasion of intimacy was near pathological. All the things he gave her—orange trees, crystal chandeliers, Louis Quinze bathtubs—only highlighted what was painfully missing. "Mick was giving of things," she said, "especially in the beginning, but there was no giving of himself."

You can't give yourself when you don't know yourself, and Mick seemed to actively avoid introspection. Despite last year's efforts of introducing him to poets and plays and the ballet and opera—and despite the fact that he'd enjoyed them—Mick's interest in this new world was transitory. His shallowness kept him from investing himself emotionally in any artistic experience. "Mick had very little insight about himself. I often heard him say that he'd rather not know what he's like. 'I am what I am,' he used to say, 'and everything just happens, doesn't it? So I let things happen to me and then react.' That's just the way Mick is." Even his interest in drugs was superficial. "He's always pretended that he's been into drugs like everyone else. It's a sham." He paid lip service to the psychedelic movement, especially when the press was nearby: "It's hard to get through the day, man, when you've let go of your ego."

But Mick was all ego, all the time. The way he, like John Lennon, avoided being alone with himself or even with Marianne by filling every minute of the day with business meetings, press interviews, public appearances, and parties parties parties, eliminating any chance for real connection. Last year it felt like she was leading the way—and she often was—photos of their '67 exploits often show Marianne a few steps ahead, and Mick lurking behind her, eager, almost boyish. Now it was Mick in front, grabbing her hand as they dashed out of a cab or ducked into Harrods. Mick in purple velvet pants holding her hand as he's about to hop on a chartered helicopter, her in a tapestry mini and bolero jacket. Marianne dragged around like a prop. Dragged around in a life that wasn't hers.

It was a life many women might have envied—the glamour, the houses, the chartered helicopters. But it was all about Mick's wishes and whims. "If he was in the country, he wanted to be in the city. If he was in the city, he wanted to be in the country. And this restless ambivalence made you feel rather strange if you were in a relationship with him."

As Marianne's loneliness took hold and grew, so did their image as a couple. Magazine editors begged for interviews, teen kids of dukes and duchesses showered them with invitations. They were courted by bankers, stockbrokers, and real estate tycoons. Designers begged them to wear their pantsuits, snakeskin boots, Afghan coats, and smoking jackets.

If Mick seemed to thrive under the spotlight, it's because he'd been preparing for this his entire life. "He instinctively knew how to deal with fame," remembered older brother Chris. "He had thought about it so much when he was poor, how he would act, what he would do when he became famous, that he was prepared for it." But Marianne hadn't dreamed of this, a life whose reality only took place in the media.

She dreamed of rabbits and hedgehogs and haunted cottages in Shropshire. She found the house of her dreams near Wales, with a trout stream, backlit from behind three mountains. Instead, Mick purchased Stargroves. Marianne planted a garden in the shape of four diamonds—two diamonds of red roses, two of white—which resembled the Queen of Hearts' flowerbed in *Alice in Wonderland*. Somewhere down the rabbit hole her dream had turned into a nightmare. Marianne was desperate to get back home.

Unhappy with the bimbo roles of 1967, Marianne took a role in Edward Bond's *Early Morning*, an experimental satire to be held at the Royal Court. The play was a mockery of establishment figures: Marianne was Florence Nightingale having a lesbian relationship with Queen Victoria. Princes Arthur and George are conjoined twins. It went beyond irreverence into the gruesome with cannibalistic orgies and firing squads.

Marianne knew what she was doing when she accepted the role—Bond's last play included a barbaric mob stoning a baby to death in its pram. This nauseating horror didn't appeal to her— she wanted Ibsen and Strindberg and Christopher Marlowe. Taking on this role was a desperate attempt to shake off the sexual stigma of *The Girl on a Motorcycle*.

Early Morning opened and closed the same day. Undercover police and members of the vice squad infiltrated the audience, pressuring the director and theater management to shut down production. Even the audience slinked out the side door, disgraced by association. It was reviewed in the *Times* as "unspeakably horrible . . . a nightmare dreamt by an overheated child."

Artistic director William Gaskill got exactly what he wanted. The play's controversy made him a momentary cause célèbre. Casting Marianne was calculated to appeal to the youthquake generation and boost his reputation amongst the rock rebel scene. She'd just been used again.

By mid-1968, Marianne seemed to be caught in some wretched cycle. She did *The Girl on a Motorcycle* to explore new artistic territory. But instead she was reduced to a helpless nymphomaniac. She was used by Mick to refine his image as elegant and cultured, used by Andrew Oldham as the "angel with big tits." Gaskill used her cultural capital to promote his own audacious hipness. All these images had been forced on her by corporate men—Mick, Decca, Oldham, Jack Cardiff, the local press, and even Scotland Yard. All of them dehumanizing, none of them really her.

Around the time of the play fiasco, Marianne agreed to appear on the BBC TV program *Personal Choice*. She relaxed into her chair as if she were with friends, crossing and uncrossing her legs, boot perched on one knee, pausing to drag on a cigarette, and leaning back on the doily-strewn upholstery. Even before she spoke, it was clear she wasn't going to spout out the perky, canned responses much beloved by publicists. Marianne was utterly candid.

First came the disclaimer, "I never wanted to talk about drugs in public because I don't want to influence anybody." She admitted to experimenting "like everybody else but not because of everybody else," called marijuana "harmless," and made some goofy remarks about LSD ("if it wasn't meant to happen, it wouldn't have been invented"). But she stopped at promoting it as a lifestyle; rather she suggested taking it one or two times to induce self-improvement. "I know so many people that before they took LSD they were such a drag, and then they took LSD. And they really opened up. And then of their own accord they stopped. Nearly everybody has stopped taking LSD. I've stopped, yeah."

She actually said, which many conveniently misheard, "It's not groovy to take it [marijuana] because it's not groovy to take anything. We should be able to be in a state where we don't need cigarettes or drink or anything like that or marijuana."

"Oh, I love death," she said breezily when asked about mortality. "It's very important to stay in the world and do things, but on the other hand, death and dreams are another thing." Murky and Keatsian, ode to a nightingale. "I'd like to go off there . . ." she drifted, nestling back in the fluffy white fur. "Off into death. I think it's a beautiful thing—just imagine if there wasn't any death."

"But you can't do that," she added hastily. "It's very wrong to make your own death."

However silly and trendy, however muddled, Marianne was promoting the opposite of suicide and drug use.

Besides, Marianne was totally genuine. She'd been romanticizing death since her convent days, roaming round the track pitch with school chums, discussing their own tubercular rock stars, the nineteenth-century poets Percy Shelley and John Keats. Why pretend otherwise?

Not everyone appreciated Marianne's frankness. Chris Reynolds of the *Evening Standard*, her hometown newspaper, ranted in his "Open Letter to Marianne Faithfull," "But, really love, you talked absolute nonsense. About marriage and children. And about drugs. Especially drugs, this was a little boy you were talking about, Marianne. A defenseless little child. I wonder if your mother, to whom you referred to as living in a tiny terraced house in Reading, felt proud of you. I didn't. Grow up, Marianne, or shut up."

An old school chum wrote in Marianne's defense, touching on her youthful openness. Chrissie Gibbs also chalked it up to Marianne's age, that her naivete and guilelessness led her into social quagmires. "I think when you are very young," he said, "your emotional life and sensual life is very confused, and she was kind of wanton." But there was something more at play here than youth: gender.

While Marianne was being publicly admonished, Mick was being hailed as the spokesman of a generation. He was listened to, not questioned—despite the debacle of last year's arrest. No one ever asked whether his mother was proud. No one told him to "grow up or shut up."

By that same year, Brian had racked up multiple arrests, drug charges, and overdoses, along with four different children from four different women, none of whom he nurtured, cared for, or financially supported. In fact, Linda Lawrence was reduced to filing in court for child support. While this infuriated parents and led to bad publicity, it didn't degrade him in any way.

"Another casualty of Redlands was my mother. It was after all the scandal that things began to fall apart for her. She started drinking heavily. She stopped showing up for work. She rarely went out of the house. She was ashamed about the Mars bar gossip and the girl in the fur rug stories in the papers."

Marianne was pregnant again. One year later, the consequences of the drug bust were becoming visible.

Ten

The Sixth Stone

I feel as though I'm rather like the sixth Rolling Stone.

Anita Pallenberg

eanwhile, Anita's acting career was faring much better. Offers poured in, and in May she flew to Slovakia for *Der Rebell*, another film with Volker Schlöndorff. Based on the novella *Michael Kohlhass*, this was a historical piece set in sixteenth-century Saxony about a merchant's social justice crusade. Anita played Katrina, a surly pipe-smoking prostitute who hung around rebel encampments razzing up the men. Filmed on the outskirts of Bratislava, the set lacked the avant-garde urbanism of *Barbarella*'s Rome. But the dirt roads, thatched-roof cottages, and ramshackle huts suited Anita just fine. She picnicked in the mud, played with the horses, and clowned around in the hay with Volker, who was thrilled to be working with her again. The film had a revolutionary spirit to it, and that came across in her performance.

"I was just blown over by her," remembered Anita's costar Anthony May. "It was mainly because of her attitude to life. She was just totally outrageous. She didn't care. She was like a real free spirit. . . . I do remember her arriving at a hotel and she was smoking a joint through a pipe. This sort of thing hadn't really hit Czechoslovakia, so nobody really knew what it was."

Whether touring with the Stones, jetting off to Paris for modeling gigs, or sprucing up Keith's Redlands estate, Anita could make any environment her own, however temporary it may have been. This time she turned her hotel suite into a veritable "Marrakech tavern" complete with a hookah pipe, clouds of incense, and silks from Morocco strewn on the bed. By her pillow, a postcard reading, "I love you—Keith."

The day Keith flew in to visit, they were filming in an old Bavarian castle, a moated fortress of heavy white limestone. "She came up to me," remembered Anthony, "and said, 'Keith's arriving in a minute.' As the Rolling Stones were my favorite band, I was very excited. We were quite high up in this castle and we saw this black car arriving and she said, 'Ah, I think this must be him,' and she ran down to greet him. As the chauffeur got out of the car, he walked around, opened the passenger door and Keith fell out into the mud. He eventually came into the castle and he said, 'Leave us alone,' and this was about nine in the morning. He passed out and they couldn't even wake him up at 5 p.m. We didn't see him or Anita for three days!"

Aside from drunken games of late-night poker, there wasn't much for Keith to do in rural Slovakia. When Volker invited him to join in as an extra, he jumped at the chance, donning a doublet and breeches, brandishing a sword with his pirate panache. From that point on, he was often seen ambling around the set sipping a Coke, trying on petticoats, or kicking around tents full of re-production crockery. Between takes Anita joined him, and they'd sprawl out in the hay with magazines and a joint. They looked like a pair of Bavarian nomads, him in embroidered poet sleeves from Chelsea antiques, her in a sackcloth farthingale, brushing her hair in the sun.

The whole aesthetic of the set—the rugged feudalism, the scruffily attractive extras lounging in groups on bales of hay—matched the ethos of late-sixties haute Bohemia. Rustic, ar-chaic, handwoven fibers, patchwork, variegated textures coarse and sheer, draping, loose strings, stray beads, and heavy-looking belts. All the actors looked oddly contemporary, the women in their gauzy smocks and wooden Dutch clogs, the men in ani-mal skins, facial hair, and occasionally tights. But even allowing for the breezy anachronism of mid-century period filmmaking, Anita's ensembles would have been more at home at Woodstock than sixteenth-century Flanders. Fold-over boots and brocade mantles, burlap vests over flimsy chemises, buckles, feather pelts, and plenty of fringe. She snuck in treasures from her own eclec-tic wardrobe, velveteen toques festooned with plumage, a rust-colored crop top of hand-dyed Moroccan wool, the same calf-high buskins she wore traipsing around Redlands. At times one couldn't tell whether she was costumed at all. One especially compelling outfit—a skimpy white bodice of cotton crochet worn with mac-ramé bracelets and ropes of metal chain mail wound tightly round her neck. She topped off the look with a necklace of her own—chunky beads and animal teeth on a black leather cord. Was this her own folkloric take on S&M party gear? Whatever it was, the look was pure Anita.

It helped, of course, that Katrina was just the cheeky sort of imp you'd find scampering around a music festival or following the Grateful Dead. But that was the thing about Anita's acting approach—she chose films for the pleasure factor. The wild Dutch hooker sporting bugle beads and feathers, the whip-cracking intergalactic queen in *Barbarella*, the modish sadism of Nurse Bullock in *Candy*, the cool-cat heartbreaker in *Mord und Totschlag*, all contain more than a bit of Anita herself or at least offered the chance to flex the more outlandish sides of her personality. She was totally uninterested in accolades, nor would she take on a dull but challenging role just to push herself or prove her acting prowess.

Filming was fun for Anita, another experience to explore and indulge in. She threw herself into her roles, which isn't the same as taking them seriously. (Just how seriously can you take a horned dominatrix who presides over a planet named Sobo?) It was all imagination, all the time, like a child dressing up as her favorite storybook heroine. The results were consistently fabulous. Anita's acting career is a glorious example of creative play triumphing over serious meditations on "craft." For Anita, living was her craft, and she did it exceptionally well.

Back in England, Anita and Keith continued their country life. They'd be seen in London now and then—at a launch party for Sir Palmer's new clothing line or stumbling around Piccadilly after the *Yellow Submarine* premiere—but stayed firmly ensconced in the nest of West Wittering. Besides, they didn't need to venture out since everyone who was anyone came to them. When Gram Parsons defected from the Byrds mid-tour, it was Redlands that became his second home. Keith took him in like a "long-lost brother," and they whiled away the summer strumming Everly Brothers harmonies or loafing around in the hammock with bottles of Rebel Yell. Wary neighbors spotted them skipping through the meadow holding hands, nails painted matching hemlock green.

Men always seemed to transform around Anita. Like Brian before him, Keith turned androgynous yet somehow more potently sexual. He'd been borrowing her clothes since the previous summer—skinny scarves, velveteen trousers, leopard coats, and bangles. Now something new was emerging—an aura of brooding malevolence—headbands, black eyeliner, spiky bracelets, and talismanic pendants. "Look at pictures of Keith before and after Anita," wrote rock journalist Rob Sheffield. "It's like the difference between Buddy Holly and Jack the Ripper."

Anita had practically destroyed Brian, but Keith bloomed in her orbit: "Keith was really a shy little guy in those days, couldn't come out of himself. And I had all this kind of Italian energy and outgoing personality, so it was really easy for me. And somehow it finally came out. He started to write songs and sing them himself. . . . I thought it was wonderful."

Keith and Anita's bond was tightening. Their dynamic even hinted at some sacred sort of pact—mystical and unbreakable, set in Neolithic rock. That summer she started commissioning jewelry, pieces specially designed for Keith by the art student David Court. "I started making jewelry for Keith through Anita. I made a skull pin, which was this carved skull with a bishop's miter of white and yellow gold with sapphires, rubies, and diamonds set in it. It was rather unusual and she said, 'Great, we'll have it for Keith and engrave on it "The Bishop of Rock and Roll."'"

Keith was coming into his own, now delving deep into his creative self. He no longer clung to Brian or Mick. He built a studio on the grounds of Redlands and began experimenting alone. Anita gave him the psychic space to think and create—and now he was laying down the bones of their next album. Keith hated the trendy psychedelia of last year's *Satanic Majesties* ("mostly shit") and was eager to move on.

Their Satanic Majesties Request was an ill-conceived flop—a flabby knockoff of the Beatles' *Sgt Pepper's*. Thanks to Anita, Keith tapped into something that would keep the band fresher and more relevant than their flower-child peers. "Jumpin' Jack Flash," which Keith wrote at Redlands, came out on May 24, 1968, with a promotional film featuring the band in necromantic makeup and gothic gear, most of which belonged to Anita. Keith wore black nail polish on the cover jacket, Anita's skull rings flashing on his fingers.

The single topped both British and American charts and airwaves. The Stones were in danger of losing their voice until Anita shone her "evil glamour" on them like the pythoness of Delphi.

It was around this time, during the creation of *Beggars Banquet*, that Anita was referred to as "the sixth Stone." She immersed them in her occult interests, her funny little rituals with runes and herbs, and the works of Aleister Crowley. They drank Anita's brew of shock and creativity and even co-opted her renegade swagger. Mick imitated her strut, Keith her signature scowl—the one that made him famous for decades. Some black magic was happening. She was reworking their destiny.

Though he resented her at first, Mick appreciated how Anita refreshed and galvanized the band. He started to pay more attention to her and even sought out her approval. Offering musical criticism to Mick, "I'd always tell him, and to my amazement he would listen," she reflected years later. "He never listened to anyone else—all those yes men. I called them shampoo people—guys with three-piece suits and curls."

Stones lackey Tony Sanchez wrote at length about Mick's need for Anita's approval: "Mick seemed to delight in Anita's sharp mind, her vicious streak that made her somehow very different from Marianne. For a while she seemed to dominate him with the same, almost supernatural hold she had over Brian and Keith. Once I heard Anita listen to a tape of 'Stray Cat Blues' as Jagger patiently waited for her to tell him (as all the other lackeys had done) how brilliant it was. 'Crap,' she said when it had finished. 'The vocals are mixed too high, and the bass isn't loud enough.' Mick, with the basic insecurity of every creative artist, was so unused to hearing someone dare criticize his work that he at once went back to the studio and had the number remixed."

In June the Stones starred in Jean-Luc Godard's new-wave documentary *Sympathy for the Devil*. Godard hung around Olympic Studios for the song's recording sessions, filming Brian, Mick, and Keith in various modes of concentration, stubbing out each other's cigarettes and scuffling over technique. But the real star is Anita, sauntering into the shot ten minutes from the end, draped in a mohair throw and dazzling as ever. She swayed to the music like the beat was in her bones, singing backup at the microphone, kissing Keith on the cheek. (It's her voice you hear at the "woo, woo" refrain—as well as Marianne Faithfull's and the band's.) By the time they finished recording *Beggars Banquet*, Anita wielded just as much power as any member of the band.

Anita saved the Stones from slipping into oblivion. *Beggars Banquet* would set off the legendary four-album run that cemented their status as the greatest rock band in the world. Mick and Keith would rise to fame as rock's favorite outlaws, but only under the tutelage of the wicked Anita, who taught them to embrace evil as a subject.

By July 1968 *Beggars Banquet* was ready for mixing, so Keith and Anita flew to LA. They spent the bulk of their time with Gram Parsons, Tony Foutz, and Phil Kaufman—executive nanny to rock and roll's children. He'd drive them around in his convertible, Keith sprawled out in the back with Gram, Anita wedged up front between Tony and Phil. Phil found Anita "lovely . . . unpretentious—just a nice person" and was happy to chauffeur her around the shops of Rodeo Drive or stand guard by the loo of the Cocoanut Grove while she snorted lines of cocaine.

Once Mick, Marianne, and Michael Cooper arrived, they agreed to make a group pilgrimage to Joshua Tree Park. Gram led the charge—it was his spiritual home after all, and besides he had the best coke ("better than the Mafia," according to Keith).

Aside from the basics—sandwiches, drugs, the requisite serape blankets—they packed up bongo drums, guitars, and telescopes for spotting UFOs.

They set up shop on Cap Rock—a monzonite formation by the San Andreas Fault with a view of the Mojave Desert. Keith tried his hand at shirtless rock climbing. Marianne whirled around the spiky yucca cacti, hair cropped short for her advancing pregnancy, paler and thinner than ever in her frilly sheer blouse. The plan was to stay up all night Stonehenge-style, and thanks to Mandrax, mescaline, and Gram's endless supply of cocaine, that's exactly what they did.

Night fell, the temperature dropped. Anita bundled up in a creamy wrap and Sherpa boots. The sweet musk of creosote bush bloomed out around them, lush and vegetal and heavy with ozone. They built a fire. The moon rose, lighting up the silvery desert holly. That's when the howling started—deep alien sounds that thrilled Marianne. Were they being stalked by spectral beasts, or had they astrally projected to the wolf forests of India? "Why, Marianne," Gram said in his Georgia drawl, "don'ja know that's just a li'l ol' coyote."

The sky turned magnesia blue, then sherbety peach. Keith hunched over his mescaline breakfast and coke, a blanket draped shaman-like over his shoulders. Marianne examined a boulder that had morphed overnight into Sitting Bull. Anita remained at her quartzy perch, for once calm and grave and motionless like some witchy Madonna of the Rocks, eyes fixed on the firmament, looking for flying saucers.

As Marianne's pregnancy advanced, she decided to relocate to the Irish countryside. In August she and Mick traveled there together in hopes of finding an appropriate home. They eventually settled on Bermingham House, near the village of Tuam in County Galway. Mick was thrilled about the pregnancy and hoped for a little girl. They'd name her Corinna, after the sixth-century Greek poet.

Marianne hoped Ireland would bring them closer. The previous summer they'd been so happy romping round Leixlip Castle, and Desmond Guinness had invited them back for another visit. But this Irish jaunt was a pale shadow of the past year's lively togetherness. Instead of frolics round the gardens and acid-laced games of dress-up, Mick played along with upper-class manners, chatting up Slim Aarons while Marianne sat wanly in a shawl. This time Mick *wanted* to hobnob with rich American socialites and Ireland's landed gentry. No giggling together over plates of cake, no inside jokes, no Turkish rugs worn as capes.

By September Mick was on his way back to London. He'd been cast as the lead in an independent film, with Anita playing the supporting role. Marianne wandered the halls of Bermingham House alone, fighting back a sinking feeling she couldn't quite explain. In the throes of a difficult pregnancy, Marianne felt more unloved than ever.

Eleven

Performance

Even before the first day of shooting, *Performance* was a seething cauldron of diabolical ingredients: drugs, incestuous sexual relationships, role reversals, art and life all whipped together into a bitch's brew.

Marianne Faithfull

nita didn't just star in *Performance*—she invented it—from the script to the characters to the concept itself. In the summer of 1966 Brian had been busy with the Stones' American tour, which left Anita free to gallivant around Paris, where she linked up with Deborah Dixon and Donald Cammell. Donald was struggling with a script about a burnt-out rock star and his equally debauched girlfriend, living in the elegant squalor of bohemian London. He'd been idling around with the story for years, and Anita was the inspiration he needed.

For Donald, she was a portal to the world he worshipped—rock stars and the druggie glamour of Chelsea. Then there was her explosive relationship with Brian Jones, whom Donald idolized. "He had all these mad movie scenarios, mostly about rock stars," recalled Anita for author Victoria Balfour. "Donald was really fascinated by the whole pop scene, and he thought these people very sexy and erotic; these young bad boys with loads of money. . . . He was completely star-struck."

She soon found herself living in a creative ménage à trois with Deborah and Donald. After a night of dancing at Chez Castel, they'd drive down to Saint-Tropez in Donald's Alfa Romeo, drink pastis at Cafe Senequier, or spend hours on the beach discussing mirror imagery in Borges. With Anita as his muse, Donald began to write the script in earnest. "Anita had a lot of influence on the way I saw *Performance*," reflected Cammell many years later. She taught him about Francis Bacon, Jean Genet, Vladimir Nabokov, and the cutup techniques of William Burroughs. She introduced him to musicians like the Last Poets, who would later find their way onto the soundtrack. Under Anita's heady influence, they pushed far beyond the usual scripted male chauvinism and sexual stereotypes and broke firmly established boundaries. Themes of gender fluidity and pansexuality occurred and recurred, radical concepts in mid-century England. "I became fascinated with some things that she was already deeply involved in, like Artaud Theatre, Theatre of Cruelty, like she'd worked before with Volker Schlöndorff on her first picture." She spent the rest of the summer with Donald and Deborah, shuttling between Paris and Saint-Tropez, fleshing out the narrative at her leisure.

The process rarely felt like work. Chrissie Gibbs and Robert Fraser would pop over for weekends, and they'd dine out on the balcony. A gathering of creative, rambunctious minds in the same glamorous setting, engaging in the lively exchange of ideas. But they were making real progress. By the summer's end there was a typed draft, which they edited daily on the beach. When the script was blown out to sea one day by a strong gust of wind, Anita ran into the Mediterranean, gathering the papers drifting in the waves. Later at home, she and Deborah salvaged the papers by smoothing them out on Donald's ironing board.

As the writing drew to a close, the girlfriend character began to take Anita's form. Her name was Pherber (a combo of Phoebe and Pilar), and she was far more than a rocker's girlfriend. Pherber was the impetus behind the action, brazen and utterly self-possessed. Anita described her as "very direct, spontaneous, pithy, funny, rather arrogant, ironic more by accident than design, and at the same time elliptical and evasive when it comes to questions about herself—sort of automatically secret." That is, much like Anita herself.

Names were thrown around when the question of casting came up—Tuesday Weld, Loulou de la Falaise, even Mia Farrow, but Donald had Anita in mind the entire time. Whether she knew it or not, she'd been writing a role for herself all along, and things would never be the same.

Two years later Donald was ready to film. Now that Mick emerged as the Stones' apparent leader, Cammell wanted him for the lead. But as much as Mick dreamed of a movie star side gig, he knew nothing about acting and turned to Marianne for help.

Marianne had a vision for Turner as a 1960s Prince Hamlet, magnetic but tragic, a bit feckless but full of menace. But Mick lacked the wounds to access this darkness. Mick was "much too straight, too strong, too together," with his neatly pressed shirts, restrained drug use, and scrupulous bank accounts. (Marianne: "There's nothing truly mythic or tragic about Mick.") First she dyed his hair a strong glossy black. She urged him to channel Brian's gender-bending, drugged-up paranoia with a dash of Keith's "beautiful lawlessness."

Marianne was in the final months of her pregnancy, biding her time in the Irish countryside. Mick spent every other weekend with her, rehearsing his lines at length. At first he looked ridiculous, prancing around with a cloak round his neck, part medieval fop, part Gloria Swanson. "He was playing a role," remembered Chrissie Gibbs, "a slightly kittenish role—somewhat absurd for those who knew him well." But something was happening in that drafty Irish castle. Marianne coached Mick until he *became* Turner, until he was believable, even to Anita. "As for the voice and the way he talked, all lah-de-dah, up in the air, it was like Brian. Brian was always a perfectionist in the way he was talking, choosing his words."

"He did his job very well," wrote Marianne two decades later. "So well in fact he became this hybrid character. What I hadn't anticipated was that Mick, by playing Brian and Keith, would be two people who were extremely attractive to Anita, and who were in turn obsessed with her."

For Anita, filming began how it always did: with Keith begging her to turn down the role, like Brian had before him. Just as he'd done with *Barbarella* and *Candy*, Keith asked Anita how much she'd be paid, then offered to match it if she passed on the role. But this time his reasons were much more complex. He knew the plot, the threesome, and the explicit group sex scenes. At the time he'd heartily approved of the script and found the whole thing "a gas." But it wasn't such a gas now that Anita was cast as Mick's love interest.

Keith feigned a blasé cool with Anita's scandalous antics but was far more traditional than she at heart. He knew she'd been sexually involved with Donald—"a razor-sharp mind poisoned with vitriol" and "the most destructive little turd I ever met."

"Cammell wanted to fuck me up, because he had been with Anita before Deborah Dixon. Clearly he took a delight in the idea that he was screwing things up between us. It was a setup, Mick and Anita playing a couple. . . . He got a hard-on about intimate betrayal, and that's what he was setting up in *Performance*, as much of it as he could engineer."

Keith's terror that he'd lose Anita to someone—or something—blinded him to her need for creative exploration.

To complicate matters further, Anita was pregnant. "I certainly did not want to get married, but I got pregnant," Anita recalled in 2003. "And then because I had to do *Performance*, I had to have a termination to do the film."

Keith couldn't help but see this as a betrayal. For decades, he would view *Performance* as the first crack in his bond with Anita.

Anita began filming on September 2. Donald rented a house on Lowndes Square, suffused with dilapidated grandeur, stuffed with dusty Dutch paintings and forgotten Magrittes. He needed it transformed into "something mysterious and beautiful and unexpected, exotic and voluptuous and far away from pedestrian; some hint of earthly paradise." Chrissie Gibbs threw himself into the task, gathering Persian rugs, exotic tapestries, and seventeenth-century Japanese dishes to tile a spacious octagonal bath. At the center, a sumptuous four-poster bed piled with velvets shipped from Morocco (Chrissie wanted to mimic "The Princess and the Pea").

The décor of Courtfield Road was Donald's other inspiration, and Anita helped furnish the set with artifacts from her own life. For silks she shopped at Chelsea Antiques. Maracas from Brazil, a tapestry from their bedroom, a fur-lined cape that once belonged to Brian. In this way and so many others, *Performance* was Anita, made piece by piece from her very cells—her hash, her records, even the script itself—blessed by Artaud, dipped in Saint-Tropez, still crusted with salt and her Bain de Soleil.

At its core, *Performance* was about discord—male versus female, dreams versus reality, London hood rat versus louche superstar. For maximum friction, he needed them trapped, hermetically sealed *No Exit*–style. Every cranny blocked, all windows cloaked in heavy blackout drapes. Drugs galore, no natural light. Dr. John's "I Walk on Guilded Splinters" playing on repeat. As one camera technician remembered the set: "You took one breath and you were stoned."

With the actors trapped in that insular world, strong personalities would clash and ignite. As a director, his key methods were isolation and disorientation.

"Donald Cammell," Keith claimed years later, "was more interested in manipulation than actual directing." He wasn't wrong. Anita's costar, Michèle "Mouche" Breton, was one of Donald's victims. A vulnerable teen from Brittany's backwaters, Mouche had been banished from home by abusive parents and thrown into the world with a hundred francs.

Young, vulnerable, uneducated, androgynous-looking girls were Donald's "number one obsession," according to an ex-girlfriend, and Mouche had the curveless thin limbs he preferred. Instead of a vulnerable child, Donald saw a potential "sexual catalyst"—the missing ingredient for his film. So he flew her to London, forging a work permit to clear her with Warner Brothers. "Besides," Donald offered by way of justification, "she was already destined for a bad end."

Keith couldn't have anticipated how far Anita would go, all in the name of gory realism. Drug-lacing, coffee-spiking, shooting up on-screen, and an eight-minute sex scene involving Mick, Mouche, and Anita herself. Lit by two enormous spot lamps shining through pink and red scarves, filmed on a 16 mm portable Bolex entirely under the covers. Donald, Nick Roeg, and even the actors themselves took turns filming.

Even for the intrepid Anita, filming *Performance* was "never much fun." Despite seeming like a sensual bacchanal, filming was strained and difficult. "It was an absolute nightmare," said Anita years later. "Donald was a real prima donna—going into fits of fury, screaming, shouting and trying to put all of these mad, deviant, perverted sexual scenarios into the movie. Nick Roeg would spend seven hours lighting one shot. We'd sit huddled together in the basement, shivering, getting stoned and waiting for scenes that we would eventually do maybe 28 times. It was all very, very messy."

Each day the set swarmed with dozens of sweaty men—gofers, PAs, and twenty-five union techs. A camerman peered up the script girl's knickers. Between the constant outtakes and sleazy assistants, the set was anything but sensual. The whole production stank of fetid sex and exploitation.

"It was like a porno shoot," recalled Anita, "and Donald loved it."

To cut the tension, Anita did what she always did on set—throw herself into the role as she had with the Black Queen. Pherber was a puckish, taunting character, always goading the others to act out. "Donald wanted my character to wind everyone else up, which I was more than happy to do."

Anita tormented James Fox, playfully pushing him to take drugs. "He refused to take a mushroom or acid. I kept on taunting him. In the morning when he had some coffee I said I'd put some acid in your coffee. Really childish stuff because I was a brat, you know."

James Fox was the typical elegant Englishman, reserved and a bit of a prude. (Donald had hired some underworld hustler named David to teach him to say "fuck" convincingly.) "I was always pretty scared of Anita Pallenberg; and I remember going with her to the German Food Centre in Knightsbridge for a sausage and thinking, 'This girl is mad and terrifying and this isn't anything I want to be connected with.'" James was already questioning his career as an actor, and filming with Anita would soon push him over the edge.

James wasn't the only one. Mick, for the first time in ages, was insecure. He was used to the spotlight of a stage but out of his depth on an independent film set. After days of shooting he'd return to Marianne, uncharacteristically shaken and feeling somewhat bruised. "He was somewhat cowed by Donald, who had a ferocious temper and would go off like a firecracker, unleashing blistering tirades. Mick found the whole process of filming very bewildering. Compared to performing in a rock 'n' roll band, it was excruciating. The repetition, the retakes, the out-of-sequence performing to thin air. Mick was losing control!"

An unlikely alliance formed between Mick and Anita. This was her world, her craft, her crowd, even, in a way, her script. But Anita had no formal training, and Mick didn't know the first thing about acting. They were both secretly intimidated by James Fox, who was classically educated. "James was such a professional," admitted Anita, "so we were all a bit intimidated by him, so we stuck more together, me and Mick stuck more together, me and Mick against James. James would be studying his script and we'd be walking around smoking joints. Just the opposite. Just to annoy him."

"It was not a harmonious shoot," Anita acknowledged. "But that's what Donald wanted: chaos, paranoia, and grief."

Anita and Mick's rapprochement did not go unnoticed. It wasn't a secret that she was playing his lover. Ex-Stone Ian Stewart occasionally worked on the set and happened to catch their infamous sex scene: "As far as Anita and Mick, I always felt there was no love lost there; they always seemed to be a bit wary of each other, but when the big sex scene of the movie was filmed, instead of simulating sex they got really into each other, and although what wound up in the picture was a lot of vague, tumbling bodies in the sheets, nothing explicit, there was a lot of explicit footage of Mick and Anita really screwing, steamy, lusty stuff."

Keith, as usual, sulked at a distance, holed up on Mount Street with Robert Fraser. Six months in prison had teased out Robert's sinister side. He'd acquired a heroin habit and happily shared his stash with Keith, who moped around listless, tormented by rumors.

Robert fanned the flames, popping by Lowndes Square during filming, then baiting Keith with scandalous tidbits: Mick was taking Anita to the basement for sex, James caught them in the dressing room three days into the shoot, Donald was fucking Anita too, and Mouche had joined in the fun. The two would laze around the flat drinking whiskey while Robert stoked Keith's paranoia. By the time Anita came back from the shooting, both would be drunk and belligerent, snarling, "What did you get up to today?"

"It was very difficult for me," remembered Anita. "Keith and Robert were both so cynical and sarcastic, slagging off the movie every day. I'd come home from filming, and they would be slagging off Jagger, slagging off everything. I was quite confused."

Despite Donald Cammell's standing invitation, Keith refused to enter Lowndes Square. He got drunk alone in the back of his Bentley, scribbling increasingly frantic notes to Anita. Going in would be facing reality, which meant he'd have to acknowledge his hurt, and he loved Anita too much to do that. So he blunted the pain, as he would for the next decade, with heroin and coke, writing love notes in the rain.

Besides, confronting Mick would jeopardize the band. It had already happened with Brian, and he couldn't risk it with Mick. He channeled his rage into their next album and started laying down the bones for *Let It Bleed*.

Rock critic Stanley Booth spent a day with Keith. He flew to London to interview the Stones during one of London's autumn storms, howling winds blowing great gales across the city. He met Keith at the pub, found him downing Bacardi and cokes and rambling on about American blues. "He was heavy-lidded and remote. We had all of our generation fallen in love with singing cowboys in westerns, in our boyhood games we had all—including Keith—pretended to be Roy Rogers, but Keith, it seemed, wasn't pretending."

Later that day Keith slapped down the hook to "Gimme Shelter." It took him twenty minutes.

Marianne understood the song as some wild omen. Their personal lives had synced up to the chaos of the late 1960s. "It turned out to be one of the Stones' most uncanny tappings into the zeitgeist. In *Gimme Shelter*, Keith's mind spun out into a mythical take on where we were all heading."

Despite the challenges, Anita delivered a groundbreaking performance—beautiful, tough, hip, and dangerously sexy, with a vivid sense of liberation and freedom. Her dialogue was illusory, with riddles, a pastiche of literary references, occult incantations, and psychological games. Pherber was the crystallographic axis of *Performance*, just as Anita was for the Stones.

Pherber wasn't the girl who hung on Mick Jagger—she was the girl who slapped a five-pound note on his bum as he climbed out of the bath. "Anita's role in *Performance* remains one of British cinema's most powerful feminist moments. Dominant, assertive, promiscuous, with the whole concept of rock-chick . . . catlike and dangerous. What she brought to *Performance* was not a performance," wrote Germaine Greer, "but herself."

They weren't just making a film about a gangster and a rock star or even a comment on the end of the sixties. They were making a film about their own lives. You could smell the sex and incense, the civet-y raunch of Anita's old fox fur. Look at the iconic bathtub scene—Donald kept the same water sitting in the tub over several days of shooting. Soap scum accumulated amongst bottles of Shalimar bath oil, Hermès Caleche, milk glass dishes, and cans of shaving foam. Stray hairs drifted in the filmy water, along with glossy pink globs of Lustre-Creme shampoo. ("Even the bathwater's dirty," observed one Warner's exec who happened to be visiting the set.) But that was the whole point—unwashed bodies mixed with the scent of unmistakable luxury, amphetamine sweat blunted by notes of bergamot, orris, and rosewood, cigarette smoke freshened by freesia shampoo.

It was this very realism that led to the outraged reception. REPULSIVENESS OF EPIC PROPORTIONS. A PRIME EXAMPLE OF THE LOATHSOME FILM. GRATUITOUS NASTINESS. AND GLORIFICATION OF AMORALITY. Whether Mick and Anita had simulated their scene was beside the point—it looked real because it was real—their real lives, their drugs, their screwed-up relationships. A little too real for the mainstream audience. Yes, she'd cracked a whip and seduced Jane Fonda as the pleathered-up Sapphic Black Queen of Sobo—but this wasn't sparkles and sanitized spaceships and trendy-looking aliens—it was all the messy narcotic confusion of the final months of the sixties, which made it worse.

Warner Brothers flatly refused to release it. There were rumors of orgies, devil worship, of tiny cameras crawling up Anita's vagina. The film went through seven editors in twenty-one months, all to placate public sensibility. The final cut was far from the spirit of the film. In the end, the explicit footage was edited into a separate X-rated short, shown all around Europe, and won a prize at the Amsterdam porn awards in 1969.

Naturally, Marianne was devastated. Despite her shock, she never blamed her friend. "I see Anita as very much a victim of all this, the vulnerable one who should have been looked after and protected. Her breakup with Brian over the previous year had been devastating. It was only natural that she would find Mick's incarnation of Turner irresistible. Their characters were propelled toward each other, and she already had a hard time distinguishing what was real and what was imaginary."

Art had crashed headlong into life, and it was a bloody massacre.

No one made it out unscathed. James Fox turned his back on acting for decades and joined an evangelical Christian group called the Navigators. Even Mick lost sight of his orderly self. He'd been smoking DMT in the dressing room, his own nod to method acting. "I really got into thinking like Turner. I drove everyone a bit crazy, I think, during the time."

Had Mick become Brian, prancing and primping and mincing his way toward a satin-lined crack-up? Or was Keith becoming Brian, spiraling out into drugs and depression—over the very same woman who'd driven Brian mad?

As for Keith, he never stopped blaming Donald for this fracture with Anita. Decades later, ten years happily married to Patti Hansen, Keith bumped into Cammell in LA. "I said, you know, I can't think of anybody, Donald, that's ever got any joy out of you, and I don't know if you've ever got any joy out of yourself. There's nowhere else for you to go, there's nobody. The best thing you can do is take the gentleman's way out."

Two months later, Donald shot himself in the head. He fired the gun at the top of his head, which meant he was conscious for the following forty-five minutes. He asked his wife China to bring him a mirror—he wanted to watch himself die. "Do you see the picture of Borges?" he asked, bleeding out into oblivion.

Twelve
The Devil Unleashed

With Anita, you knew you were taking on a Valkyrie—she who decides to die in battle.

Keith Richards

For Anita, when the film wrapped the affair was over. There was no residual emotional link. "Mick wanted to do another movie with me and for us to be a couple, and other people made offers for us to make films together. But I just didn't want it. Mick just wanted to walk around and show me off like he did with all his women." She ignored Mick's romantic overtures and recommitted in earnest to Keith, who she sensed "needed a more human kind of attention and care and love."

Keith justified the betrayal with casual male bravado: "It was like Peyton Place back then. I mean, hey, I'd stolen her from

Brian. So you've had Mick now; what do you fancy, that or this? I heard rumors, and I thought, if she's going to be making a move with Mick, good luck to him; he can only take that one once. I've got to live with it. Anita's a piece of work."

As if to cement their love, Keith bought a townhouse on 3 Cheyne Walk, just doors down from Mick and Marianne. The five-storied building of stately red brick dated back to the early eighteenth century. Unlike Mick and Marianne with their elegant antiques, Keith and Anita rejected the building's historical roots. They adorned their new home in ornaments of dark fantasy—oak-paneled reception room perversely draped in black velvet, black Lucite candlesticks glowering over an original Queen Anne fireplace. No chairs in sight—just floors strewn with rugs, animal prints, batik pillows, cushions from Tangier, and wool-woven tapestries of nomadic desert scenes. A psychedelic piano dominated the drawing room, along with a giant hookah and glittering disco ball, which Anita helpfully constructed to guide acid trips.

With Mick in London wrapped up in *Performance*, Marianne spent most of her time in Ireland zonked out on barbiturates. "Things were already beginning to go wrong," said Chrissie Gibbs, who visited her in Tuam. "Marianne was falling about a bit, taking too much of whatever she was taking. We went across in a little boat to the Aran Isles. We climbed about and went to this great fort on top. We then went to some holy well, and Marianne threw her cigarette into it. It wasn't the sort of thing she ever did. She always had a great sense of place and sanctity, but something was getting to her and she was beginning to get into a muddle. Obviously the drugs and her relationship with Mick were interdependent, but I think it was the drugs thing more. The pressures and anxieties of the affair and the availability of dope conspired to pull her down. She took refuge in drugs, I suppose, because she realized that the relationship wasn't progressing or fulfilling either of them like she dreamed it might."

Sometimes Marianne wondered whether their baby was just publicity for Mick. He'd already made her pregnancy public, blurting it out to reporters camped outside Cheyne Walk. "It's real groovy. . . . We'll probably have another three. But marriage? Can't see it happening . . ." Mick *had* wanted to marry Marianne— especially after the drug bust. But now he realized the bad boy status was working to his advantage.

On October 12 Mick took a film break to appear on *Frost on Saturday* alongside David Frost, Diana Dors, and Mary White-house, the spokesperson for the Clean Up TV pressure group. Mick sashayed in wearing his typical finery, his shoulder-length hair dyed Turner-black, a white camellia pinned to his velvet lapel. He kept his signature cool, pointing out that *her* church accepted divorce: "It may even accept abortion," he continued. "Am I right or wrong? I don't see how you can talk about this bond which is inseparable when the Christian church itself accepts divorce." Mick was prodded, but his adversaries remained respectful. He wasn't told to shut up, and he certainly wasn't asked if his mother would be proud of him.

When the BBC announced Marianne's pregnancy, she faced even more public condemnation. Within hours, reporters swarmed the village of Tuam to scrounge up gossip. The archbishop of Canterbury begged his diocese to say intercessory prayers on Marianne's behalf.

When *Performance* wrapped, Mick began preparing Cheyne Walk for Corinna, hiring decorators, buying more Regency beds. Marianne flew back to London on November 19, hoping to enjoy her last two months of pregnancy at home. But her doctor worried about her anemia and checked her into a maternity clinic in St John's Wood. Mick sent her flowers, baskets of chocolate and fruit. On November 22, she miscarried at seven months.

Marianne was devastated. And guilt-stricken on top of all the heartbreak and loss. "What really hurt me terribly was that I was told that I had lost the baby because of drugs, because I was a junkie. The doctor who had attended me was the same doctor who had taken care of me when I was pregnant with Nicholas. But then, you see, I had been living a four-square life with my husband, John Dunbar, and I was a proper mother. Now I had run away with the bad man of rock and roll."

To make matters worse, Mick carried on as if nothing had happened. He threw himself into his work, which was easier than ever now that Keith lived next door.

"I think Mick and I could have overcome all our problems if I hadn't had a miscarriage in my seventh month and the baby hadn't died," Marianne said years later. "I wasn't far from becoming a real person at that point. I hadn't yet attained that status, however, and I was still very much under Mick's thumb and still a nasty, resentful, jealous little girl, full of anger and hostility, all of which I kept bottled up inside." And then there was that deeper unspoken hurt—Anita. "That was real betrayal. She was my closest friend. She was my only friend!"

Under the ruthless tyranny of cool, Mick refused to show any emotion at all. His acknowledgment of Marianne's pain was limited to gifts, usually roses or jewelry. But these were cold comforts for Marianne: "I always lost the jewelry and I've never cared much for out-of-season roses."

Mick and Marianne were living two different lives during the last few months of 1968—months marked by heartbreak, affairs, miscarriage, and loneliness. Together they would leave it all behind. Filming was over, and it was December now. Brazil seemed like a good idea.

Anita and Keith—who'd heard all the glories of the previous year's Brazil trip—were eager to join. The South American hinterlands were known for supernatural sightings, and Anita hoped to spot geoglyphs, UFOs, and the Nazca Lines.

On December 18—Keith's twenty-fifth birthday—the two couples met at Heathrow for a midnight flight to Lisbon, where they'd board a ten-day cruise to Rio de Janeiro. They wanted to travel "in the old style," and they certainly looked the part—or at least their version, edgy parodies of old-school cruisers—fedoras, fur pelts, boots with hooked Victorian gaiters and crocodile skin. They stalked through the terminal like glammed-up grave robbers, mesmerized reporters trailing at their heels.

Keith acted as spokesperson for the party, taunting the press with fanciful half-truths. "We have become very interested in magic, and we are very serious about this trip," he declared with the seriousness of a campaigning MP. "We are hoping to see this magician who practices both white and black magic. He has a very long and difficult name which we cannot pronounce—we just call him Banana for short."

The ship was 1930s glam, like Noël Coward could have popped up on the deck. Anita fit the part in cruise-wear white, while Keith dressed "deliberately outlandish" in a diaphanous djellaba, Mexican shoes, and a tropical army hat. He mingled at the bar with upper-class English passengers, guzzling pink gins, pink champagne, and chatting about life "before the war."

Anita spent her time filming loungers and shuffleboarders with her Super 8 Cine Camera or scandalizing other passengers with her madcap antics. This was just before anyone had sunk deeply into opiates. (Keith: "If any of us had been seriously hooked by then, we wouldn't have taken that form of transport.") But Keith and Marianne indulged in drugs at sea, numbing the pain of their partners' affair. They smoked potent Brazilian weed and filched codeine-laced cough syrup from the ship's infirmary.

By the trip's end Anita was battling waves of nausea. The ship's doctor prescribed narcotics, including laudanum and blends of various painkillers. Once she even scored a shot of morphine, much to the delight of Marianne and Keith. "I remember that Keith and I were very proud of her in that idiotic junkie way."

They disembarked in grand style—and checked into Rio's Copacabana Hotel. From all appearances, their time at the Copa was quintessential Rio, with poolside drinks and patio parasols, wide-brimmed straw sun hats in pinks and blacks, Marianne in head-to-toe white on a chaise. Beach afternoons drawing faces on the sand, piggyback rides for little Nicholas, while Anita did topless handstands in the surf.

These moments were captured on the Super 8. Marianne could have been any happy young mother, but Anita's brisk flamboyance jumped off the screen—stopping traffic to try on matador gear, twirling through courtyards in a silky orange cape. She was the real bird of paradise there, perched like a macaw in the spiky green foliage, her red and yellow boas against the bright pink oleander, signet ring and giant hoops flashing gold against her tan.

The sunny photos masked Marianne's piercing melancholy. This trip to Brazil was nothing like last year's. It had all the trappings but none of the magic: "The subsequent trip was much more controlled and of course a lot less interesting. It was really just like being in London or Rome or anywhere you like. Our little group on another set; only the scenery had changed." Their problems had followed them all the way to the Tropic of Capricorn.

Anita's nausea continued in Rio. She hemorrhaged in her bed late one afternoon, staining the sheets red with blood. In a move that typifies her insouciant autonomy, she slipped away from the others and quietly found a doctor alone. When she returned that evening, she told Keith she was pregnant.

Between the tenor of the times and Anita's essential toughness, there was no question of her abandoning the trip. They continued on through Brazil, traveling unrecognized, and arrived at a ranch in Mato Grosso where swathes of cattle pasture met thick jungle canopy. Steeped in the lawless spirit of frontier boomtowns, the region was known as Brazil's own Old West, with its abandoned logger outposts, old dust roads, and the phantom glitter of miner's gold. Mick and Keith bonded like the cowboys of their youthful fantasies, "boots on the rail, thinking ourselves in Texas," laying down the bones of "Honky Tonk Woman" to the thrum of locusts and bullfrogs.

They'd never stayed in such primitive lodgings—no room service, no air-conditioning. Blind black frogs leapt from the toilet when you flushed. Mosquitos the size of thumbs descended nightly, prompting Keith to embark on a futile nightly blitzkrieg, whacking through the house with a rolled-up newspaper. "By the end of our stay, even Keith capitulated," remembered Marianne. "We just sat on the porch covered in them."

Yet somehow, Anita managed to thrive, navigating early pregnancy on a Wild West road trip, conquering nausea with elegance despite the unbearable heat. Completely unfazed by her recent affair with Mick, Anita didn't worry whether she'd threatened her bond with Keith, not to mention her friendship with Marianne. She remained as close to Marianne as ever. The night of Nicholas's birthday, they filled the swimming pool with flickering candles. For Anita this wasn't cognitive dissonance. Conventional codes of conduct were irrelevant to her. Sheepish self-consciousness was not in her nature.

Besides, like all her affairs, Mick had been a fling, and when it was over that was it. Unfortunately Mick didn't feel the same way, and the shadow of *Performance* cast a pall over the trip. Mick flirted heavily with Anita, whispering in her ear, ogling her at breakfast over coffee and cornmeal cake. And though she rebuffed his sexual advances, she happily entertained his bawdy innuendos, including thinly veiled allusions like "You Can't Always Get What You Want."

"I did not want to be his girlfriend. I never did. But Mick and me still had this kind of secret, or thought we did, so for me it was exciting because I thought I was in the middle of this high drama. And Keith was willing to go along with it." Thanks to Keith's stoic passivity, their flammable quadrangle quietly fizzled out.

For Marianne, an explosive finale would have been almost better. She tried to make the best of it, ignoring the come-ons Mick whispered to Anita. The harsh landscape matched her alienation. Dry dust caught in her throat, triggering a bout of bronchitis. She borrowed Anita's widest-brimmed hat, draped it in cheesecloth, and floated round the grounds in her red ankle boots, pricking burrs caught in her gauzy white trains. After three or four days of mental and physical hell, she packed up Nicholas and left.

"In Brazil," Marianne wrote years later, "the situation among Mick, Keith and Anita seemed to boil up into a lethal brew. . . . I felt I was there for some psychic reason, but what the hell it was I never understood."

Anita, Keith, and Mick traveled on to Peru, flying to Lima, then Cuzco. They checked into Hotel Bolívar, altitude eleven thousand feet, where oxygen tanks lined the lobby along with carts of coffee. Anita navigated the shift like a pro, smoking nonchalantly while Mick and Keith gasped for air. When she woke during the night and found the toilet broken, she simply hopped up to pee in the sink. It collapsed under her weight and shattered on the floor, water blasting everywhere from a massive pipe. (Keith: "Real Marx Brothers, slapdash, carry on . . . stuff some rags down there, call the people.")

They chewed coca leaves, dined with military governors, and eventually made their way to the remote town of Urubamba, miles away from any hotels. Eventually they found a tiny bar, played a few rounds of "Malagueña," and the bar's landlord offered them rooms upstairs. It was a perfect example of Keith's wild gallantry, the traveling minstrel winning a bed for his pregnant girlfriend.

By the time the trio made it to Machu Picchu, drugs and music eclipsed their search for UFOs. Mick was focused on a new song—"You Can't Always Get What You Want." In this light it emerges as a twisted love anthem—Mick's itinerant desire for women who reject him. And in that bittersweet song we also sense his relief—Mick knew he couldn't handle a woman like Anita.

"We went in search of flying saucers," Anita said years later, but did they really?

Marsha on tour in 1972 with sixteen-month-old Karis in tow. *(Photo courtesy of Getty Images)*

Marsha performing on the Isle of Wight, August 1969. "I was bopping like a thing possessed and feeling at the end of it as if I'd been in a dream." *(Photo courtesy of Getty Images)*

Marsha modeling for *Vogue*,
November 1968.
(Photo courtesy of Getty Images)

Marsha with baby Karis in freshly starched frock.
(Photo courtesy of Getty Images)

Luciferian lovers Keith and
Anita, December 1969.
(Photo courtesy of Getty Images)

Twenty-year-old
Marianne in 1967,
four months into
her relationship
with Mick.
*(Photo courtesy of
Getty Images)*

"Over on the wedding day," Mick and Bianca minutes before
taking their vows in Saint-Tropez, May 1971.
(Photo courtesy of Getty Images)

Mick and Bianca's swashbuckling
style on the Goodbye Britain tour
in Newcastle, March 1971.
(Photo courtesy of Getty Images)

Tangier or bust. Marianne and Anita strut
through Heathrow Airport in March 1967.
(Photo courtesy of Getty Images)

Anita sprawled out on the set of *Der Rebell* in Slovakia, sporting her own "barbaric" tooth and leather choker. Late spring 1968.
(Photo courtesy of Getty Images)

Keith dotes on Anita at the Lido in Venice, September 1967.
(Photo courtesy of Getty Images)

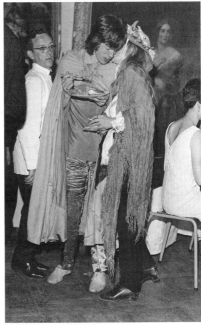

Cake, LSD, and milkmaid hats—Mick and Marianne mortify Desmond Guinness at Leixlip Castle in August 1967.
(Photo courtesy of Getty Images)

Waiting for the maharishi—and the Beatles—in Wales, August 1967. *(Photo courtesy of Getty Images)*

"Maybe the most you can expect from a relationship that goes bad is to come out of it with a few good songs." Holed up in Heidelberg in 1967 while Marianne films *The Girl on a Motorcycle*. *(Photo courtesy of Getty Images)*

Fifteen Tuinals down, a bottle more to go . . . Marianne hours before her suicide attempt in Melbourne, Australia, July 1969. *(Photo courtesy of Getty Images)*

Anita holds court with
Marianne and Brian
in Heathrow Airport,
waiting for their flight to
Gibraltar, then Tangier.
*(Photo courtesy of
Getty Images)*

Anita plumps up
Mick's pout on the
set of *Performance*,
September 1967.
*(Photo courtesy of
Getty Images)*

He's with me . . . Anita and
Keith in Cannes, May 1967.
(Photo courtesy of Getty Images)

Anita, Keith, and Marlon at Mick's wedding with Tommy Weber's sons, Jake and Charley.
(Photo courtesy of Getty Images)

"Children are the best thing
I ever had . . ." Marlon in the
stylish arms of Anita on the
1970 Scandinavian tour.
(Photo courtesy of Getty Images)

Thirteen

Sister Morphine

"Sister Morphine" was my *Frankenstein*.

Marianne Faithfull

By 1969 Marianne was drained. Creatively she felt shackled. *The Girl on a Motorcycle* had been an embarrassment—the *Times* panned her performance as a "panting ball of fluff." Marianne didn't even attend the premiere. But her debut in *Three Sisters* earned her accolades and respect. So at the start of the year she tried stage acting again—this time as Ophelia in Tony Richardson's *Hamlet*.

Hamlet opened on February 2 at the Roundhouse theater in Camden Town. "When I did *Hamlet*, that was pure joy." Marianne loved everything about the role and relished each line, those Anglo-Saxon words like "primrose" and "hellbane." Lead actor Nicol Williamson was "delightfully mad and possessed," and Marianne began sleeping with him midway through rehearsals. Between acts she'd make love with Nicol in his dressing room, slip off to snort a quick bit of heroin, then rush onstage in time for the mad scene, sprigs of rosemary knotted through her tangled hair. "In a way, it was like being in a contemporary drama, at least that's the way it affected me, as if I were the Ophelia of the sixties."

And she was. Past portrayals of Ophelia were chaste and demure, but Marianne shed all that virgin timidity. Her powdered skin implied late nights and hedonism, with pompadour hair, smoked-out eyes, and a *mouche* that hinted at sexual experience. Hair piled high in Bardot flax, sprigs of thyme and purple daisies tucked behind her ears, then loose for the mad scene like a Hyde Park hippie. Half lush voluptuary, half late-sixties twiglet, Marianne paved the way for decades of eroticized Ophelias.

Marianne tapped into the character's subversive potential. Her Ophelia scoffed at the paternalism of her father, Polonius, and brother, Laertes. When Laertes warned her of toying with Hamlet's affections, she laughed in his face, pulling him close for a transgressive kiss. She smirked at the prayer book Polonius pushed on her, mock-reading while lounging odalisque-like on pillows. There was no girlish reserve in the way she handled Hamlet, slipping off his gifted rings with nonchalance, responding with the self-assured banter of any experienced lover. In the mad scene she taunted the older generation, handing out posies of fennel and rue with the rebellious whimsy of a fifteenth-century flower child. Marianne's anemic pallor heightened Ophelia's uncanny wantonness. "I had not learned how to be an actress, so instead of being able to plug into something I became Ophelia. I had to do it in a primitive way, like a child would."

Primitive or not, the critics found her mesmerizing. Donald Zec at the *Daily Mirror* called her performance "disturbingly brilliant." *Time* magazine: "Marianne Faithfull's Ophelia is remarkably affecting. She is ethereal, vulnerable, and in some strange way purer than the infancy of youth." But insecurity had already taken hold. Marianne was grasping the last shreds of her vitality. "When I performed Ophelia, I still had it and I fought bitterly to keep it."

Marianne drowned out her inner critic with heroin. She'd done it just once before, a sort of fluke between acts while performing *Three Sisters*. She threw up backstage and never tried it again, until now.

Heroin worked for this specific role, adding a glassy-eyed realism to Ophelia's despair. (Perhaps too real—prudish reviewers complained of Marianne's "druggy" performance.) "What nobody realized then—I wasn't playing Ophelia—I *was* Ophelia. It may sound silly now. But night after night I felt myself becoming more and more withdrawn and agitated. Her suicide deeply affected me," she told the *Daily Mirror* on November 23, 1970. Offstage she indulged in lurid fantasies of drowning in the Thames, mermaid hair and deep-circled eyes, floating down the river like London's Lady of Shalott. One night she slipped out of the house alone and stood along the Chelsea embankment. "I felt myself being drawn closer and closer to the water's edge. Somehow the tragedy of Ophelia and all the unhappiness in my own life seemed to merge. I was so close to throwing myself in the river," she said to the *Mirror*. She'd morphed into her role—just like Anita in *Barbarella*. But she was no interplanetary dominatrix queen—she was utterly powerless.

Years later Marianne admitted to being bewitched by the drug's romanticism. All those years reading Baudelaire, De Quincey, and

Keats left her "half in love with easeful death." Soon she started mixing heroin with Mandrax, phenobarbital with sleeping pills, Percodan with cocaine. She was seen leaving Cheyne Walk after another drug bust, dead-eyed behind her oversized aviators, wearing a wool cape in June, her blonde crop growing out in tangled wisps. "For years I had been babbling about death in interviews. That was playacting. There came a time, however, that it stopped being a performance."

Mick was around less and less since her miscarriage. He threw himself into work, and now he was writing his best songs ever. He'd wake up sometime in the late afternoon, read the papers, catch a play in Covent Garden, then work in the studio with Keith until morning. Mick's days fell into an effective routine, but hers stretched out before her, hollow and wanting.

She toyed with reviving her singing career, though her last hit song was now four years old. Decca threw together a compilation album, which sold poorly thanks to her plummeting public image. Not that she had any interest in the label's fluff ditties. Marianne wanted to write her own songs now.

One night she sat on the stoop of Cheyne Walk, strumming Mick's guitar. She was fiddling with a riff he'd invented two summers ago in Rome, a mournful, simple melody he eventually tossed aside. A montage of images flashed through her head: their recent Brazilian holiday, the boat, the drugs, Anita bleeding out until "the clean white sheets stained red." It quickly evolved into a hospital scene, an accident victim crying out for more morphine, desperate for the night nurse to relieve her pain.

On her first studio visit in nearly two years, Marianne found her singing voice had totally changed. The plaintive songbird sweetness had been replaced by the husky rasps of a well-traveled witch. Decca released "Sister Morphine" on February 21, 1969. Two weeks later they pulled it from the shelves, citing the "scandalous" drug content.

Marianne was crushed. "I could see now that I was trapped. . . . I wouldn't be allowed to break out of my ridiculous image. I was being told that I would not be permitted to leave that wretched, tawdry doll behind." She begged Mick to plead her case to Decca. He made one attempt before backing down. Two years later he recorded Marianne's song and released it on *Sticky Fingers*. Credited to Jagger-Richards the song was a hit, and no one batted an eye over the drug references. (Aside from the original UK Decca single, where it was the B side to "Something Better," Marianne was not listed as a cowriter of "Sister Morphine" until *Sticky Fingers* was remastered and rereleased in 1994.)

Meanwhile, Mick and Marianne drifted further apart. Not only did she feel betrayed by Mick, she felt diminished by the sexism inherent in the music industry. What was the point of writing songs that would never be heard? "I lost heart. I couldn't stand it and broke away. . . . I could see that the undisputed champion and winner of the rock 'n' roll stakes was going to be Mick. I could never compete. I would just have to accept my fate and be Mick's muse. The role of a muse is one of the acceptable ones for women, but it's terrible. Being the kept plaything of this great rock star wasn't in my destiny—I knew that."

"Sister Morphine" was the death knell of her relationship with Mick. Their sex life had all but vanished, and Marianne numbed the sting with a string of affairs. Her girlfriend Sadia was a fun, if drug-addled, romp. Then there was her tryst with Stash

Klossowski, who climbed the wisteria on the wall to reach her balcony, then tumbled into the bedroom wearing a cape. Their relationship deteriorated into "chronic retaliation," a series of betrayals until no one wins.

Marianne soon found herself bored and listless, with more and more time on her hands. With Keith next door Mick was working nonstop, and the nature of their recording sessions had taken a disturbing turn. No girls were allowed, and even Anita found herself excluded. "I'd be pacing around the house alone or with Anita, both of us bored to tears and feeling rather useless and ornamental." Sometimes Mick and Keith would throw money at the girls and tell them to go shopping for clothes and drugs in Mayfair. "It's a bit like life in the seraglio," joked Anita years later. "Luxury, drugs, and a lot of waiting around for the sultan to make an appearance!"

The prior year Mick had remixed songs on Anita's advice, but now she was banished from the process entirely. "We were not really allowed into the recording studios," Anita remembered. "It was kind of a macho male thing. When the boys were busy—the girls were sort of thrown together—and we didn't know what to do with ourselves."

The two descended deeper into heroin and learned the art of skin-popping. "Marianne Faithfull and I were always left alone," said Anita in 2016. "Keith and Mick were recording and we were friends. We hung out together, taking drugs together, and we went to John Paul Getty's house, the Rossetti house, because he was the last resort and he always had some drugs."

For Marianne, Anita's friendship was a relief from the emptiness of pop stardom. "I had a great deal more in common with Anita than Mick," wrote Marianne, though she admitted they had very different personalities. "Anita was really sophisticated and elegant. . . . I was a bit hopeless. She would put me together, tell me what to wear, get me to look right. I'd give her books and she'd like that." Soon they were spending entire afternoons talking about moon phases, alphabet dolmens, and mnemonic finger poems, or reading aloud from Robert Graves's *White Goddess*. "That was our stuff. We didn't speak about it in front of other people."

Somewhere between trying on clothes and taking baths together, the two became casual lovers.

Both shared a secret aversion to men—Anita had been assaulted by an older man while studying art in Munich: "I went totally anti-men. I found them very obnoxious, so I just ignored them. I went with women. In Italy it's like a pastime, especially in the summer when the sun shines out. Everybody does it!" Marianne's mother had been raped by Russian soldiers in the wake of World War II: "I think my mother—the way she was—she had this unconscious unspoken loathing of men—and it was a big problem for me."

Marianne's ambivalence toward physical intimacy was no match for the pressures of the permissive sixties. "I'm not that interested in sex, and I've noticed that this upsets men," she wrote. "They want women to think about sex a lot, and always be wanting it." Like many women she was coerced into sex she didn't want and never really enjoyed it until her early fifties.

Years later Marianne admitted to having loved Anita ("I would have done anything for her"). When she confessed this to her old friend three decades later, Anita merely nodded "like some great old cat being brought her tribute. Another rat tail to nail up on the barn door."

Fourteen
On the Outside Looking In

First of all, I think women rule the world, period.

Marsha Hunt, Interview in *Melody Maker*, 1973

Marsha Hunt grew up in North Philadelphia—steeped in doo-wop, Philadelphia steak sandwiches, and the bad boys she loved. Raised by three women—her librarian mother, her glamorous Catholic aunt Thelma, and her grandmother Edna, a bold Southern woman. Whether bringing home a paycheck, shoveling snowbanks, or stoking the clanky furnace in winter, her "three mothers" did it all and never expected otherwise. She didn't even know that women cried.

As a first grader in St. Elizabeth's Catholic school, Marsha was happily studious and the only Black girl in her class. Aside from the pleasantries exchanged with local white shopkeepers, the only whites she really "knew" were Fred and Ethel and Lucy and Desi. Between street pressures on the edge of the crime belt and her education-minded mother, six-year-old Marsha navigated a world where neighborhood kids teased her for "acting white." Yet her white classmates wouldn't hold her hand during fire drills.

Despite all this she had a happy childhood—the sweet summer scent of wet grass and asphalt after the rain, the jukebox at the end of Twenty-Third Street that played "The Glory of Love" if you fed it a nickel. A backyard garden with hollyhocks and marigolds, pushing Fluffy the cat in her doll carriage. There were penny candy stores with Mary Jane toffees and loose potato chips scooped into brown paper bags. But at five she knew people who'd been beaten and stabbed on the streets or scalded with lye.

Music was Marsha's salvation. Church gospel was the backdrop each Sunday morning. But the a capella doo-wop boys were the ones who stole her heart, harmonizing on street corners, strutting down the alleys with flashy hats and fancy footwork. Music was everything.

The family's move to Philly's Mount Airy neighborhood took Marsha out of physical danger but away from the street singers she loved. Radio provided her musical landscape until the launch of *American Bandstand*, a music show broadcast live from Philadelphia.

With *Bandstand* you could actually see the music, and for Marsha that changed everything. She'd race home from school to catch the first half hour, dancing in her braids and gingham, imitating the pony, the bunny hop, and the mambo. The cameras scanning the audience—who danced to the music— captured real teenagers. *Bandstand* attracted the local kids, both white and Black. The Platters were just as welcome as Bill Haley and His Comets. And though *Bandstand* featured all kinds of acts, what Marsha loved most was the music of her heritage, the familiar sounds of street harmonies—Little Anthony, Frankie Lymon, the Flamingos.

At ten she was captivated by the teen dancers, many of whom looked just like her. She watched their variations of spins and twirls and imagined herself in their bobby socks and backward cardigans, her mind swirling with earth angels and blue moons. Puppy love lyrics and a 4/4 dance beat meant being "A Teenager in Love," or so you hoped.

In that era the very concept of the "teen" was new and glamorous, creating a generation of girls who celebrated Clearasil and hairspray. As for so many of her peers, pop music launched Marsha into adolescence. She tossed out her ballet shoes for a pair of Cuban heels, hitched up her pencil skirts on the school-bound trolley, and slicked her lips with Westmore's Oooh La La Orange. She'd saunter past the playground with a wiggle in her walk, hoping for glances from the boys playing basketball. All she really wanted was a little bit of kissing with this week's love of her life.

Bandstand put Philadelphia on the pop culture map. Life was great. But in 1960, Marsha's mother decided it was time to move west. Being plucked out of the city she loved was unbearable. No more *Bandstand*, street singers, or dancing the pony with friends. Her diddy-bopper days were over.

Oakland was a culture shock, especially its music scene. California teens didn't dance on the street, they went surfing and partied around bonfires on the beach. But Marsha found work in a late-night coffee bar—the Egg Shop and Apple Press—and quickly fell into the local poetry scene.

Soon she was hanging around North Beach in San Francisco, a hub of jazz clubs and bookshops light years away from gum-snapping Philly. She ordered a pair of handmade sandals and bought dangly wooden earrings from a local street vendor. Grandma Edna sewed her a poncho out of a square of Mexican wool, and soon Marsha looked the part of a West Coast bohemian, at least enough to be welcomed into the Cabale Creamery on San Pablo. She far preferred R&B's warm familiar beats, but luckily the Chambers Brothers broke up the daily folk grind.

She found herself a regular at Cabale Creamery parties, parties where you immediately understood that the less you said the better. Marsha hid her discomfort by chain-smoking Kents, flawlessly parroting their *cool*s and *way out*s while deftly avoiding the passing joints. She didn't have the same freedoms as these white beatniks, who bitched about their wealthy parents while spending their money on weed. And dodging sexual advances was a daily hazard. Marsha's sexual inactivity wasn't modern. Though she had no practical need for it, Marsha was the first of her friends to go on the pill. You had to disguise yourself as a married woman back then, and she did.

Marsha enrolled at Berkeley in 1964 during the peak of student demonstrations. The Free Speech Movement sprang up her very first semester, kicking off waves of student activism nationwide. Three months later was the occupation of Sproul Hall—five thousand students sitting cross-legged on the floor, watching movies and singing folk songs led by Joan Baez. Her sophomore year they marched against the Vietnam War—a black coffin to the draft board, ten thousand participants, and the first of its kind in California at a time when anti-war sentiment was suspicious and rare.

Despite this activity restlessness got the better of her. She hopped a bus to New York, then moved on to Boston, passing evenings in coffee shops listening to folk singers. But out East a girl on her own was a target, so Marsha fled back to the relief of Berkeley, where boys took you home to smoke joints and talk politics and your biggest worry was the guy perched in a cherry tree by your open window playing a Dylanesque harmonica while you tried to study French.

Yet even back at Berkeley something gnawed at her, despite her effortless bouncing between campus cliques. To stamp out that great empty, Marsha focused on her studies. She hoped to specialize in psychological anthropology, then attend grad school at Ann Arbor. Hell-bent on proving she was a serious student, Marsha joined in the lunchtime arguments over Kant and Kierkegaard, read Genet, and snuck into Michael McClure's lectures at the College of Arts and Crafts. She didn't hate those things, and at times she even liked them. But there was a performative element to all that fervor. Surrounded by friends whose passions were academic or political, Marsha doubted she fit in at Berkeley at all.

Excited as she was about progressive ideas, waving placards on the terrace left Marsha unfulfilled. There were drugs of course—amphetamines for cramming, acid for parties, and sweet Mexican weed that looked like catnip. There was her heartthrob English lit professor, who rode to class on a Harley and wore leather jackets. There were trips to San Francisco to see Lenny Bruce, or LeRoi Jones's *The Toilet* three nights in a row. There were boyfriends like Joe from the Free Speech Movement and nights reciting *The Waste Land* while getting drunk off mulled wine.

And there was always music, a love she kept hidden from suitors and friends. Berkeley's intellectuals didn't like rock and roll, and had little interest in rhythm and blues. Despite the school's reputation for diversity, campus musical tastes were uniformly folk. Marsha nourished her love of R&B in secret, playing records in the privacy of her room. Ruth Brown, Mary Wells, and the Supremes provided sweet relief after overdosing on Bob Dylan, Phil Ochs, and Joan Baez.

Marsha felt the pull of R&B deep in her bones. She recognized it in the thump and blare of Martha and the Vandellas during a screening of Kenneth Anger's *Scorpio Rising*. She was desperate to dance but the others sat motionless—for them the pop soundtrack was serious cultural commentary. She stayed glued to her seat, unable to admit her passion for pop and not yet aware that her passion was valid. Soon she'd understand she had no need to hide it.

But music changed faster than hemlines that year—on a monthly basis and sometimes even weekly. In 1965, Motown went mainstream, and bands like the Stones put their blue-eyed spin on soul. Gradually, she found friends who tuned into pop music, which was rapidly morphing into psychedelia-spiked rock. There were concerts at the Fillmore and dance parties at Longshoremen's with smoky strobe lights and chic London deejays. But the dancers at these parties moved with studied affectation, flailing wildly to prove that they were out of their minds on drugs, not dancing for the simple joy of the music.

Unsure of what she wanted but sure of what she didn't want, Marsha couldn't retreat to the protest scene with its painfully earnest singers with socially relevant lyrics.

She was alone in her room dropping acid when the idea came to her, watching the snowflake pattern on her wallpaper melt into itself like ice cream. The masquerade and posturing were over. Suddenly it was obvious—she had to sing. And the best way to do it was to move to Europe.

Fifteen

Icon

You're kidding yourself if you think you're going through the front door on your own terms, because the world's been going on too long on someone else's terms.

Marsha Hunt, *Melody Maker*

It was February 1966. Marsha took a cheap flight to Heathrow and hitched a ride to London. Broke and exhausted, she slept in Waverley Station. Yet she remained undaunted, excited even.

The next night Marsha crashed in Holland Park with the brother of an anthropology classmate. In the morning she wandered down Kensington High Street, bundled in box-shouldered fox fur from the Second World War, a last-minute thrift find before she left Berkeley. The sky hung low over Central London, smoky gray sky without a sliver of blue, belted raincoats, and cherry-red lorries. She was broke, knew no one, and had no clue what to do, just some vague girlish dream of singing. That courage—the senseless guts to leap before looking—was far more common in the sixties than now. You just took it on faith that things would work out then—and they sometimes did. There was a transatlantic network of international students, and Berkeley was the master key. Bumming penniless through Europe earned you respect, especially with Berkeley's activist pedigree.

This underground chain made anything possible. You could wander alone into a Camden pub and leave with a bedsit at David Hockney's. Marsha spent her first week with this web of rebel orphans, warming up together under gas stoves and quilts, sharing hot water bottles, contacts, and cash. She found London kinder, easier than California, where everyday racism kept her on her guard.

Marsha basked in her first London spring, the cool rain, apple blossoms, Regent's Park rose gardens, how the warmth melted that English restraint, injecting Oxford Street plodders with lunch hour giddiness. She made friends quickly—American but especially English—drifting happily from one pad to the next. She bided her time babysitting for designer Alice Pollock, who owned the Quorum Boutique with Ossie Clark on Kings Road. Privately, Marsha still nursed a secret hope to sing.

The Beatles and the Animals didn't appeal to her—she never rushed to see them on *Ready Steady Go!* She caught the Stones at Royal Albert when they played with Tina Turner—whose frenetic onstage vigor left her reeling. Marsha longed to dance like the coquettish Ikettes, shimmying their way through the stroll, skate, and camel walk.

Performing live had as much to do with image as voice, so Marsha straightened her hair into a Sassoon bob, bought red block-heeled pumps and plastic hoop earrings. Alice and Ossie lent her minis from Quorum, and she practiced singing alone by the cupboard door mirror.

Soon enough Alexis Korner picked her up for his blues trio. Shyly at first, self-conscious cigarette dangling from her mouth, Marsha sang her way around London's blues scene, meeting other performers along the way. One of these musicians was John Mayall, and their brief love affair provided the space for Marsha to take her art seriously. John plunged her into that professional milieu, artists who lived for the pure joy of music, no "message" necessary.

While touring with Alexis she met Long John Baldry, who asked her to audition for his band Bluesology. (Elton John—then known as Reggie Wright—was the keyboardist.) She jumped onstage in her Sassoon cut and fox fur, buzzing with the white heat of Kings Road hipness. She offered to sing a cappella—like the boys on the stoop—and before anyone could stop her—launched into "Love Is a Many Splendored Thing" by Little Anthony and the Imperials, with all the vocal twists and turns he'd done in 1958. Marsha got the job. London was swinging just for her.

Now Marsha was singing at the Flamingo Club, Studio 51, and the legendary Marquee. Soon she was touring England with Bluesology, speeding up and down the roads in the band's red Commer van, stopping for beans on toast or fish and chips in the "trannies"—transport cafés. They played town halls, college campuses, smoky clubs, and seaside dives, and she loved exploring the country's small towns, its nooks and brooks and funny little hamlets. She even loved the foreignness itself—another country, another race. Immersing herself in British English like a foreign-language student, reveling in the nuances between Liverpool and Birmingham, the working-class cool of roadside

Cockney, how they'd sidle up and greet you with "How the fuck are you," almost as a compliment. England's highways were buzzing with vans in those days, stuffed with pop girls, Merseybeats, and American R&B. Months ago at Berkeley, she could never have imagined opening for acts like Jimi Hendrix and the Kinks.

Marsha never doubted her ability to thrive. But her own vocal cords left her ambivalent. Motown's explosion set the bar impossibly high—Diana, Aretha, Tina, Martha, and Mary. Her audience assumed she'd hit and hold those high notes simply by virtue of being a Black woman. But those treble tones were simply out of her range. She questioned whether singing was the right path for her and even considered quitting Bluesology. Before she was forced to make a decision, the band broke up on its own.

Within a few months her visa would run out, and she was having trouble getting it renewed. Ever resourceful, she proposed to her friend Mike Ratledge of Soft Machine, and they married in April 1967. (They're still married, though they have yet to kiss or hold hands. Marsha's secret to a happy marriage? "Separate immediately.")

After her six-month stint with Bluesology, Marsha briefly joined the band the Ferris Wheel. Rehearsals were repeats of the same old assumptions—no, she couldn't sing "Respect," and she didn't do gospel. When glandular fever forced her to drop out, Marsha felt almost relieved. She spent the summer sinking deep into her thoughts, planning her next move or collaboration. As fun as touring was, she wasn't making real progress as an artist, not nearly enough to justify dropping out of Berkeley. Instead of singing someone else's music, it was time to write her own.

John McVie lent her a bass and promised to teach her a few riffs. But she needed money for an amp and headed to Portobello Road, hoping to run into some friends who could hook her up with an au pair job. Instead, she ran into aspiring director Roger Croucher, who suggested she go to the West End and audition for the musical *Hair*.

The Shaftesbury claimed to have one slot left. She walked several blocks through a thick mist of humid rain, panicking over the inevitable effect on her hair. Taming it took a Herculean effort, and by the time she reached Shaftesbury, it had tripled in size. Self-conscious but determined, Marsha went through with the audition.

Little did she know the rain had been a godsend. Marsha's untamed halo of hair was seen as the embodiment of Black beauty—and an even chicer statement than long hippie locks. Not only did she get the role, the stage manager insisted she go natural for the show.

Hair opened in September 1968. The content—nudity, drugs, and songs about sodomy—drew enormous crowds and mass-media coverage. London went wild. Only when the roof of the Shaftesbury Theatre came crashing down did the musical finally end in 1973.

Marsha was very much in sync with the musical's ethos. The brief flashes of nudity were less about eroticism and more about self-acceptance. "You couldn't be a woman in your 20s in London at that time and not be part of the sexual revolution. I was all t**s and bum, and that was an expression of liberation. I thought it was my duty to take my clothes off, to show that women no longer had to hide."

Despite having only two lines of dialogue, Marsha attracted a huge portion of the media attention. "They came down to take pictures after a show and there were a lot of kids who were all dressed alike, but I happened to have more hair than anyone else onstage so all the photographers went for me . . . I was one of the few people here who pictorially they were able to exploit with the hair. They thought I looked like what black America was all about."

Martha was interviewed, photographed, and ferried around to clubs, film premieres, and soirées with Princess Margaret. She tempered the thrill with commonsense humility: she wasn't singled out for charisma or talent, she was the only cast member sober enough for early morning photoshoots. Much of the cast was far too stoned to wake before noon, but the only thing Marsha was shooting up was vitamin B to boost her energy.

Designers sent her dresses, producers slipped her their business cards, newspapers begged for her opinions. The morning after opening night, Pamela Colin from *Vogue* called. They wanted a photoshoot with Patrick Lichfield—not just some anonymous head shot but a four-page spread. The accompanying text declared: "People stare at Marsha Hunt on the London streets. She knows it. She doesn't mind. Who cares? She's she. She's free." Days later flowers arrived with a note from Diana Vreeland herself. Marsha was flabbergasted. She never dreamed she'd be embraced by the chilly arms of haute couture.

It seemed 1969 would be a banner year for her. She was *Queen* magazine's first Black cover girl, gleaming Christmas balls strung all over her hair on their December issue. Her *Vogue* photoshoot— with clothes and without, save for the wooden bangles she wore on set for *Hair*—was noticed by Paramount producer Richard Roth. Marsha was flown to LA for a TV screen test. When she showed up at Paramount, Roth whisked her away to a Hollywood dentist who snapped a plastic cap over her gappy front teeth. Next was a wig fitting at Hollywood and Vine—Marsha hated wigs and refused to even straighten her hair—she was pleased when they couldn't find anything big enough to cover it. The worst was the pasty pancake makeup they used to lighten her skin and the fussy blue shadow they painted on her lids.

When Paramount's limo arrived to drive her back to LAX, Marsha breathed a sigh of relief. She might be American, but London was her home now, and Track Records was waiting for her with an appealing contract. She recorded Dr. John's "I Walk on Guilded Splinters," a spooky soul number that flew up in the charts, and was soon asked to perform on *Top of the Pops*. She wore hot pants and a tight bolero top, which unbeknownst to her revealed her breasts each time she raised her arms in a sexy voodoo dance.

Press photographers pounced at the chance, pointing their camera lenses straight at her breasts. "I was showing cleavage, but instead of it being top cleavage it was bottom cleavage. And suddenly every gig I did after that was like 'What are you doing in jeans? We expected you to be wearing the suit you had for *Top of the Pops*.'" She'd been stamped with the label of wayward, wild, bad girl. But Marsha had expected this. "The pop business has always exploited sexuality," she told *Melody Maker* in 1973. "You either go into the business knowing that's going to happen or you naively confront the business thinking that you aren't going to be exploited on that level."

The publicity was darker this time around, with none of the hippie lilt of *Hair*. But Marsha had made a deliberate choice: "One reason why I did what I did was because I was tired of English roses, I mean the sweethearts who sit in front of the microphone and it's all civilised."

It was this departure from the English Rose chanteuse that caught Mick Jagger's attention, and he asked her to pose in promotional shots for the single "Honky Tonk Woman." His concept was a scantily clad (preferably Black) woman, perched in a bar flanked by the Stones.

Marsha refused.

Mick—always encouraged by a woman's refusal—was hooked.

He showed up unannounced at her Bloomsbury flat after midnight, grinning sheepishly in the doorway, hands shoved in the pockets of his black peacoat. He drew one from his pocket and aimed it at her like a pistol.

"Bang."

Her response was far from overwhelming lust. The fluorescent strip lighting cast sickly shadows on his English pallor, and he had visible spots, which he later apologized for. After the Adonis-like looks of her ex Marc Bolan of T. Rex, Marsha could hardly consider Mick beautiful. But his infectious grin—boyish, candid, guileless, and direct—won her over right away. He seemed like a lost schoolboy you'd invite in for tea, which is exactly what she did.

They sat on her leather Chesterfield sofa, drinking tea and smoking. Mick knew her musical mentors like Alexis Korner, and having grown up worshipping blues musicians, he had an impressive knowledge of Black roots and blues music. She found him eager to discuss politics and culture, alert and engaged. "He was educated. He was a radical. He was not the man people think they know now. Somehow, that all gets lost over time."

That night they laughed so much she feared they'd wake her roommate—the sort of laughter that had long been absent from Mick's life. His past several months had been fraught with problems—Brian, legal issues, Marianne and her drugs. He seemed inexplicably lost, and she could tell that Mick Jagger, the most famous rock star in the world, was desperately lonely.

It wasn't simply loneliness that endeared him to Marsha—it was that he was so unashamedly open about it.

The sky lightened, Mick's harsh London accent growing gentler by dawn. When he walked out her door at six in the morning saying he would call, Marsha never expected to see him again.

Why was Mick so open with her when he'd turned so cold with Marianne? Was it because of the drugs? Marsha was completely straight; she didn't even drink. She certainly—at this point in her life—was more independent than Marianne. Whatever the reason, Marsha sensed that Mick needed to confide in her.

Why did Marsha feel so responsible for the feelings of this wealthy white man? She saw celebrity as superficial and never took her own rise to the charts—let alone Mick's astronomical fame—that seriously. And though she'd been sleeping with Mick since night one, she ultimately saw him as more of a friend than a lover. Her lack of passion for Mick allowed her to treat him with magnanimous, coolly detached, disinterested compassion, and she always left a door open for him. Mick admiringly referred to her steadfast reliability as "butch," and in turn Marsha saw him as a "golden eagle with a broken wing."

Whatever his reasons, the side Mick showed Marsha was gentle, humble, vulnerable, and sincere. For now.

Sixteen

Black Magic

Danger is great joy, dark is bright as fire.

Marianne Faithfull

Always ten steps ahead of the zeitgeist, Anita was bored by the final year of the sixties, all hippie clichés and futuristic jabber. She despised those ersatz bohemians loping around Chelsea in bare feet and dirty smocks. "I could never understand why people walked barefoot down the King's Road," she said. "For one, it was filthy. And why deny yourself the most beautiful part of a woman's wardrobe?"

Anita's passion for the occult had not faded, and the ancient practices of Saturnalia and Beltane were bracing antidotes to pop culture platitudes. While others tuned in and dropped out, she was busy reading books by Aleister Crowley or painting Egyptian hieroglyphs on her oak-paneled stairwell.

"I had an interest in witchcraft," she recalled later, "in Buddhism, in the black magicians that my friend Kenneth Anger introduced me to. The world of the occult fascinated me." Kenneth—a West Coast Crowleyite and avant-garde filmmaker— met Anita at Robert Fraser's on Mount Street. Steeped in black magic and Hollywood gossip, he dazzled the Chelsea set with his shamanistic credentials.

Like Crowley, who reveled in his sinister reputation—he was known posthumously as the "the wickedest man in the world"— Kenneth proudly declared himself "the most monstrous moviemaker in the underground." Whether shock tactics or genuine nods to Satan, Anger's films were riddled with demonic symbols— sex rituals, sadomasochism, and crucifixes. He shared Anita's occult obsessions. They talked long into the night by her Queen Anne marble fireplace, chatting about *The Golden Bough* and the Mass of Saint-Sécaire. He told her all about his current project, *Lucifer Rising*—a mini-epic about Egyptian gods who summoned up the rebel angel. Anita immediately hopped on board as a producer and introduced him to Marianne, who would star in the film as Lilith.

Charismatic Kenneth lured the men in too, charming Mick with sordid Hollywood gossip. Mick saw star potential in *Lucifer Rising*, and eventually agreed to play the devil himself. Keith thought this new prince of darkness was a hoot and called himself the filmmaker's "right-hand man." Kenneth soon became a frequent guest at Redlands, running rampant through the Tudor home's haphazard bedrooms, sketching film concepts on the whitewashed walls of clay daub, tracing pentagrams in chalk all over the stone floors. Neighbors would spot him pacing the green at dawn, surveying magic circles he'd constructed at night.

With Anita he fostered the deepest connection. It was Kenneth she turned to when midway through pregnancy, she wanted to sanctify her bond with Keith. Conventional marriage was out of the question, but she was open to the pagan rite of handfasting. Kenneth offered to officiate the ceremony, but only after painting the door of Cheyne Walk gold. He left to procure a magic paint spiked with herbs, and Anita and Keith went to sleep. When they woke, the door's inside had been painted gleaming gold. What's more, the paint was already dry.

The oak door had been bolted with multiple locks, and Kenneth had never been given a key. Anita thought he flew in like a witch in the night.

Kenneth's explanation is slightly more believable. "They had forgotten they left the door unlocked for me, so I got in with paints and so forth. I turned up inside their house, but there was nothing mysterious about me somehow breaking in or anything. It was because, frankly, they took so many drugs they tended to forget things. It was a heavily-drugged period."

Which is not to say he didn't believe in enchantment. If anything, he thought Anita was the witch. "I believe that Anita is, for want of a better word, a 'witch,'" Anger commented years later. "The occult unit within the Stones was Keith and Anita and Brian."

Stash Klossowski dismissed all that. "It's pretty ridiculous this 'Anita and the occult' or 'Anita the Witch Queen' sort of thing. I was one of the people who knew her well at that time and I can tell you, it's all rubbish. . . . This whole thing is just someone's Halloween dream." Tony Foutz agreed. "Everybody had a fascination with Aleister Crowley at the time," he stated, "but Anita wasn't a necromancer or a witch or any of those tags that they put on her now; it's just so odious. In Rome, I spent a lot of time with

Anita when she was alone, and there were none of those characteristics of the dark side."

But maybe Kenneth had hit on a deeper truth. Like the high priestess Pythia, men perpetually turned to Anita for guidance. More Delphic Oracle than languid muse, Anita held sway over everyone she met. The Stones turned to her for everything from lyrics to cover art to final remixes. "Anita was like a life-force," wrote Stones' drug dealer Tony Sanchez, "a woman so powerful, so full of strength and determination that men came to lean on her."

Spring turned to summer 1969. Marianne felt "something very nasty coming." She worried about Brian, who was ousted from the Stones two weeks prior. It had been coming for years, poor Brian stumbling around on hog tranquilizers while Mick and Keith pounded out pop songs. But this had long been the Stones' dynamic—ego battles and schoolyard brutality. Even Keith had joined in, jeering as Brian fumbled over his guitars in pathetic drug-induced stupors. It was bone-chilling how swiftly they dropped him once they saw him as a drag.

So one night in late June she threw the *I Ching*—DEATH BY WATER. She threw the coins once more—death by water again. "Look, we have to do something," she pleaded with Mick, who was beginning to feel a bit spooked himself.

That weekend they drove to East Sussex. Brian had recently moved from Courtfield Road to Cotchford Farm—the former home of *Winnie-the-Pooh* author A. A. Milne. He was touchingly thrilled to see them both, but Mick, whose disdain was pure muscle memory, insulted the steak dinner Brian prepared. The would-be rapprochement ended in a fistfight, with both Mick and

Brian tumbling into the moat. (In those years English rock stars always had moats.)

It was a mismatch, with Brian sluggish, weakened from years of booze and pills. Marianne felt sorry for him, gentle Brian alone in his Winnie-the-Pooh palace. There was something sweetly child-like about his excitement over buying Cotchford Farm—like the way he'd lie on his stomach playing with his beloved train sets.

Would Brian die? Would she be next? Perhaps that watery death in the cards was hers.

On July 2, 1969, Brian spent the day nursing a bottle of vodka. After a few sunset Quaaludes, he went for a midnight swim. He jumped off his diving board, then flipped onto his back to float in the deep end of his pool. Cobalt tiles shimmered in the twi-light, casting shadows on his white skin and bleached-out hair. Brian drifted alone in the floodlit water. "I love this place," he murmured softly, eyes flickering to a close.

After all their fights and reconciliations, Anita blamed herself for not being the one to catch Brian when he fell, the one to pull out his inhaler, the one to turn him on his side to keep from choking in his sleep. Survivors' guilt hit her hard. She'd pore over his trib-utes in newspapers and magazines, then clip out his photos and paste them all over her walls. Marianne compared her to a manic Camille Claudel.

"I'll see him again," she announced, almost like a threat. "We promised to meet again. It was life or death. One of us had to go."

The Stones gave a tribute concert in Hyde Park four days later. Dressed in a gauzy white frock, Mick read Shelley's "Adonais" to a crowd of five hundred thousand, while three thousand white butterflies were released onstage.

Anita sat cross-legged in the tiny VIP area, draped in a silky maxi-dress and coin-spangled headdress. Something about the concert sent chills down her spine. "The concert was quite a frightening event," she recalled. "You can see that in our eyes. I was incredibly pregnant at the time and was standing on the rails at the side of the stage. The people [were] getting closer, and then suddenly, I saw all the Hells Angels and said, 'Oh, my God, this is going to end up really bad.' Then they told me that they were the security people, but they were pretty rough and during the concert were climbing on me to get a better view. . . . I had to climb a tree to escape the crowds and hide."

Marianne clutched Nicholas and wandered dazedly through the crowd, her eyes pill-glassy, her skin dull and mottled by heroin-induced acne. She looked obviously and extremely out of it, but not too doped up to miss Marsha Hunt, whom Mick had perched on a scaffold right next to the stage. As if his betrayal wasn't blatant enough, he ended the set by belting out "I'm Yours and I'm Hers." By now, Marianne was too numb to feel heartbreak. "There was Marsha bursting out of her white buckskins. She was stunning. If I'd been Mick in that situation, I might have done exactly the same thing."

Marsha swayed in her custom-built scaffolding, gorgeous and distracted. She'd never been a Stones fan, and even with the added jolt of her romance with Mick, she had a hard time psyching herself up for their songs. Besides, she was thinking about her show that night in Manchester.

Mick came to see her at home that night. He was leaving in the morning for Australia. Tony Richardson had offered him the lead in *Ned Kelly*, and filming began in two days. Rain came down harder than she'd ever seen in England. When she felt that lump rising up in her throat, she laughed off his goodbye kiss and shooed him away. She always hated goodbyes.

Seventeen

Death Is the Ultimate Experience

You want pain and suffering? I'll show you pain and suffering!

Marianne Faithfull

Mick seemingly couldn't board the flight to Sydney fast enough. He was no doubt thrilled that his acting career had "caught up" with Marianne's. They'd be working together, with Marianne in the role of Ned Kelly's sister. Australia seemed like a welcome break from London, especially while collaborating on a film.

But now the whole plan seemed horrendously grotesque. Brian's body was barely cold, and Mick was already on to the next flight, the next press event, the next new project.

That was the way the Stones operated—don't look back, keep it moving. What passed as ambition and good business acumen

181

now appeared as sickening coldness. Far from showing regret or remorse, Mick seemed relieved to shake off the weight of his dead friend. Would he do the same with Marianne?

In a desperate state of numb resignation, Marianne agreed to board the plane. She popped fifteen blue Tuinals on the long flight to Sydney, then staggered into an airport besieged by paparazzi. Dressed in a suede pantsuit and Biba heels, she clung to Mick's arm, dead-eyed under the brim of her wide-brimmed floppy hat.

They checked into the Chevron-Hilton, overlooking Sydney Harbour. Mick fell asleep immediately. Marianne rang room service for a cup of hot chocolate, then happened to glance in the vanity mirror. "I saw a thin, frightened face. I'd cut my hair, I was anorexic, and my skin looked cadaverous. I saw someone literally falling apart." It was Brian Jones staring back at her. Marianne was Brian, and she was already dead.

She sat down at the vanity with the hot cup and saucer, reached into her purse for the bottle of sodium amytal. She took one tablet after another, sipping on the chocolate and staring into the mirror. Brian flashed before her, half-drowned and haggard, waterlogged blonde hair darkened to tarnished brass. Or was it her as a mid-century Ophelia, a Biba-clad zombie floating down the Thames? The more tablets she swallowed, the more she longed to die—she'd have thrown herself into the harbor had the windows not been sealed. By the time she crawled into the bed next to Mick, the bottle was empty.

Marianne closed her eyes and found herself lost in a blank gray expanse, no sun, no horizon, no sense of warmth or cold. Just Brian in Valenciennes lace and yellow striped pants, hair dyed green like a leprechaun. He was his typical effusive self ("Thank god you're here, Marianne . . . thank god you're here").

He took her arm and they began to skate, long looping glides on a plane of silver ice. Brian moaned about the lack of drugs in the afterworld, what a "drag" the place was, no Valium, booze, or smokes. The landscape shifted to a misty Dulac fairy tale, and Brian cheered up enough to chat about his coronation miniatures, complete with Beefeaters, coach, and horses. He asked for books about railway bridges, guides to switch boxes, George MacDonald's fairy stories, and *Foxe's Book of Martyrs*. Marianne promised to buy them for him once she got back to London.

Suddenly they stopped at the edge of a cliff. There it was, that flat gray abyss again. "I'm so sorry, Marianne," Brian apologized, backing slowly away from her toward the cliff's edge.

"Death is the ultimate experience," he said with a wink, then jumped off into oblivion.

Brian was buried on July 10, 1969. It felt like some late-sixties adaptation of Racine—the fourteen-car cortege, the hearse mobbed with sobbing fans, the Ossie Clark–clad girlfriends weeping arm in arm—all model-thin blonde doppelgängers of Anita. The wreath of lilies spelling out "Gates of Heaven," courtesy of the Rolling Stones. The silver and bronze casket sent by Bob Dylan, with Brian enclosed, in his powder-blue jacket and freshly bobbed hair.

Bill and Charlie were the only Stones in attendance. Keith claimed studio commitments, Mick left for Australia. Anita was riding out the final weeks of her pregnancy, and Marianne lay intubated at St Vincent's Hospital ten thousand miles away.

Brian's coffin was lowered into a grave twelve feet deep to keep him safe from morbid fans. An unknown woman threw down a single yellow rose. Just as the gravediggers began shoveling dirt, one lone policeman gave a silent salute.

COLLAPSE! DRUG SQUAD AT HOSPITAL screamed the Sydney *Daily Mirror*. Rumors flew that police confiscated two bottles of sodium amytal. Detectives and customs officials hovered by the hospital door. The drugs were illegal, scored in the back alleys of Rome; the drugs were prescribed by a posh Knightsbridge doctor; the drugs had belonged to Brian Jones. Marianne found Mick in bed with a woman, or Mick himself had stuffed the tablets down her throat. They were only compounded by Eva Faithfull's midnight flight. ("I'm on a mission of mercy," she'd told the press, sweeping through the Sydney airport swathed in her signature black.)

Mick rushed to the hospital after filming his hanging scene. At bedside the mournful mother, the repentant boyfriend, scurrying nurses. The local priest performing an extreme unction—the sacrament, the jeweled cross, anointing her forehead and palms with oil blessed by the archbishop of Sydney and reciting a liturgy—to save the patient from losing "hope in God's justice, truth and salvation."

Journalists swarmed from all over the world, paparazzi dressed as doctors pushed past the nuns and stormed through her door. They shoved cameras inches from Marianne's face, which soon appeared on the *Sunday Mirror*'s front page—unconscious, clamped down by restraints, head skewed to the side, oxygen pumps, and tubes shoved down her throat and up her nose.

The narrative followed a familiar trajectory, the room filling up with bouquets and phone calls. Hundreds of get-well cards. Thousands of fan letters. Heaps of tiny snowdrops from John and Yoko. The scent of honey blossoms laced with phenobarbital. Perhaps she wasn't all that bad, just a twenty-two-year-old girl caught in the agony of pop. All the while the nuns kept their vigil, whispering prayers for their dear little Marianne.

"Marianne is a delicate woman," Mick explained to the press, blaming her collapse on the long flight to Sydney that pushed her into a state of "exhaustion." He sent her letters almost daily from the set, letters full of remorse: "Please forgive me for causing you all this pain. . . . I'm utterly devastated to realize that you felt you were in such agony you had to kill yourself." And she wanted him to feel that way. "I know that when I took my hundred and fifty sleeping pills, I did it out of revenge."

Andrew Oldham capitalized on the gruesomeness by releasing a greatest hits album immediately, the cover framed in black with ominous gothic typeface. The *Sunday Mirror* dove into the whole sordid tale, including a picture of Anita and Keith with her plumed regalia (*It's my baby*, says Keith). Car wrecks, drug busts, sudden deaths and mystery babies—just the latest episode in the Rolling Stones saga, which inevitably revolved around their women. Then came the official opinion of the *Mirror*'s in-house doctor: drugs had cut off the blood supply to Marianne's brain, leading to a loss of functioning that "could be permanent."

When Marianne woke up, Eva transferred her to Mount St Margaret's, a private clinic run by the Sisters of the Little Company of Mary. The ideal setting for a repentant convalescence—more nuns, hushed corridors, her mother saying the rosary in the east wing. Marianne was forbidden to speak for two weeks—her throat had to heal from the hospital tubes. She communicated with Eva by writing notes.

Her voice came back in late July, and she gave her first interview since the overdose. "Sun Shines Again for Marianne," declared the *Daily Telegraph*, with photos that framed her as a resurrected angel walking the hospital grounds attended by nuns, her freshly washed hair glinting with light. There were shots of her picnicking outside with Mick, as if she now deserved this bucolic paradise. The press vacillated between these redemptive narratives and more sordid ones.

After three weeks of hospitalization, Marianne was well enough to fly back to London. She signed autographs at the airport, wrapped in a trench, her face prednisone puffy. Reporters barked out the million-dollar question: "Why did you do it, Marianne?"

"Tell everyone in Australia I love them and want to thank them for being so kind," she said, Eva shuffling her along the tarmac. In her hand she clutched a toy koala and a copy of *Australian Women's Weekly*, her own face plastered on the cover.

While Marianne recuperated, Mick phoned Marsha constantly and bombarded her with letters scrawled in his messy left hand. He called her "Miss Fuzzy," and she remembered the letters as thoughtful, playful, innocent, and sad.

On July 20, 1969, while Marianne was still hospitalized, Mick wrote Marsha a gentle letter from Australia titled "Sunday and the Moon" when the world watched the televised landing of America's three astronauts on the moon, 239,000 miles away.

Eighteen

Boots, Birth, Breakups

Women in pop are in much the same situation as blacks have been. You've got to slip in through the side door ... and once you're in, then you do your damage.

Marsha Hunt

arsha busied herself in the recording studio, cutting singles and collaborating with musicians like Pete Townshend and Ronnie Wood. But her manager, whom she shared with the Who, was a terrible match. Kit Lambert was a bully, too caught up in machismo and studio power games to give Marsha the attention and respect she deserved. He'd show up to recording sessions hours late sans apology, leaving Marsha seething and her backup singers exhausted. Both Kit and his partner Chris Stamp dismissed Marsha's ideas and threw her shabby material they wouldn't dare give their male bands. They refused to recognize her pop music's worth.

She'd already proved herself on the charts, and on the stage of *Hair*—that should have been enough hype for the record business.

They put her down for rising up in fashion and theater. Yet here she was, one of the only women in London fronting a hard rock sound. In the ultimate snub, they pawned her off on their own receptionist, David Ruffell. Marsha was relieved—David was far more competent than Kit and Chris—and he genuinely cared about her work. Still, she knew they did it to humiliate her.

Like Marianne, Marsha distrusted music industry moguls, who seemed determined to label her based on race and gender. Chris Stamp—self-appointed authority on who qualified as Black—was one of the worst offenders. Black militancy was fashionable after all. Marsha's elusive independence grated on him—the way she'd always turn down a joint or bump of coke. She remained unfazed. Just another test.

At the peak of her success, Marsha found herself alone in a space that was almost exclusively white and male. She'd always be an outsider in this "brotherhood of English rock," which in the late sixties resembled a "drugged soccer league." Yet she managed to carve out a space for herself. She found a backup band from Glasgow called White Trash, and cultivated an edgy new stage persona—tough, boot thumping, but undeniably femme. "I think maybe that women came to see me because it was like a breath of fresh air," explained Marsha years later. "I was doing something apart from standing there and singing. I was asserting something. I mean, I wasn't carrying any flags across the stage, but I was getting up there and doing what I wanted to do. . . . When I came along I didn't think there were any other chicks doing what I was doing."

That summer, Marsha went on her first independent tour. She witnessed all the daily delusions, weekly overdoses, and the potent narcotic of audience worship. But it wasn't all bad; in fact, she loved the camaraderie of the musicians, techs, managers, and roadies. There was an easy egalitarianism to the business back then. Road crews helped out with each other's bands, lead singers filled in on their rivals' set list. Marsha's conga drummer was detained at the border after flying to Belgium for the Bilzen jazz festival. Peter Frampton himself came to the rescue, tapping out a beat as she sang her chanson cover "My World Is Empty Without You Babe."

Marsha never saw touring as work—it was instead a glorious education. She valued creative freedom far more than glitter. The heady buzz of learning, improvising, and performing kept her naturally high with no need for drugs or even booze. That summer she was too high on life to sleep, except when chauffeured around in the back of her white Citroën.

All of this culminated at the end of August on the Isle of Wight, during a three-day music festival—the largest open-air concert in the history of rock. Marsha was the only woman billed with the Who, Joe Cocker, Bob Dylan, and the Moody Blues.

She came on just before the Who, dressed in a ripped tee, black leather shorts, and matching gloves with heavy rings. She looked out into the audience of 250,000—a horde so large they were no longer people, just a hazy gray expanse blending out into the sky. "Fuck me," her bassist gasped in disbelief.

Marsha opened her eyes to the cheering crowd—hundreds of thousands of music lovers, flower children, free spirits, and dissenters.

Full of hope and possibility, she threw herself into the music.

Marlon was born on August 10, 1969, at King's College Hospital in Camberwell, South London. The press swarmed outside the hospital walls, and Anita and Keith emerged in their desperado glory—Keith in flowered shirt and waistcoat, silver-studded trousers and signature snakeskin boots; Anita in a crushed velvet dress, cradling the baby wrapped in a fringed piano shawl.

Keith was ecstatic, with none of his usual surly reticence. "Anita's an amazing lady. There are some people who you just know are going to end up alright. That's why we had Marlon because we knew it was just the right time. We're very instinctive."

"I want more babies." Anita beamed. "I'm going to have a thousand more. I think having babies is a wonderful thing."

The press couldn't resist hounding them about marriage, but Anita and Keith were too happy to be baited.

"I'm very happy," said Keith, "but this makes no difference to my marriage plans. There aren't any. I'm not saying marriage is out, but it's not in, either. Neither of us is talking about that at the moment."

"I agree entirely with Keith," Anita added.

As they made their way to the car, a photographer called for a shot of Keith holding the baby.

"I don't dare," Keith said, steering Anita into the Bentley. "It's a woman's job."

A welcome ceremony awaited Marlon back at Cheyne Walk, including a musical tribe of mystics from Bangladesh. They chanted as the baby was brought into the house, dropping rice and rose petals from the oak balustrade. Robert Fraser was there with a crib hand-painted in psychedelic colors.

"Everybody was slashing me when I had Marlon," Anita told Victoria Balfour, "saying, 'You must be crazy to have children.'" They criticized everything, even the milk bottles she used to feed him.

Keith had an easier time. "Keith would pick him up from his crib and whisper to him about all the things they would do together one day once he got a little bigger. 'You and me baby. . . . We've got the whole world together. We don't need nobody else."

But Keith's time with the baby was cut short. He was needed in LA with the rest of the band to record their new album, *Let It Bleed*. And the Stones' American tour—their first in over three years—was due to start on November 7, 1969. A fragile newborn couldn't join him on the road. Keith would have to leave his lady at home.

Keith hated abandoning Anita at this hour. They'd been doing so well together, and last year's heartbreak seemed forgotten and resolved. Now his heart broke again over the looming departure, and he poured all that longing into writing "Wild Horses." "I wrote this song because I was doing good at home with my old lady," he would tell Stanley Booth in December 1969. "I wrote it like a love song."

Keith ignored the troops of groupies that trailed him that tour. "Whenever we got to a hotel, he was calling her," confirmed Sam Cutler. "He desperately missed Anita. He pined for her. . . . He was never unfaithful to her. I was with him every minute of the day of the 1969 tour and he was never with any other women. He was a one-woman man—a great romantic and a gentleman."

Though nominally still with Marianne, Mick continued his romance with Marsha and promised to call her on tour as much as he could. She was blasé about Mick's inevitable backstage flings, and she knew there would be many. This was the heyday of rock groupie culture, with Miss Pamela Des Barres leading the charge.

But Mick needed a woman by his side to ease him through the pressures of recording. So he sent for Marianne, who was convalescing from her overdose in a Swiss clinic.

It wasn't Mick who met Marianne at LAX but the tie-dyed, mustachioed Phil Kaufman, who drove her to a detox bungalow in Hollywood Hills. After four days of vitamins, Percodans, fruit juice, and massage, she was delivered to Mick—fresh-scrubbed and heroin-free, in a much more manageable state.

Phil drove Marianne to Laurel Canyon—where the Stones were remixing *Let It Bleed* before starting their American tour. The Canyon was a haute hippie enclave nestled in the hills above Sunset Strip. Locals called the neighborhood "God's Golden Backyard" for the music, friendly vibes, and year-round wildflowers. Folk rock drifted through perpetually open windows, along with cannabis and camphor-y eucalyptus. The Stones were staying with Stephen Stills on Shady Oak in Studio City. Honeysuckle and wild jasmine climbed the trellis. Bougainvillea tumbled from the bower bridge that connected the mansion to the two-story pool house, which the Stones had taken over as their recording studio. You could breakfast in the solarium on mimosas and cocaine, along with fresh baguettes and tortas de papas. You could doze off in the hammock under a canopy of palms or head down to the cabana for naked tarot readings, courtesy of a blonde local mystic named Angel.

Marianne spent her time alone by the pool. She'd wake up, stumble into the limo with the on-call chauffeur, cruise around and score some acid, then head back to the Shady Oak house to trip. Sometimes Pamela Mayall (John Mayall's ex) would join her by the pool for cocktails and cocaine, then hit up the "air-conditioned bars" of Sunset Strip. She made a point to see very little of Mick, and even distanced herself from Keith. She'd shared everything with them over the last years—acid trips, drug busts, courtroom dramas, partner switches, pregnancies, miscarriage, creative exploration—and now she couldn't speak of these two recent tragedies, of her suicide attempt and the death of Brian Jones. She needed to share those visions of Brian, the ones she'd had during her own brush with death. It seemed right to resurrect him, if only in memory.

"I was bursting to tell all my friends about my extraordinary experiences in a coma, but no one wanted to hear about it." Any mentions of ice-skating with Brian half dead in Australia were immediately shut down. "They considered it, I imagine, an indiscretion on my part."

There it was, that maddening English froideur again. They simply couldn't acknowledge Brian's death, let alone her melodramatic overdose. And then there was guilt. Rather than face their own culpability, it was easier to dismiss Marianne as insane. "It was around this time that people started to think me completely mad, and due to the Undead Brian business, I've been considered pretty much mad as a hatter ever since. But I don't really care. It did happen, and I'm not going to change my story just because it doesn't suit other people's views of reality."

Marianne dreaded the menial rigors of touring, the early flights, lost room keys, keeping track of boots and makeup bags. Suddenly Mick's entreaties to come along rang hollow. A retinue of groupies was waiting in the wings. She glimpsed some hanging around Laurel Canyon, in top hats and glitter tights and bright unjaded eyes. They traveled in packs and strummed guitars stuck all over with stickers, like teens doodling in their history notebooks. They were green to the rock game but knew how to play.

Miss Pamela had her eye on Mick, and the Dynamic Duo had already moved into Shady Oak—a set of identical twins Stills kept on hand for "back rubs."

In America, Mick and Keith shattered the glass ceiling of fame. Marianne saw it the night she joined them at the Roxy: "We walked in, and it was like the Aztecs seeing their first horses. A hush fell over the room. The band stopped playing. Like that moment in *The Day the Earth Stood Still*." Mick cut the tension with a campy little curtsy, but one thing was clear—the Stones weren't just rock stars. They were "gods of deliverance." They were gods, while she was just another figurine in this garish tableau.

Marianne felt the heaviness of the moment—her relationship with Mick had slipped beyond repair. "You Can't Always Get What You Want" (she'd hear them recording it in the pool house)—those mournful chords would open, and she'd burst into tears every time. She knew it was about her romance with heroin, and Mick no longer believed she could kick it. One day Mick found her in a bedroom alone, silently listening to "Sympathy for the Devil." He sank to the floor, resting his head on her knees. She petted his head as if he were a child. "He was trying to hold on to me. . . . I was retreating, and he knew it."

That Santa Ana breeze spiked with electric sex—she felt it that night at the Roxy—she sensed it in the jasmine-y air of the Canyons, rich, terpenic, heavy with indoles. Some dark madness was brewing outside the Hills' rarefied haven. While Mick lounged by the pool, "all that Gimme Shelter stuff" was coming home to roost. Love-ins had given way to bloodlust in California, and nihilistic fringe groups hailed Mick as the devil incarnate. In Oakland their pamphlets were already circulating, anticipating the Stones' American tour. They invited the Stones to play their "splendid music in factories run by the workers, in the domes of emptied city halls, on the rubble of police stations, under the hanging corpses of priests." Just as the pamphlets promised.

Of course Mick was never their "comrade" in arms. He preferred chinoiserie to communism, and the Stones were fast becoming the establishment themselves. Mick and Keith joked about the so-called revolution, that American tendency toward extreme credulity. English hippies only cared about drugs, art, and shopping, and any talk of the coming apocalypse was laughed off. Marianne understood what the Stones could not. "They had no idea of the demonic forces that were gathering."

But this wasn't Marianne's story, and she wasn't sticking around to watch it play out. By the time Mick returned to England in the final week of the sixties, Marianne was already gone.

Nineteen

Not Fade Away

Maybe the most you can expect from a relationship that goes bad is to come out of it with a few good songs.

Marianne Faithfull

Anita's postpartum months were bleak. "After Marlon was born, it was a very heavy period, and I suffered a lot for about three months. . . . Then when Keith went on his American tour that was very hard for me because this is the time when the father should be with the child and I felt completely forgotten. So I just started taking drugs again, and then I smothered all of my feelings with drugs."

And then there were the letters from the British Home Office, which arrived weekly and threatened her with immediate deportation. The caveat: they'd extend her visa, *if* she married Keith. After the ups and downs of 1969, Anita's "paranoia meter" blew through the roof. By the time Keith finished his American tour, Anita was addicted to heroin.

Keith flew back to London on December 8, reeling from the horrors of the Altamont show. Reporters flooded the gates of Heathrow, ready to capitalize on the concert's bloody wake. They found Anita waiting for Keith at customs, Marlon on her hip, wrapped in marmalade fox fur once owned by Bette Davis. She railed about the Home Office, who now were threatening to confiscate her passport. "I'm not going to get married in order to suit them. . . . It's just like living in a police state."

Mick called Marsha immediately after Altamont. He wanted to fly her to Provence, where he was checking out real estate. As much as she wanted to see him, Marsha declined. Plus, she thought he had split with Marianne and needed some time to adjust.

But Mick had not split with Marianne. In fact, he'd been calling her every day on tour, and occasionally even sent her on special little errands. That black studded belt he brandished onstage during "Midnight Rambler"—Marianne found it at Chelsea Market and had it shipped to the States. But Marianne was lonely, especially with Anita preoccupied with three-month-old Marlon. Never one to abandon a friend in need, Anita called Marianne to ask a little "favor." Her ex Mario Schifano—the "Italian Andy Warhol"—was coming to town. Could he crash with Marianne?

Right away, Marianne knew that Anita was setting her up. Sympathy tears over breakups weren't Anita's style. She got right to the heart of the matter and solved it by sending over her infamous, drug-addled ex. ("Anita was probably thinking, 'poor Marianne, so lonely and in need of a good fuck.'") But this was a genuine act of Pallenberg kindness, and Marianne recognized it as such. Within hours Mario was installed at Cheyne Walk, and he and Marianne became lovers.

Mario Schifano was addicted to cocaine and by 1969 had racked up a litany of arrests. In Italy they called him "the damned one." But that's why he appealed to Marianne. She found him "terribly intense and serious . . . trying to find in people deeper levels of self." Mick cringed at discussing anything emotional, let alone a breakup, an affair, or a miscarriage. And as a wealthy European intellectual, Mario appealed to Marianne's "last residue of cultural snobbery." Even better, he was destructive, out of control, and cursed—the complete opposite of Mick, who postured as a revolutionary but spent his one protest signing autographs in Grosvenor Square.

In a desperate move to break free from her old life, Marianne ran off with Mario to Rome. They holed up in his medieval quarter flat, a decrepit rat hole with a burnt-out fireplace and lines of coke laid out on half-painted canvases. Little Nicholas played on the rickety staircase. A far cry from her Roman summer of '67, chasing the ghosts of French courtiers through the Villa Medici. Here, she hoped to nurse her drug habit in private.

But the press inevitably found her, cackling over her squalid conditions. In late November she granted an interview to *The People*, who sent a journalist to catch up with the couple over breakfast. Mario remained obstinately mute. When asked about their future, he gave a Continental shrug, silently winding his fingers through Marianne's hair. But Marianne waxed poetic about her new lover. "Mario is charming, kind, talented, loveable, and terribly intense and serious. . . . He is a serious man, not at all of the pop world, but of the political world."

Marianne was understandably defensive. Three years prior she was pilloried for her association with the Stones. Now she had to defend herself for breaking up with Mick. Dating an Italian leftist really ruffled the feathers of British xenophobes.

But it wasn't just that. Mick—once thrown in the clink for three tablets of speed—now dined with dukes and hobnobbed with MPs. The conservative echelons of British society might not have liked him, but somehow he managed to earn their respect. Marianne was the butterfly broken on the wheel.

"Does it really shock people," Marianne asked rhetorically, "me stealing out of England with a man like Mario?"

"Stealing out of England" like a thief in the night? As if it were a prison break? As if she belonged to the British public and press, the pundits and opinion makers. Did they have any compassion for the girl? At nearly twenty-three, she *was* still very young, despite one marriage and separation, her singing and acting careers, one child, a miscarriage, several arrests, and addictions.

Mario was helping Marianne into his brand-new Jaguar when she turned to the reporter with one last remark: "I no longer want to hurt," she said, swaddled in the sable coat he'd just given her. "I shall NEVER return to England."

More reporters hounded her and under the guise of patronizing concern filed lurid reports of her living conditions. But Marianne met them with proud defiance: "The people in Britain imagine they have some form of right to me. They must realize I am not their property and what I say, do, or think is absolutely no business of theirs. I love Mario. I am happy with him. But this is all very delicate, and a girl's private affairs have to be seen with some compassion. There is a curiosity about me. People's real interest in me is morbid, the girl who tried to commit suicide. They never see a woman with body and soul with private difficulties. They will never let such a person be. I am happy. I am absolutely penniless. I am going to start from scratch. People can help me by just forgetting me."

She needed to murder her English image, the one curated by male music moguls then bashed by the media for her link with the Stones.

Marianne softened when speaking with Italian reporters. "It was thanks to Mario," she told a magazine in Milan, "that I took hold of myself again." Desperate to believe in a future of some sort, Marianne set up Mario as some sort of savior, refashioning him as a Byronic hero. "It's strange—I never believed in fairy tales. But at this point I feel like Sleeping Beauty in the arms of her Prince Charming."

Whether desperate delusion or simple lust, Marianne hoped to begin a new life in Italy. But poor Nicholas was suffering cruelly. "He loved Mick and my betrayal of Mick was terrible for him. The crunch came one day when Nicholas was in his room. We were in another part of the house, a huge place in the country. It was winter and an electric fire was on. Mario had given me a sable coat (or got somebody to give it to me) and Nicholas took the fur coat and put it on the electric fire and stood there to watch it burn. And just after it caught fire, Helen, our nanny, walked in, thank God." She knew she had to leave—but where exactly was home now? There was Yew Tree Cottage, a sixteenth-century thatched-roof Mick bought for her mother the previous year. Marianne flew back to England with Mario in tow, just in time for Christmas.

Headlines like "Marianne's New Fairy Tale Prince" and "Marianne Talks of New Love" made their way to America, where Mick learned of Marianne's defection on tour. Humiliated rather than hurt, he dreaded the prospect of an empty house. By now he was more invested in Marsha, who agreed to move into Cheyne Walk for a while.

By the time Mick met Marsha, he was already pure product—he needed someone he could be a *person* around. Marsha didn't cater to him, flatter him, or judge him, though she was well aware of Mick's less attractive qualities.

What could he offer her? That wasn't even an issue. She was thriving independently and happy to nourish their friendship. It was Mick who had slinked into *her* life, not the other way around. And why ask him to relinquish his freedom when she had no intention of giving up hers?

Mick told Marsha he'd spend Christmas with Keith, and Marsha spent a cozy holiday alone with her puppy, then moved into her new Knightsbridge flat.

Meanwhile, Mick called Marianne nonstop—things would be different now, at the very least they should give it a try. Marianne ignored him. She knew it was time to let go, and she suspected Mick knew it too. Winning her back would spare him from public humiliation. He couldn't bear for it to look like *she* left *him*.

On Christmas Eve, he tracked the couple down to Yew Tree Cottage, spoiling for a fight. At this point Marianne didn't know who she wanted: the "unknown quantity" of Mario Schifano or the devil she knew—Mick? As flattered as she was to see him show up, she knew he was there to defend *his* honor—which meant exchanging blows with Mario. Exhausted, ambivalent, Marianne slipped off to bed unnoticed. She swallowed a sleeping pill, switched off the light, and let the men duke it out on their own.

She woke up to Mick sleeping soundly beside her. Mario crashed on the couch and slunk off at dawn. She first felt relief— much more sexually drawn to Mario, she was still more comfortable with Mick than anyone else. A killing sort of comfort she longed to escape.

If she kept slogging along as Mick Jagger's girlfriend, Marianne knew for a fact she'd wind up dead. Sometimes survival means going up in flames—killing that "angel with big tits" once and for all.

Twenty
The Outer Circles of Hell

If your life is not going as you like it, pretend it's a movie.

Andy Warhol

Despite the distance that separated them during the Stones' American tour, Mick and Marsha were closer than ever. During dinner at Mr. Chow the day after Christmas (mere hours after reconciling with Marianne), Mick told Marsha that he loved her—and that she'd be the perfect mother. He wanted to have a baby.

Marsha was taken aback—Mick was a notorious womanizer. As much as she enjoyed their quiet nights in St John's Wood, she couldn't imagine herself as Mick Jagger's life partner—or any man's for that matter.

Still, she could tell that on some level Mick was sincere. His longing was obvious, and Marsha wasn't exactly opposed to the idea. She knew she didn't want to marry Mick or even live with him, but it was the dawn of 1970 with the sexual revolution in full swing. All kinds of alternative lifestyles were possible, and Marsha's views—while not mainstream—were moderate compared to those at hippie sex communes. She herself had been raised by three women, and living with a man hardly seemed necessary.

According to longtime Stones friend Spanish Tony, Mick did love Marsha and considered proposing but quickly decided against it. For all her intelligence, compassion, and obvious beauty, Marsha did not fit Mick's "romantic ideal."

Apparently, the feeling was mutual—Marsha was never in love with Mick. She agreed to have his child not out of some glommy-eyed infatuation but in the spirit of the free-love ethos that had guided her through the sixties.

While fantasizing about new-age parenthood with Marsha, Mick was patching things up at Cheyne Walk with Marianne. Of course, he'd been sleeping with groupies on the American tour. But the prior twelve months had been a litany of betrayals—Mick with Anita, Marianne with Stash, Marianne with Nicol, Mick with Marsha, Marianne with Mario, Marianne with the magician. They had far bigger issues than after-party dalliances, and, as Marianne reflected in her memoir, "getting upset about a little bit of fucking around was unhip and middle-class."

But this time was different. In LA girls with names like Susie Suck, Suzie Creamcheese, and Kathy Kleevage hovered backstage in their feathers and Lurex, ready to pounce during "Midnight Rambler," watching Mick whip the stage with his Chelsea Market belt. These girls made a living out of sleeping with rock stars, and there was something perversely organized about their approach. From the roadie-blowing underlings to the dick-sculpting Cynthia Plaster Caster, to the undisputed groupie "queen" Miss Pamela Des Barres. In fact, Mick romanced Pamela right after Altamont, including two attempted threesomes and slow dancing in Keith's closet. (To the tune of George Harrison's "My Sweet Lord.")

As pathetic as she found these fawning "wahinis," Marianne was somewhat rattled. Not only were they catering to Mick's fantasies, their very concept of sex lacked any sense of boundaries. "I knew I couldn't compete with groupies, for Chrissakes. I didn't even give anyone a blow job until my late twenties." The groupies introduced Mick to ice-cream-flavored douches, which he suggested to Marianne once they were back together in London. Indignant but secretly curious, she inquired at her local chemist, who brought out some ghastly rubber contraption, more surgical than sexual. Not to mention the cheap chemical taste of coke and cash and bubblegum and Clorox. Marianne substituted jasmine bath oil ("I don't think Mick noticed").

When he wasn't on tour or in the studio, Mick was hobnobbing with aristocrats, an activity Marianne couldn't stand. When the Earl of Warwick invited Mick to dine at his castle, Mick insisted on dragging Marianne along. "I didn't care a flying fuck about him," said Marianne. "He was a raging bore. It was an insufferably stuffy evening and I soon found myself swooning from boredom." Marianne took five Mandrax tablets and passed out in the soup. Mick had to carry her home.

"I remember going to a dinner with British MP Tom Driberg and the eminent poet W. H. Auden. In the middle of the evening Auden turned to me and, in a gesture I assumed was intended to shock me, said, 'Tell me, when you travel with drugs, Marianne, do you pack them up your arse?'"

It was one thing to be mocked by puffed-up aristocrats. But humiliation from a poet was more than she could bear.

If he was going to treat her like a whore, she might as well act like one.

Marianne was miserable, and she no longer bothered to hide it. She cried constantly, bursting into tears at star-studded events like the premiere of *Candy*. To outsiders she was still Mick Jagger's girlfriend living a rock and roll fairy tale—every teen girl in Kansas wanted to be her. Marianne's anguish was practically an insult—how dare she be so ungrateful and sad? Even Eva threw up her hands in vexation. What was wrong with this spoiled, sick girl?

She might not have known it at the time, but she wasn't just sad—Marianne was angry. And like so many women she turned her anger inward, by pommeling her mind and body with more drugs.

Drugs—once a source of experimental fun—turned to escape, then addiction, then blatant self-abuse. Opiate paraphernalia became her closest companions, syringes, tinctures, and tiny glass vials, heroin kits courtesy of the NHS, tablets in powdery pinks and robin's-egg blue. But for all the pretty trappings, it was impossible to pretend she was Samuel Taylor Coleridge or Elizabeth Siddal. Her hair hung lank, her ashen skin broke out in spots. "There sure was nothing Romantic about it, and the journey finally led you into hell. It wasn't at all like Baudelaire or De Quincey or Oscar Wilde. It wasn't even like Dorian Gray."

As skilled as Mick was at ignoring the obvious, Marianne unraveled rapidly. He'd come home to find her in a stupor, or asleep in their Louis Quinze bath. Overdoses, suicide attempts, empty bottles of sleeping pills. Mick was worried, then frustrated, then disgusted, then indifferent. One day Atlantic Records' Ahmet Ertegun stopped by for a tête-à-tête with Mick. "She could jeopardize everything," Ahmet whispered darkly. "It's a bottomless pit, and she'll drag you into it unless you let her go." Marianne heard it all—a child eavesdropping at the top of the stairs. She packed up Nicholas along with two Persian rugs and snuck out the next morning while Mick slept.

Marianne decamped to Yew Tree Cottage. She played with Nicholas while Eva went to work, Hank Williams and Robert Johnson spinning endlessly on the turntable (the only two records she had at Yew Tree). Few friends came to see her, and she almost didn't want them to. She felt a giant gulf between herself and her past.

In a flash of cruel irony, Marianne's divorce case went public days after she left Mick for the final time. John was finally divorcing her, accusing adultery and naming Mick as the correspondent. MARIANNE WASN'T FAITHFULL screamed the papers. "More heartache for that beautiful girl whose life has been one long turbulent chapter." Her personal life played out in a familiar scene, the court battles, the custody tug-of-war. Marianne clung to six-year-old Nicholas. "He's all I've got worth fighting for," she offered weakly to the press.

Mick continued to pursue Marianne half-heartedly, while she flirted with squires and trendy antique dealers. She managed to kick heroin for some months but replaced it with methadone, ale, and Eva's Yorkshire pudding. By the time Mick finally came to see her at Yew Tree, Marianne had gained five stone. With one look he recoiled in horror, and Marianne knew he was finished. Never mind all of her affairs and addictions—weight gain was another thing entirely. After Mick made his hasty adieu, Marianne toasted herself with a glass of sherry. She chuckled to herself, relieved to be finally, irrevocably alone.

Marianne clung fast to her dream of acting. In fact, it grew even stronger post-Mick. She played the lead in a BBC adaptation of Somerset Maugham's "Door of Opportunity" and was cast as Desdemona in a rock musical based on *Othello*. But after one day of rehearsals in Birmingham, news broke of another drug-induced coma. Marsha Hunt ended up taking the role.

She landed a part in Thomas Middleton's *Women Beware Women*—a part she quickly lost to an in-flight panic attack. Gossip rags rattled away with half-truths—Marianne stumbled through auditions stoned out of her mind, Marianne blew a role with Roman Polanski. Each slip, each arrest was gleefully reported, along with all the comas, the collapses, the comebacks, and the courtroom dramas. There were multiple reports of her lying to a Heathrow customs official over the price of a mink coat. She hoped to dodge the press by staying out of London, but the mob hunted her down to the little hamlet of Aldworth.

As Mick's star power rose, Marianne sank deeper into the muck. Her image was as tattered as her relationship with Mick. The media rehashed her Australian overdose and spun it as a selfish plot to sabotage Mick. The Mars bar rumors were brought up again, allowing "every sadistic little creep in England to vent his vileness" on her. Back in '67 she was nineteen, naive, ensconced in the soft glow of Mick's exuberant love. Now she was alone and too weak to fight back. "I was anorexic, I was doing drugs. The energy you need to oppose an assault like this is phenomenal. You need a huge amount of psychic stamina just to withstand a pressure as unyielding as that, never mind combatting it."

The media continued to savage her, documenting her disarray and drunkenness, every rough and rangy moment, each topple in a tangle of unwashed hair and lipstick. In flares of masochism she played it up for the press, babbling about drugs and sex and death in televised interviews. Tabloids pounced in barbaric delight: GIRL ON MOTORCYCLE LOOKS LIKE SHE'S BEEN RUN OVER BY ONE.

Then there were the "personal" notes—hate mail, obscene letters, pornographic accusations—hussy, brazen tart, trollop, the scarlet woman of Rome (often underlined, always anonymous). This started back when she left Mick for Mario, and it hadn't let up since. Hordes of reporters still stormed Yew Tree Cottage, furious their pop princess had run off with an Italian. She heard them beating on the door one day: "Where's Marianne? We've come to get even with her." Some threatened to kidnap Nicholas and save him from his degenerate mother.

Marianne's fall from grace was complete. Her own career long forgotten, she was now nothing more than a drug-addled groupie. The same music execs who once lauded and praised her now called her a parasite and a drag on Mick. Ahmet Ertegun, who had just agreed to give the Stones their own record label, again urged them to cut ties with Marianne entirely. Mick, ever the careerist, did as he was told.

In the end, the forces that demonized Marianne and exalted Mick were one and the same. It wasn't just moral panic over "degenerate youths" or pearl-clutching *Post* readers. It was rock culture itself.

Twenty-One

Dead Flowers

I promised myself I was never going to be treated like a second-class citizen.

Bianca Jagger

One bright March morning in 1970, Marsha discovered she was three weeks pregnant. She met Mick in Hyde Park to tell him the news, and they both gamboled about happily in the sun. Marsha had assumed Mick might change his mind, but here he was, downright giddy at the prospect of parenthood.

The reality of pregnancy crept up on Marsha slowly. She quit smoking, cut out junk food and all-night jam sessions. Her belly swelled against her leather shorts, forcing her to switch to loose skirts and dresses. The worst was breaking the news to her band.

Her first fight with Mick broke out when he threatened to send their baby to Eton. (Why did Mick assume he was having a boy?) When he suggested naming the baby Midnight Dream, Marsha saw trouble ahead. All the more reason to maintain her independence—and keep the paternity of her future baby a secret.

Marsha did go public with the pregnancy itself at a charity benefit that summer. Dressed in a Thea Porter maternity gown, she confirmed to the press that she was indeed pregnant, without revealing the name of the father. She was nonchalant about the announcement—and the press surprisingly kept their cool too. After all, Vanessa Redgrave had just given birth to Franco Nero's son. But would Marsha be granted the same sort of freedom?

Throughout the year of 1970, Anita's drug intake continued to skyrocket. Barbiturates for breakfast (usually Tuinals, pierced with a needle to speed up efficiency). Mandrax or Quaaludes with afternoon tea. And of course, speedballs of heroin and cocaine. Keith was right behind her. To supply their habit, he found a married couple—both registered heroin users—and moved them into the Redlands staff cottage. Twice weekly the couple would take the bus to Chichester, fill their heroin prescription at the local Boots, and share their stash as a substitute for rent.

They weren't the only new faces. Now that the Stones had their own record label, new executives and tour crews shuffled in and out of Cheyne Walk. Manager Michael Chess camped out there for a year, cooking weekly Sunday fry-ups in the kitchen with Anita. But less savory characters conned their way into her home, including the drug dealer Tony Sanchez. He "worked" as Keith's bodyguard for £250 a week, plus free room and board. This became something of a trend in 1970—drugged-up freeloaders flopping around like they owned the place. These men were nothing like Anita's old friends—the coltish, picaresque Stash or the lovably affable Tony Foutz. In '68 she'd presided over a veritable rock salon—but now instead of writers and filmmakers, she was surrounded by grimy toadies slavering over Keith. "There were so many creeps in the house," she recalled later, shuddering at the memory.

Despite having invited these hangers-on himself, Keith spent most of his time at home shooting up in the bathroom. Post-tour adrenaline, Altamont flashbacks, and guilt over Brian hammered away at him, along with the pressures of success. "I felt I had to protect Keith," Anita admitted years later. "He was flying so high in the music world. He couldn't recognize a face or anything. He sat for hours and hours on the toilet. He used to play guitar and write in the bathroom. And then when the evening came, he just got very nervous and didn't know what to do with himself, basically, because he had this routine of being onstage. It was very hard for him."

Keith was deep in the "honeymoon phase" of addiction. ("I found smack made it much easier for me to slow down.") Swaddled in its narcotic cocoon, he was able to focus solely on music and was once again writing the best songs of his life.

Anita had no such outlets. Her acting career stalled out with motherhood, her old salon had fallen away. Bereft of any chance to channel her creative energy, she plummeted further into drug abuse.

Planet Stone had become grotesquely corporate—thirty-man entourages, T-shirt vendors, giant blow-up lips—and all the businessmen, leeches, and sycophants that went with it. These new yes-men were far worse than Andrew Oldham. She had power back in the early days—those "shampoo people," they were all intimidated by her. But now, the corporate misogyny rolled right over her.

She found herself longing for her years with Brian. It wasn't Brian himself but the independence of her modeling days, before she'd even moved into Courtfield Road. The twelve-hour rendezvous, flying alone to meet Brian in Munich or Milan. "In the early days it was kind of fun," she remembered later. "But then when things started to get bigger, I didn't enjoy the lifestyle at all. I didn't like the whole scene. Honestly, I can say now if I knew they'd become that famous, I'd have moved out and disappeared long before."

Making her own money, throwing her things in a bag and jetting off to another European city alone, no one to answer to, her luggage stuffed with leather, silks, and lace she bought herself. A snakeskin jacket, a Whitby brooch, button-hooked boots she found in Milan. So many lost now, so many treasures lost on the road. "With my lifestyle, I lost everything," she'd muse. "Especially the things I liked."

By late August Keith was preparing to tour again. Anita would join him—with Marlon in tow. She faced the usual backlash. "How can you have a child on the road?" But Anita had no use for public scolds. "I thought it was better to be with the parents than by himself."

Their first European tour since 1967 was more frenzied than ever. This was Altamont on steroids—riots, tear gas, arson, arrests. Fans flailed in the floor seats like some sweaty devil's pit. Grown men wept at the sight of Mick gyrating in mesh crop tops. In Paris one leapt onstage during "Midnight Rambler" and dropped to his knees, begging to be whipped. "It was like the holy fucking virgin," said lighting artist John Dunbar. "Horrible shit."

As usual, Anita looked amazing, striding through Helsinki Airport in pinstripe flares and platforms, Marlon propped in one arm, vintage chain-strap cocktail bag dangling from the other.

Leather hot pants over lattice-patterned tights, velveteen body-suits under Ossie Clark snakeskin. The wide-brimmed fedoras replaced with newsboys, floaty minis now heavy ankle-grazing layers swishing over witchy lace-up granny boots. Gypsy caravan spiked with goth.

Everything about them was unconventional. Instead of relaxing in hotel bars and lobbies, they lounged on the rocky hardscape by Finland's Hotel Kalastajatorppa. Baby Marlon sat merrily amongst rubble, in woolen stockings and a Tudor-style smock of woven velvet like a little page in training. Anita stretched out next to him, smoking her Dunhills, in a black long-sleeved maxi-dress emblazoned with a giant fleur-de-lis.

But some fresh blight darkened these tender moments—heroin. Navigating a tour through the perils of addiction was a full-time job. Packing up and relocating every forty-eight hours, sneaking your stash past international borders, scoring in a foreign city thirty minutes before call time—it was a lot of work. Keith had purchased his own bespoke drug "smugglers"—a shaving foam can hollowed out for heroin, a fountain pen that carried up to two grams of coke. Starstruck promoters foraged for last-minute emergencies. Anita and Keith had long been the Stones' social fulcrum. But this time they traveled apart from the band—just Marlon, his nanny, and saxophonist Bobby Keys.

Anita blazed on with her usual wild antics—chugging glasses of aquavit at promotional dinners, making out with Keith in front of Swedish dignitaries. Police would be called after scenes at local bistros, tour managers would peel her off the hotel lobby's floor. Anita seemed to lack her trademark self-possession. There was something desperate about her intoxication, as if she were lurching deliberately toward oblivion.

Anita's daily cocktail of cocaine, Quaaludes, and heroin left her in worse shape than Keith. As Astrid Lundstrom would later say, "I remember being impressed with how strong Anita seemed when she got pregnant with Marlon. When I saw her again at the airport in August 1970 as the Stones were about to go on tour in Europe, I was blown away because she was totally strung out and a mess."

Midway through the tour a woman caught Mick's eye. Raised in the twilight of Nicaragua's crumbling oligarchy, Bianca Pérez-Mora Macías was as far from the sixties zeitgeist as you could get. No interest in acid, druids, or mysticism. Everything about her was angular and severe, from her cheekbones to her politics. It was as impossible to imagine her in grimy hippie layers as it was to imagine Anita at the opera.

Mick met her at a party in Paris, on the arm of aging billionaire Eddie Barclay. She came off haughty, pretentious—the wrong kind of snob.

She was everything Anita couldn't stand. Mick fell in love instantly.

After the tour Mick flew Bianca back with him to London and quickly installed her at Cheyne Walk.

Bianca was different from any girl Mick had ever been with. She had none of Marianne's sleepy permissiveness or Marsha's idealistic acceptance. The blatant vulgarity of rock culture shocked her—she spent her first fifteen years planning to be a nun. She quickly caught wind of Mick's twisted droit du seigneur and hated the rumors that he'd "fucked all the other Stones' wives except for Charlie's."

She was also the first of Mick's girlfriends to openly identify as feminist. "I left my native Nicaragua to escape its narrow perceptions of women. . . . Little did I know, when I entered my well-known marriage to Mick in 1971, that Nicaragua and the 'enlightened' world had so many discriminatory attitudes towards women in common."

Marsha was seven months pregnant when Mick left for the Stones' European tour. Telephone calls became less frequent, but he always made her laugh about roadside mishaps or whose girlfriend he just slept with. He talked about band issues or regrets with Marianne. Most of all he talked of feeling lonely. Then one day in September, he told her he'd met Bianca. Gradually Marsha noticed a rift. Mick continued to phone, stayed friendly but cool, as if they were discussing the weather or a set list, not the birth of their child.

Once he got back, Mick vacillated between brutal coldness and bursts of affection. He'd declare his love at one moment and shout at her the next. He grumbled about the pressures of a child, and Marsha found herself reminding him that it was far too late for reconsideration. Even worse, Mick seemed to have forgotten that the baby was his idea.

For her own sake and the baby's, Marsha kept her cool and hoped that Mick would turn around once the baby was born. By the time her due date arrived, Mick was back in London but expressed no interest in being part of his child's birth. He did send £200 and a brief note saying, "I know I haven't done right by you," and a ring (on loan) for her to wear during labor.

Marsha gave birth to Karis Jagger in St Mary's Hospital on November 4, 1970. She went through labor alone—no one pacing the waiting room or rubbing her back through contractions. Immediately restlessness began to set in. She didn't like being treated like an invalid, didn't like the hovering male doctors lecturing her on how to hold the bottle or fold the nappy in a certain way. Worst of all was the claustrophobic maternity ward, with its cooing and tittering over rattles and bonnets, doting husbands, and nosy mothers-in-law. Once again, Marsha felt like an outcast.

With swollen, burning stitches, Marsha slid into her red slingback pumps, swaddled her baby in a Kaffe Fassett sweater, and took a taxi home.

Karis was ten days old before Mick decided to pay them a visit. By now, Marsha was in no mood to fake it. She was too tired to care about his latest sex exploits, too tired to feign interest in his band or fights with Keith. This time, she cut off Mick's banter and faced the ugly truth: Karis was their child, his child, a child he'd begged her to have, and he was too busy with Bianca to give a damn about either of them.

A switch went off in Marsha's mind. She'd fallen for Mick's gentleness, his honest vulnerability, which for men of that time was radical and rare. Now the smoke screen had faded, and Mick was mercenary, cruel, and utterly banal.

Twenty-Two

Save the Tears

Life is a shipwreck, but we must not forget to sing in the lifeboats.

Voltaire

Keith and Anita spent Christmas at Redlands, still nursing their heroin addictions. The junkie "renter" couple still installed in the cottage. In the spirit of the new year 1971, Keith decided to detox off heroin. So Bill Burroughs sent over his favorite nurse, to administer apomorphine therapy in the privacy of Cheyne Walk.

For seventy-two hours, Nurse "Smitty"—a somewhat sadistic woman from Cornwall—tended to Keith, along with Gram Parsons, who was taking the cure as well. The two sweated it out together in Keith's four-poster bed, vomiting into a pail they passed back and forth. "Oh no," they'd shudder at the sound of pounding

221

footsteps, "here comes Smitty." The woman would shoot them up with apomorphine ("the time, boys, the time"), then loom over them. "Stop sniveling, boy. You wouldn't be here if you hadn't screwed up." Verbal abuse was part of the Bill Burroughs cure.

This masochistic detox did not appeal to Anita. Besides, Keith was using again within three days. They'd soon be on the road again for the Goodbye Britain tour—their last stop before exile in the sunny Riviera.

Marsha found herself alone those last long nights of 1970—save for the baby and her nanny, Maria. No stage, no photo shoots, no tour bus, parties, or recording studios. No more whimsical dreams of coparenting with Mick. Her own family seemed light-years away in Nixon's America, where gentle hippie laughter had given way to dark cynicism.

But Marsha wasn't lonely. Karis was "a thrill a minute," radiating "the purest baby love." Marsha threw herself into motherhood with her usual mix of optimistic curiosity and never lost her keen sense of play. At times it seemed like she really was in a play, scrubbing Playtex bottles alongside Maria, starching snow-white onesies like she'd done it all her life. A housekeeper joined them a few days a week, and Marsha found she'd created a cozy little matriarchy. She'd feed or bathe Karis, while Maria and the housekeeper argued in Spanish, their contention adding a welcome little "zing" reminiscent of backstage banter. At night the nursery became a dance hall, Marsha swinging her baby around to the voice of Aretha Franklin. A dance demanding respect and freedom.

Freedom. Like Marianne and Anita, Marsha needed freedom—more than she needed love, companionship, admiration, or even success. And how could you have freedom under the shadow of the Rolling Stones?

The Stones kicked off their British tour on March 4, 1971. The Goodbye Britain tour was a throwback to the old days. "They hadn't toured England in so long," said rock journalist Robert Greenfield, "it was kind of like a high school reunion." Once again, Anita and Keith isolated themselves, forming a little troupe within a troupe with Marlon, Gram Parsons, and their new puppy Boogie, an adorable little cavalier spaniel. (Keith refused to put him in the storage keep on flights.) "Boo-gey, boo-gey," Anita would croon, petting the dog's silken head.

Though no longer the band's social center, Anita still reigned as queen of the Stones. She marched down tarmacs like a blonde Mata Hari, blasting through the North's coal towns in pleather push-up bras and silver hot pants. "She'd be dancing onstage every night with Marlon in her arms—Bianca never would have done that. Anita *was* rock and roll."

Bianca was one of the few people Anita failed to impress. Mick made it clear that she must accept Anita: "Anita is one of the Stones now. . . . Put up with her as best you can." But the differences between them were simply too vast. Anita's laissez-faire sloppiness repelled Bianca, not to mention the blatant drug abuse. As for Anita, she hated "the stuck-up bitch" on sight. "Fuck-eeng bourge-oise cunt voo-man," she hissed, when Bianca stepped in front of her backstage before a show.

Unfortunately for Anita, Bianca wasn't going anywhere. She'd already replaced Keith as Mick's confidante, and he relied on her support. The Goodbye Britain tour was ramshackle rough—just the way Anita and Keith liked it. But Mick needed consistency and control. The shows themselves were wildly erratic, thanks in part to Anita and Keith's escalating drug use. They'd miss a train from London to their next gig in Liverpool, charter a private jet and miss that flight too, resulting in five-hour delays and angry, booing audiences. Mick would feign nonchalance for the benefit of Keith ("I don't care. I don't give a shit"), then privately collapse into Bianca's arms. Mick was able to show his vulnerable side only to women, as he had with Marianne and Marsha during trying times before.

Three months later Mick would marry Bianca—in a star-studded glitzy televised extravaganza. Marsha caught Maria watching the wedding on TV—the Saint-Tropez setting, the throng of paparazzi, the pregnant bride glowing in glossy white Saint Laurent. To Marsha's surprise, Maria was crying.

After sliding back into heroin during the Goodbye Britain tour, Anita and Keith both needed immediate detox. Keith tried the Burroughs cure again, then flew to the French Riviera with Marlon, where he settled into Nellcôte, his new home in the fishing village Villefranche.

Anita went a more conventional route—a chic private clinic in North London. For weeks she languished in the cushy Bowden rehab, detoxing from heroin. Sleeping pills and methadone eased her through the initial withdrawal. She missed Keith and Marlon but fell in fast with Puss Coriat—a gorgeous heiress and fellow patient who became Anita's friend and lover. The two amused themselves with romps around Bowden's luxurious grounds, all-night Ouija board sessions, and singing along to the Shangri-Las' "Leader of the Pack." Sadly, the cure never took, thanks to Spanish Tony's weekly gifts of flowers stuffed with packets of heroin and cocaine. Anita was discharged from Bowden with more drugs in her blood than she had on admittance.

Nevertheless, she flew to Marseille to meet Keith and Marlon, just in time for Mick's wedding in Saint-Tropez.

Despite her pregnancy and traditional Catholic upbringing, Bianca was in no hurry to marry Mick Jagger. "As far as marriage was concerned, I was frightened of the whole idea. It's Mick who is the bourgeois sort. . . . He insists on having a proper ceremony and becoming man and wife in the traditional sense."

But Mick had his way, and they planned a civil marriage at the Saint-Tropez town hall, followed by a Catholic service in a nearby hilltop chapel. Despite Bianca's wishes for secrecy, the British press descended on the town weeks before the wedding, along with chartered planes carrying guests like Paul McCartney, Ringo Starr, Eric Clapton, and Ossie Clark. Among the fray were two small children strapped with half a kilo each of cocaine— Keith's wedding gift to the bridegroom, which he fully intended on consuming himself.

The real trouble started the morning of the wedding, when Mick blindsided Bianca with a prenup-wielding lawyer. Horrified by the transactional gesture, she immediately pled to call the wedding off. Mick refused with customary stoniness: "Are you trying to make a fool of me in front of all these people?"

Bianca backed down, and the little hall filled with actresses, heiresses, and assorted rock royalty. Keith Richards, who arrived in tights and a tunic, was initially barred from entry and nearly arrested for throwing a junkyard sheet of metal at the gendarmes. Bianca arrived late in a low-cut suit by YSL with a floppy-brimmed hat and short white gloves. To her horror, hundreds of photographers had pushed their way into the building. She sank into a pew, yanked off her gloves and lifted her veil. The paparazzi went wild—what could be hotter than a beautiful woman, weeping bitterly on her wedding day.

The press blasted the news all over London: MICK ROCKS HIS OWN WEDDING . . . MICK WEDS IN HIPPIE CHAOS. The last to find out was Marianne, who spotted the headlines in Paddington Station. She took a Valium injection, stumbled to her favorite Indian restaurant, and gulped down several vodka martinis. She began to lose consciousness, and the waiter called the police, who arrived to find her facedown in her curry. She spent the night locked up and wasn't recognized until morning when the constable asked whether she'd kindly sign their guest book.

Twenty-Three

Off the Rails Rococo

It's such a lonely existence, living with a rock n' roller. No matter how much he loves you, he will always love his music more.

Anita Pallenberg

As the Stones' official French headquarters, Nellcôte would serve as their recording studio and, since Keith was king of the castle, a party mecca for decadents. Musicians, designers, heiresses, and drug dealers all made their pilgrimage down the jagged roads of the shimmering Riviera, to a Romanesque villa whose doors were called the "Gates of Heaven."

Nellcôte was just like Anita—rangy Old World glamour mixed with casual excess. Towering French doors opened to sky-high ceilings and giant chandeliers dripping with crystals. Sunlight glinted from the gilded mirrors and bounced off herringbone floors, palmetted floor-length curtains, and crumbling crown molding. Two courtesan sphinxes watched the side entrance, which Anita dressed in black taffeta bonnets. Like Maleficent's palace, nestled among thickets of cypress, pines, and baobabs. Palms and banana trees swayed and tangled, fresh vines sprouting each day like some deranged fairy tale.

Anita played bouncer to the dozens of guests—and there were dozens—swinging through the massive glass doors. She served lunch on the verandah at 5 p.m. daily, when the butter-soft morning light had hardened and fractured, glittering on the sea like sharp shards of glass. Gram Parsons slumping over his coquilles Saint-Jacques. John Lennon rapidly downing a bottle of red, then vomiting on the marble steps before he got to the loo. "Too much sun," Keith affably allowed, though it might have had something to do with the methadone. Anita presided over the mayhem as lady of the manor, barking out orders in her leopard-print bikini, legs flung over the arm of a Louis Quinze chair.

An old harbor town near the Italian border, Villefranche-sur-Mer was steeped in outlaw spirit—sailors, mobsters, gangsters, French Corsican bandits. Keith—especially suited to gunslinger lawlessness—took to the heated atmosphere like a pirate himself. You never knew when a fender bender would escalate into a fistfight, whether Keith would pull a German hunting knife from his leather satchel or point Marlon's toy pistol at the harbor master of Beaulieu. Then there were "les cowboys" who frequented Keith's favorite café, a gang of cigarette smugglers he later hired as Nellcôte's cooks and gardeners, whose other duties included scoring heroin in Marseille.

Coke-smuggling dilettante Tommy Weber assimilated easily to the ethos of Villefranche. After impressing Keith with Mick's two-kilo wedding gift, Tommy won Keith over further with VIP passes to the Monaco Grand Prix. The day before the race, he escorted Keith and Anita through Monte Carlo, in a manner, according to Robert Greenfield, "that blew even their minds." The threesome walked the entire circuit—up the hill to the casino, down past the Metropole—passing back and forth a giant bottle of tequila. That was the thing about Tommy—no one outside of Mexico drank tequila in 1971. Anita delighted in flaunting the rules and scampered around the race cars cackling, taking deep swigs from the bottle in the blazing May sun.

It was a bit like the court of Henry VIII—young libertine nobles vying for the sovereign's attention. "The entire South of France was on its knees for the Stones." They invited the mayor to Sunday dinner, slipped the local cops money to turn a blind eye, and ordered off-menu at their favorite café.

And then there was Nellcôte itself. "People acted differently when they came to that house," says Robert Greenfield today. "You couldn't walk in and not be wowed—it was kind of like walking around a small palace." Paneled walls framed by lacey painted flourishes, tables topped with inlaid gold and trimmed in scrollwork. A massive marble staircase with wrought-iron balustrades with black-and-gold filigree welcomed the often-intoxicated courtiers. It was like their own Hall of Mirrors, where Anita could lounge on a tapestry settee, one chunky sandal digging into the silken upholstery.

It wasn't as if they were trashing the place; this was simply the way Keith and Anita lived everywhere, as offhand hippie regality, making themselves at home. Gold ormolu writing desks next to Marlon's wheeled feeding chair. Cigarette packets scattered on eighteenth-century marble. Chipped Limoges dishes stacked high with sugar cubes, sea anemones strewn on old silver platters, along with stale baguettes, beer cans, sheet music, and baby bottles. Old farmhouse tables set with crystal coke cruets, one of Keith's switchblades, and a half-empty bottle of ouzo. A toy wagon might be spotted on an Aubusson rug. Anita placed a nude life-size cutout of Mick on the mantel, a fixture for the duration of the summer.

It was turning out to be a sweltering summer even by Riviera standards. Anita spent weeks in her leopard-print bikini. This was France, where it was not unusual to sunbathe topless or even naked. But she knew she was somehow sexier, more powerful in that leopard bikini. Robert Greenfield remembers a smitten delivery boy, who fell into Anita's thrall on each weekly visit. "Every time he came over, she backed him into a wall, intimidating him, the guy was helpless. . . . She *was* the Black Queen."

Recording hadn't started yet—Keith was having too much fun. At the moment he had kicked his own drug habit and was waking up before noon for the first time since grade school. Nellcôte even had its own little harbor, accessed by treacherous steps carved into rock. He bought a motorboat, which Anita christened the Mandrax, and they'd jet off to Italy in the morning for breakfast. Keith spent most evenings on the terrace with Gram, getting drunk off pastis and harmonizing on "Cathy's Clown."

Guests continued to pour in by the hour, among them Gram's girlfriend Gretchen, pianist Nicky Hopkins, and sax player Bobby Keys. There were faces from the past like poor Michèle Breton, and future drug dealers like Jean de Breteuil. Anita's literary mentors made the pilgrimage too, Terry Southern and William S. Burroughs. There were actors she never cared for and barely even knew, like Alain Delon and Catherine Deneuve, and close friends like Deborah Dixon and Prince Stash.

Photographer Dominique Tarlé arrived for what he thought would be a two-day shoot. "At the end of the afternoon, they invited me for dinner," he recalled. "After dinner, I thanked everybody for a beautiful afternoon, and it was Anita who said, 'Where are you going? Your room is upstairs.' I ended up staying for six months."

Even if guests had wanted to leave, Keith basically forbade them to, despite his lifelong ease with solitude. Once the Gates of Heaven clanged shut behind you, there was no going back. Unless of course you were banished or dismissed, events that happened with increasing frequency as the summer wore on.

Aside from the Stones and their families, there were journalists, roadies, and various hangers-on, all vying for the attention of the rock and roll monarchs. And the children—Marlon and Tommy's two sons, Charley and Jake. "The house was very kid-centric," remembered Robert Greenfield. Marlon, Charley, and Jake ran loose through the villa. Keith loved his son's feral nature and encouraged it all: sticking his fist in the butter at dinner, eating ants from the overgrown garden. ("He wants to eat fucking ants? No problem. Let him eat what he wants.")

Which is not to say Marlon was neglected—far from it. Keith and Anita had no nanny: they fed and bathed Marlon all on their own, read him stories each night, and put him to bed. Keith built him a sandbox next to the marble staircase; Anita sang to him in French by the dusty dwarf palms.

They even took over parenting Tommy's two boys, bringing them to the beach or on trips to the zoo. In snapshots you'd think they were Keith and Anita's, the way they held them so naturally, packing them sandwiches of sardines and olives, buying them comics, dancing with them to "Midnight Rambler" late into the night. "They treated those boys like their own—they were incredibly loving to them." Keith affectionately named Jake and Charley "the rollies"—their nimble baby fingers could roll out the tightest-packed joints.

Despite their rebel nature Keith and Anita loved family life best—no bedtimes, late breakfasts, their own wild-spun cocoon. In France their warmth bloomed and flourished. "It was just a happy family," remembered Dominique Tarlé, "as simple as that."

Anita and Keith were still solid that May, giggling to themselves as Mick walked down to the altar, speaking in their riddled code no one else understood. Robert Greenfield saw their closeness the first time he interviewed Keith: "I'm on the steps with Keith and Anita comes down and sits right there and Keith says, 'Ask Anita. Anita's seen it all—she's seen everything.'"

Their love was comfortable and nourishing as the late spring sun. Dominique caught it one brilliant sunny afternoon, when Keith serenaded Anita on the terrace: "These two love each other and don't hide it. It's not their style." By now they were the great outlaw couple of all time. "Anita and Keith . . . resonating in perfect harmony."

In a way, the cozy minimalism of Bowden house triggered less anxiety than the sprawling rooms of Nellcôte. "She was running the house," Tarlé remembered. "In the morning Anita would be getting everything ready because they had houseguests. She'd be working with the people in the kitchen, choosing the food. In the afternoon, she'd look after Marlon."

Now Anita was responsible for everything, including all negotiations with the staff. The kitchen—which had been closed for half a century—now needed to feed a house of twenty. Within days Anita had it reopened and decorated, fired up the AGA and hired a chef named Fat Jacques. As the only one fluent in their languages, it was up to her to communicate with the French cook, the German housekeeper, the Corsican bandits moonlighting as gardeners.

"Ten people for lunch . . . twenty-five for dinner," Anita complained two decades later. "The food was actually a major problem. You couldn't always just run into town and buy food for all those people, you know, everybody would be hungry at different times. Sometimes there'd be twenty people sitting down." Anita made sure the fish was fresh; that Keith had his fry-ups, shepherd's pie, and mushy peas; and that the silver came up the Victorian dumbwaiter.

"I didn't realize at the time what a responsibility and what a frustration she had every day at Nellcôte with everyone coming over," said Stones' assistant June Shelley. "When she was short-tempered with me or the cook, or frustrated, it was because she was dealing with roadies and engineers and the rest of the Stones who were treating the place like a twenty-four-hour restaurant." Sometimes she'd wander into Villefranche alone and sit for hours at Café Albert or wander the Italianate Église Saint-Michel.

"Just about everybody we knew from London turned up at one point or another to check out what we were up to," reported Anita to writer Sylvia Simmons. "Some stayed the weekend, some stayed longer, some wouldn't leave, some we had to make leave. We had no privacy. It was exhausting."

Passive Keith leaned on Anita as bouncer—a role she played through gritted teeth. "I remember throwing loads of tantrums—all the stress of these people walking in, and I couldn't say, 'You can come, you can't come.' There was no way of stopping this flow of people, and at the end of the day it got irritating. I remember having a fit with Nicky Hopkins, the piano player, when he came down; I treated him pretty badly. So I did have my bad moments I must say." Not only did she man the gates for their own friends but the shady freeloaders who infiltrated the villa. Keith seemed incapable of telling anyone no.

Resentful of being cast as the harridan, Anita would occasionally lash out at Keith. "One time, I got furious because he wasn't listening to me. I took his guitar and crashed it on the floor. Keith didn't even look at me. He took the phone and called Stu, his man Friday, 'Come here, one of my guitars has had an accident!' And I became even more furious! There was always a competition between the guitars and me. Keith wanted the best place for them on sofas and armchairs."

The mood shifted darkly as recording began, which took place each night in Nellcôte's muggy basement. It was an underground maze of tunnels and rat holes—wicker trays of bread and milky coffee, crumpled packs of Marlboro Reds, and empty bottles of Dom Pérignon.

Mick shuddered each time he walked into the basement. He thought it was "disgusting" and "looked like a prison." He couldn't adjust to Nellcôte's grimy rhythms—Bianca had him eating vegetables and going to bed at ten. When recording, Keith rarely rose before four and was not fully conscious until close to midnight. Mick would show up ready to work promptly after lunch and lash out at Anita when Keith went missing: "Where the fuck is he, what the fuck is Keith doing?" Keith would be holed up in the bathroom playing guitar on the toilet or disappear for hours "putting Marlon to bed." But Anita had no escape. She was saddled with everything from supervising the cook to making sure *les cowboys* didn't end up robbing them blind.

By now Nellcôte was riddled with thieves, and Anita fretted that burglars would ransack the villa. She had the groundskeeper install a chain-link fence around the house and rang the local zoo to put monkeys in the bread trees. Among the humid haze of excess, sense and time was unraveling. And Anita wasn't the only one who felt it. "Mick wanted to call the album *Tropical Fever*," remembered Robert Greenfield, "and that's what it was like."

Still, a perverse organization remained, and just like during the fall of an empire some things still ran like clockwork. Each evening at seven the children ate dinner, before the adults' shift around eight-thirty or nine. Then Keith and Gram played their nightly duets, jacked up on coke and backlit by cherubs, practicing glissando.

Everything was changing. Mick, jealous of Gram, sensed Keith was coming into something different. But Mick himself had caused much of the shift by isolating himself with Bianca. She couldn't bear the grime of Nellcôte and insisted on a mansion in Antibes. The other Stones were scattered all over Provence. Charlie in a farmhouse six hours away, Mick Taylor in Grasse, slowly sinking into addictions of his own.

In nearly every way France was not what they thought it would be. Whether they knew it or not, they'd entered a completely different era of their lives. Just two months prior, to avoid the high taxes they'd bid goodbye to Britain, where Anita rattled her tambourine onstage in Brighton, shaking Marlon on her hip with two drinks and a joint. Now Anita was drifting further from the axis, the sun-center she'd been since 1965. She made the band the gods that they were, blessed them with Lucifer, and anointed them with charm. But she took a back seat to the corporate behemoth. If the Beatles were "more popular than Jesus," the Stones had more power than the devil himself. "But she was Anita and she was in the moment," remembered Robert Greenfield, "and she was going to make it an Anita moment—that was her power."

Heroin found its way back to Nellcôte. Keith needed it to blunt the pressures of recording, Anita needed it to blunt the pressures of the house. Between the drugs, late hours, and stress of recording, Keith—whose libido wasn't high to begin with—simply didn't have the leftover energy for sex. "Keith was not fucking her," said Robert Greenfield. "He was on smack—or up all night playing with Gram."

From the beginning, it seemed inevitable that Tommy Weber would go for Anita. "You would not believe what he looked like," said Robert Greenfield. "Immensely charming, courtly, civilized." Blond like brother and sister, just as she was with Brian.

"Behind closed doors they were Lancelot and Guinevere." Tony Sanchez witnessed "moving sheets" in the bedroom, and reported Anita's betrayal to Keith. Tommy was terrified—would Keith come after him with one of his knives? On the surface, Keith didn't seem to care. "They didn't have any kind of conventional judgment," said Greenfield. "It was like the Court of the Crimson King. . . . What goes on at court only makes sense at court." Even Keith's stray comment to Tommy had the air of Wolf Hall to it: "I don't know why you say you're vegetarian. You've been helping yourself to my meat."

The closest Keith came to "settling the matter" was the Riviera version of a duel—racing go-karts under the blazing hot sun. "Keith drove straight at me," said Tommy. "That's how much he loved Anita. It was murder. Barefaced murder."

Keith's go-kart flipped and smashed into Tommy's. Both men were injured, but Keith was dragged several yards, "his back scraping along the tarmac and opening up like a steak."

With nearly all the skin torn off his back, Keith was in need of serious pain relief. This is when he began using heroin again in earnest. With a local doctor already making weekly house calls to Nellcôte to shoot up its occupants with vitamin B_{12}, a heroin prescription was easily obtained.

Keith began his French summer clean, at least his version of it, which still allowed for cocaine, Dom Pérignon, and copious amounts of Tommy's tequila. Anita's slide back to heroin distressed him, as he saw her diving headfirst into addiction. Talking to her had always been a labyrinthine experience, but now her riddles went from sphinxlike to psychotic, chanting a single phrase on repeat until the words had zero meaning. Conversations sounded increasingly like demented nursery rhymes. Keith worried about her immediate safety. Most alarming was her candle obsession, which she arranged round her bed like a funeral mass. Twice her bedding caught fire and encircled her in flames while she dozed in a boozy slumber of pills.

Like an addict's desperation for that elusive first high, Anita longed to go back to her first years with the band. Before she and Keith were parents, before the Stones morphed into a corporate powerhouse. Was that what she tried to do in Villefranche—recapture the freshness and fun of those years? Perhaps that's why she took up with Tommy—things had lost their luster and newness. In another attempted strike against anhedonia, Anita started sleeping with Mick shortly after his wedding.

Anita always invented her own reality and confused you so much you had no choice but to live by it. Robert Greenfield remembered Anita at Villefranche: "You were very well aware that this person's sensibility was from another planet."

Nellcôte was perched so high on the hill, you could almost see inside the yachts on the bay. (Keith bought a pair of high-tech binoculars to peer into their windows.) One night Anita looked through them and swore she spotted a pirate galleon. Keith dismissed it as one of her outlandish ravings, but Tommy was game for any of Anita's antics. She handed him the binoculars, and to his astonishment, he saw a ship rocking spookily at the harbor's edge—"the real-life incarnation of the Flying Dutchman." "We've got to get on it," he said to Anita. "That's exactly what I was thinking," she beamed, thrilled to have lured in an attractive accomplice.

They drove to the harbor in the middle of the night, where the cowboys broke loose a little fishing boat. Then they all got in and set out to sea, where the galleon drifted at anchor in the black water.

Halfway out the harbor they ran out of petrol. So the cowboys took the oars, and they pushed on ahead, until they reached the mysterious galleon.

The ship, more than fifty feet long, rocked back and forth in the choppy waves. An old-fashioned lantern clanged through an open hatch. Tommy and Anita banged their oars on the sides—presumably to get the pirates' attention. No sound.

Anita wanted to shimmy up the side of the galleon. This was too much even for Tommy, who with no petrol, black night water, possible pirates, and a rapidly rising tide wanted to retreat. But Anita was determined to board the ship. Tommy now faced Anita's wrath and ridicule: "She began calling me 'une lache,' which is French slang for coward." Leave it to Anita to insult in native tongue.

Eventually Anita relented. The cowboys rowed them to shore, and they slinked back to Nellcôte. The sun had risen by the time they returned, and Keith met them at the door, demanding answers. Her song and dance about a pirate ship was too much for Keith to stomach. After another explosive argument, Anita fled for the hills with Tommy, with Marlon, Jake, and Charley in the back seat. They made their way into the foothills of the Alps, where Tommy kept a little chalet he used for secret trysts.

Anita had little, if any, plan. She soon found herself bored and frustrated by Tommy, a boredom she tried to alleviate with insults. "I don't know what we're going to do about your dick," she'd say, after a heated session of lovemaking. "The greatness of Anita is her telling him he's not big enough. She's fucking him and slagging him at the same time. She was trying to get in his head—but she would have anyway—she was that powerful."

Soon Tommy realized Anita was "way out of my league" and was using him "as a goad to get Keith to pay attention to her."

Once back in Villefranche, with Tommy finally banished, Anita still had problems. Her next target was Bianca. She resented the fact that Mick had married her in the first place: she assumed Bianca had pushed hard for the marriage, though it was in fact Mick's idea.

Much of Anita's unease was justified. "Bianca hated the way Keith and Anita lived," said Robert Greenfield. She had to grow up fast in battle-scarred Nicaragua, where war was not an abstract concept and politics were more than trendy slogans. The dissolute grime of Nellcôte was more than she could bear, especially during a hot summer pregnancy. The few visits she made were spent hiding in the bathroom for hours with her makeup kit.

"She'd go in with this huge, massive makeup bag," recalled Anita, "and she came out and she looked totally the same! She always used the makeup to perfection, but you didn't see that it's makeup. It looks completely natural, that fantastically careful makeup that looks like no makeup at all."

It wasn't just Bianca's airs that rattled Anita—it was everything she stood for. Bianca clashed with the rugged rock and roll ethos that stood at the very heart of the Stones. She pre-ferred lawyers and agents to artists and musicians. It was all about power, status, and money; she cared little for the music, just the adjacent fame. Social-climbing snobs horrified Anita, and with Anita, there was no middle ground. Bianca was a threat that must be annihilated.

Keith wanted to stay out of the fray, so Anita enlisted Spanish Tony to help with her schemes: "That chick is going to break the Stones up just like that other chick broke up the Beatles. We've got to do something for the sake of the band." Anita started with rumors. First, Bianca was lying about her age. ("She says she's 25, but I'll bet a million pounds she's 35 if she's a day. She's just an old bird pretending to be young. I'll bet her tits are all droopy.") Then Bianca was a man who'd had a sex-change operation. "She believed what she believed. Anita was so out there, you couldn't bother to argue."

Anita's tactics grew crazier and crazier. Knowing Mick's affin-ity for Black women, she plotted to have Angela Davis released from prison. She planned to fly her to France, so Mick would di-vorce Bianca and marry the "sweet black angel." In Anita's mind, this seemed like a reasonable plan. When it failed to material-ize, she resorted to voodoo: "It doesn't matter anyway," she said nonchalantly. "I've put a curse on her. She won't be around much longer." And sure enough, Bianca was soon packing her bags for Paris. ("I never want to see that cow Anita again.")

In their haste to blame each other for their thwarted dreams and fear, did they forget the two men who were the real cause of their misery? Perhaps they would have understood how much they shared that summer—two lonely queens in isolation who both deserved far better.

By the end of July, Anita knew she was pregnant, this time unhappily so. She'd been thrilled with Marlon, but the reality of childcare was brutal for her. Keith had been on the road for half of Marlon's first twenty-four months and in and out of the recording studio for the other. Gone was her carefree, capricious existence and her budding movie career, and she knew another child would make it worse. But Keith, for whom parenting meant teaching math by letting the baby dial for room service, desperately wanted another child. No matter that their relationship was deteriorating quickly—he'd slipped back into heroin and spent most of his waking hours recording in Nellcôte's cauldron-like basement.

One complicating factor was the father—there were three men in question. Not only Keith and Tommy, but now Mick.

By the end of August, Anita could no longer ignore her pregnancy. Quite alone at this point, she confided in German to the housekeeper Elizabeth Heiner. Elizabeth turned to June Shelley, who recalled a "split feeling" between her sympathy for Anita and her loyalty to Keith. The first and most pressing obstacle was how to afford it. Unlike Anita, June had her own credit card and could theoretically call an Italian travel agency and book a trip for Anita without Keith ever knowing. Liz Heiner begged June to hurry up and do it ("Help her, Madame June, you must help her"). Still, June deferred to Keith. By this time Keith was beginning to suspect that the baby was Mick's. "Go ahead," he muttered with bitter indifference. "Buy her a one-way ticket to anywhere she wants." On four separate occasions June bought Anita tickets to Paris, London, and Switzerland. Each time Anita overslept and missed her flight. She was simply too disorganized, too lethargic, and too hopeless to go on her own. Soon June realized that Keith knew all along—Anita couldn't possibly pull herself together to make a flight on her own, which is why he approved the ticket in the first place. It's hard to believe that Anita, who could sell a diamond, fire the cook, and order two kilos of coke in one morning, needed Keith's permission to have an abortion. She may have dominated Brian, but like it or not she was under Keith's thumb.

Twenty-Four
Give My Love to London

Fate, I respect it a lot. I never regret anything.

Anita Pallenberg

Despite those stressful steamy hours spent at Nell-côte, Mick gradually relaxed into his Riviera summer. He finally wanted to spend time with little Karis, so he asked Marsha to fly with her to Provence. She assumed she'd be staying with Mick and Bianca—an awkward situation Marsha was happy to navigate, if only for the sake of baby Karis. But when Jagger's driver Alan met her at the Nice Airport, he drove them straight to Mick Taylor's house outside Grasse.

Their house was beautiful, surrounded by lavender and flower farms. Marsha liked Mick Taylor—they'd crossed paths in '67, both in the ever-shuffling Bluesbreakers lineup. She'd been the one to introduce him to the Stones when they needed a new guitarist. Seeing Mick Taylor teetering on the edge of heroin addiction shocked and saddened Marsha, but she kept those thoughts to herself.

That evening Alan drove Karis and Marsha to Bastide du Roy, a sixteenth-century villa passed from Bourbon kings to French fashion designers straight to the prince of rock royalty himself. Mick was renting from the Prince of Polignac, whom he occasionally invited over for an afternoon of falconry on the bastide's acres of manicured gardens and lawn. Marsha couldn't help but flinch—here Mick was, residing in sun-drenched baroque splendor, yet he couldn't spare a penny for his infant daughter.

At dinner Mick and Bianca nuzzled over the fish, giggling and whispering to each other in French. Marsha endured it for the sake of Karis—she didn't want Mick to miss out on her babyhood. But why should she care when Mick didn't seem to? Here he was catering to Bianca's every whim—spotless white furniture, bowls of organic produce—yet he seemed cruelly indifferent to Marsha and Karis. After suffering through the excruciating dinner, Marsha squelched her pride and asked Mick for a loan—a paltry £200. (She hated to ask, but knew he'd never offer.)

Back in London she faced serious money problems. She'd kept herself afloat the past six months—a play here, a soft drink commercial there—but she fell behind on rent and was forced to let go of her housekeeper and nanny. Navigating auditions was an ordeal without childcare—she'd push Karis in her chariot through London's West End, audition with the baby bouncing on her knee. As Karis's sole caretaker and provider, she struggled to maintain her performing career, losing contracts, acting, and singing opportunities—including an audition with Sidney Poitier. Marsha sensed her luck would change for the better, though she had no clue when or how. The affair with Jagger had diminished her in the eyes of the public. "I'd been to university. I had opinions, beliefs, intellectual strength. But, because of what happened, people thought I was some dunderhead. I was dismissed as a rock chick. You know the thing. You say my name and they think 'hot pants, Sixties, Jagger' all that s**t" (*Daily Mail*).

Mick continued to ignore his daughter while living his jet-setting life with Bianca. To remind herself of Mick's goodness, she'd reread his old letters—only two years old but time capsules from an innocent haze. Was she wrong about Mick? Had he changed? It wasn't nostalgia, or to rekindle a love lost, but reassurance that their friendship had been real.

Marsha's luck did change in 1972, when she joined a Scottish band called 22. They signed to Phonogram, cut an album, and by May were ready for a summer tour in Germany. She hired a nanny to help with Karis on tour—a qualified one who charged accordingly. Unfortunately, that meant calling Mick.

She hated asking Mick for money. It wasn't just pride—she was thinking of Karis and her future, which was more important than Mick's immediate support. Marsha waited as long as she possibly could, and eventually tracked Mick down through his office. He didn't respond. Days later he flew to America for the Stones Touring Party—expected to gross $4 million.

The German tour couldn't come soon enough. Marsha slipped happily back into the rhythms of touring. By late June they reached their final destination—an open-air concert in Nuremberg.

They arrived early, at a corner café for tea. Marsha wedged in a booth with the rest of the band, Karis tucked in the corner beside her. The tea was set down at her end of the booth, and Karis reached for the tea glass before Marsha could stop her.

Karis pulled her little hand away from the hot glass, which tipped it over, spilling the boiling water all over herself.

The searing pain was so great Karis couldn't even scream. Marsha pulled at the baby's long-sleeved dress, which was quickly melting into her steaming skin. "Wasser!! Wasser!!" The panicked band yelled. A waitress eventually rushed Karis to the kitchen and held her under the sink's cold tap. Johnny, the pianist, drove them to the American hospital—a tiny army facility with no emergency services. All they could do was bathe Karis in pHisoHex—they didn't even offer a hospital gown.

Shrugged off by doctors and desperate for help, Marsha fled to the Frankfurt Airport, leaving the band with instructions to call Bianca in London, who arranged for a hospital and driver to pick Marsha up at Heathrow. For ten days Marsha slept on a hospital cot, while little bandaged Karis healed from her wounds. Marsha phoned Mick to send half the hospital bill. Despite multiple messages, it never arrived.

Once back in London, Mick called Marsha playfully, joking around as if nothing had happened. Marsha made a simple request. Karis needed an emergency fund for medical bills in case of other accidents. Mick laughed it off and joked that she'd "spend the money on shoes."

On October 21, 1971, Bianca gave birth to her daughter Jade. One month later the entire Stones crew flew to Los Angeles to finish *Exile on Main Street*—a process that would take nearly four months. By now Anita was midway through her pregnancy—she vowed to quit heroin at the five-month mark. But how could she in the gloomy rental bungalow she shared with Keith in Bel Air, with Gram or John Phillips always stopping by with their stash?

When her due date drew near, she flew with Keith to Switzerland, where they both endured harrowing detoxes. In April, Dandelion was born in a clinic in Vevey, just weeks before Keith left for California with the rest of the band to promote *Exile on Main Street*.

The North American tour of 1972 was unprecedented in terms of scale, vulgarity, and groupie exploitation. Documentarian Robert Frank captured it all on film—from the roadies pinning down naked groupies, intoxicated women, to the foot-long lines of cocaine. This was the Stones—and seventies rock culture—at their very worst.

It had been decided early on that "the women" would not join them. Anita—jaded about the rock scene in general—resigned herself to staying in Switzerland with Marlon and her newborn girl. Bianca was furious. One year into marriage and Mick was already leaving her to preen about onstage, take joyrides on Hugh Hefner's plane, and cavort around the Playboy Mansion. She had her hands full with baby Jade and couldn't help but feel hurt and abandoned.

But Bianca would not play by Mick's rules. She called him on tour, interrupted recording sessions, and ripped up his precious collection of expensive silk ties. Worst of all she talked to the press, especially about Mick's less-than-flattering qualities. "Mick screws many," she'd shrug with her signature icy hauteur, "but has few affairs." From the very start she never stroked that massive Jagger ego.

By 1972 there was an even younger crop of groupies, who had to content themselves with roadies, techies, or at best saxophone player Bobby Keys. The Stones themselves wanted women who were on their level—they always had. Charlie was ever faithful to Shirley, Bill insisted on bringing Astrid, and Mick was still sleeping with friend Chris O'Dell. And despite his disintegrating relationship, Keith longed to return to his family.

As sixties idealism gave way to seventies excess, the Stones and their image were steadily commodified. The focus shifted from records to concerts, now heavily marketed products of sex, money, and corporate power. Anita would have hated the grotesque spectacle—the whole crew tagging along—Dick Cavett, Zsa Zsa Gabor, Princess Lee Radziwill, Truman Capote.

Keith was ready to snap, punching clerks, smashing a bottle of ketchup against Capote's door, calling Stevie Wonder a "bloody cunt." Their equipment truck blew up in Montreal courtesy of a bomb set by French Canadian separatists. Hells Angels sent them death threats in New York, and like fugitives they hopped from hotel to hotel. Keith went under his favorite pseudonym—Count Ziegenpuss.

Both Anita and Keith hoped to settle in Switzerland after 1972's American tour. "After the baby was born," reflected June Shelley, "I remember Anita asking the doctor in this little-girl voice, 'Is Switzerland a good place to raise babies and children?' and he said, 'Yes, it's a wonderful place,' and it was almost as if her face lit up. They rented a chalet in the mountains above Vevey, and she was going to have her teeth fixed. It was almost as if they were going to start afresh; they were going to have a second chance without drugs and raise children."

Their chalet looked out on Lake Geneva, and Keith even learned to ski. Blue Lena was flown over from England, and they bought a bright-yellow Ferrari Dino. Anita remembered Switzerland fondly, a happy sanctuary far from the "creeps" of Cheyne

Walk: "It was actually quite nice. We had this little chalet and we used to ski to the front door. . . . [W]e used to drive around in Ferraris and Bentleys. . . . It was fun. We always had people in the house and friends would come visit us."

In Villars they forged genuine friendships with like-minded people who didn't care about their fame (or infamy).

Keith thrived in the Alps and enjoyed the luxury of anonymity. But he and Anita found themselves caught in a sort of vicious cycle—Anita would get clean while Keith was on tour, only to plunge back into heroin whenever he returned.

"It should have been a good time," Anita later reflected, "but it was difficult having children and belonging to Keith's world. We were both still on heroin, and then he'd go off to perform and I'd have to stay there by myself stuck on heroin. I had kids to take care of but couldn't do a good job of it. I was more interested in getting my supply than I was in looking after them. People started to condemn me as a bad person, neglecting my kids, only interested in feeding my habit. Instead of getting them dinner, I'd go out and wander around and meet some people and spend the night in the park looking for flying saucers." Looking for UFOs and ley lines, just like she'd done in West Wittering. Only this time, she was alone.

On December 14, 1972, a judge in Nice charged Keith and Anita with drug possession. They fled to Jamaica and spent the New Year withdrawing from heroin on Mammee Bay.

Meanwhile, Mick and Bianca were in Managua distributing typhoid injections and medical supplies. And when Nicaragua was hit by a devastating earthquake in December 1972, Bianca urged

Mick to set up a benefit concert—a project he happily took on. One of the first examples of celebrity philanthropy, where international glam meets developing nation charity.

Bianca filled their home with antiques and orchids and cooked his favorite Japanese food. They had dinner parties, attended movie premieres, spent Christmas in the Swiss Alps. Summers were spent in Montauk at Andy Warhol's cottage, lounging in his sauna and private wrap-around beach. Evenings they feasted on littleneck clams and chilly vodka martinis—often joined by Lee Radziwill and Dick Cavett—the very same celebrities Anita despised.

While Bianca lived the luxe (if empty) life of rock royalty, Marsha was reduced to living on welfare. Mick still refused to acknowledge his child, and while Marsha had no interest in any sort of relationship, she needed some financial support—at least that emergency fund for Karis. As much as she loathed the idea of a paternity suit, Mick left Marsha with no other choice. News of the suit quickly went public, shattering her professional image. Within two years, she went from being "the girl from *Hair*" to "the girl who was suing Mick Jagger." Marsha, who cared nothing for money and fame, was accused of squeezing Jagger's bank accounts and latching on to his name. Mick attacked with his own team of lawyers, dragging her humiliation even further. "Why did Marsha have to be so bloody silly," Mick whined to the press. "It wasn't as though I was going to leave her and Karis to starve."

Karis would be twelve by the time Mick reentered his daughter's life. "She was twelve—formed—when they got to know each other. What are you going to do to a child of twelve? You are going to have some influence, but there is already some core stuff pulled together by then . . . I know that she would be a different person had he been around all the time, and, in a way, with hindsight, I can say, 'Wasn't it lucky that he wasn't there'" (*Daily Mail*).

In January 1973 Keith left for the Stones' two-month Pacific Tour, leaving Anita alone in Jamaica. Her nightly parties with local Rastafarians attracted the disapproval of their wealthy white neighbors, who eventually notified the police. They raided the villa and handcuffed Anita, who naturally resisted arrest, reeking of marijuana and shouting wildly in Italian (they nicknamed her Mussolini). They dragged her to a cell and charged her with everything from drug possession to "practicing voodoo." Keith, who by now was back in London, pulled some strings and had her released. He met Anita at Heathrow Airport, where according to Tony Sanchez, she "ran into his arms, sobbing like a lost little girl."

Anita and Keith moved back to Redlands, so rich with memories of their wild early love. But malaise and addiction followed them to West Sussex. "By then we were both pretty heavy into drugs," remembered Anita, "and our communication was pretty low. Really, I mean we hardly even talked to each other if it wasn't about drugs or 'Have you got anything?' or 'Let's go get something.' So it was very sad."

They were both in their own private stupors when Redlands caught fire one night in late July 1973. Marlon managed to rouse his parents, and the three fled to safety as the thatched roof blazed above. The paparazzi arrived soon after the firefighters, who were still hosing down the embers as dawn began to break. Anita watched mutely, a baby chair of Marlon's dangling from her hand. On her head was one of her old fedoras, wilting under the weight of time.

After the fire Keith and Anita retreated to Switzerland, where they continued to drift apart. "People who used to be friends began to get very bitchy toward me. Keith had this entourage of hangers-on who were always around the house, came for a weekend, stayed on for weeks and months, always a house full of freeloading sycophants, 'Yes, Keith, yes, anything you say, Keith,' no private life, no time to talk, the suppliers bringing us the heroin, but that's all we had in common."

In 1975 Anita discovered she was pregnant with their third child and on March 26, 1976, gave birth to their second son, Tara Jo Jo Gunne. When little Tara was only four weeks old, Keith left for the Stones' European tour.

The Black and Blue Tour of 1976 featured lotus-shaped stages, inflatable phalluses, and naked groupies swinging from crystal chandeliers. Once again, it was decreed that the women would stay behind. Once again, Anita had an infant to care for. Not that she had any interest in joining this Coca-Cola-sponsored sham.

Two weeks into the tour the baby died in his crib of SIDS. Keith and Anita plunged into despair. And while the two remained at least nominally together, their high-voltage love had burnt itself out.

While Anita and Keith pulled apart in their grief, Mick and Bianca continued to fight over groupies and infidelities. Back at home Mick tried in vain to keep Bianca in her place. She'd bound out of bed for an 8:00 a.m. dance class and leave him sulking all morning. The worst was when she told him about a book she was working on about nutrition in America: "I thought he was going to say, 'That's wonderful.' Instead, he said, 'Why do you need to write a book? Why throw away a year of your life?'"

Bianca saw why Mick was drawn to vibrant, creative women. He wanted to suck up all their genius—he didn't want them working on projects of their own. Like Marianne, she likened herself to Zelda Fitzgerald and determined that she wouldn't suffer the same fate: "I don't approve of what Scott did to Zelda. He used her through all his books, and when she started to write herself, he said it was all his work and got her locked up."

"Mick is in some ways a misogynist," she admitted. "I don't know if he'd be too happy if I were that successful. Men don't want you to be independent because then you will escape them." Already she realized what Marsha and Marianne had figured out before her—there was nothing revolutionary about Mick. He may have written "Street Fighting Man," but at his core he was just a "very conservative Englishman who thinks his wife should take care of the children."

Backstage in 1976, Mick met Texas model Jerry Hall. Blonde, compliant, and only nineteen, the band was thrilled to see Mick move on with a woman less "trouble" than Bianca.

Bianca, like the women before her, refused to be made a fool of. In addition to her fling with Ryan O'Neal, there were galas with Euro heartthrob Helmut Berger, White House dinners with Jack Ford, and late-night phone calls with Warren Beatty. Dressed by Halston and dancing with Warhol, Bianca dominated New York's parties on the back of a wild white horse. She was history's youngest member of the best-dressed hall of fame. Halston thought she should aim higher than fashion and think about acting: "She has a great star quality, a voice like Tallulah. She could bring back glamour to Hollywood."

Halston wasn't the only one who thought so. Bianca signed on with agent Henry Ufland, whose clients included Jodie Foster and Robert De Niro. Her first role was in a film called *Flesh Color* with Dennis Hopper and Veruschka von Lehndorff, playing an icily faithless Mafia wife. Soon another offer of an Italian project called *Trick or Treat*, which she ultimately pulled out of. "I refused to do things not in the script—lesbian scenes were later written in, and I refused to do nude scenes at all."

In the end, it wasn't fashion or film that inspired Bianca, it was human rights and feminism. "I was brought up in a terrible way," she told *People* magazine in 1977, "brainwashed by the sexual repression of my native country. But here today, women are still in a state of crisis." She called out the music industry in particular for its misogyny. "It's terrible. It's debasing how young girls are used as sexual objects in videos—we have to stop it. We have to object to it." Bianca had no qualms about appearing extreme or "difficult" and had no interest in sugarcoating her beliefs. "I believe in women's liberation," she explained, "but I do prefer the term 'emancipation.'"

Toward the end of the interview, her thoughts drifted ominously to her marriage. "Mick and I will have been together seven years," she mused. "I hope we make it."

Bianca filed for divorce in May 1978. Two weeks later the Stones unleashed their most sexist album of all time—*Some Girls*. The title song was a litany of demeaning racial and sexist stereotypes, including the line "Black girls just wanna get fucked all night." Reverend Jesse Jackson denounced the song as a "racial insult" that "degrades blacks and women." Mick railed about censorship and free speech, but he needn't have worried. Record labels and radio stations were blasé about misogynist hate speech, but the mere mention of a morphine drip sent them scrambling for their pearls. Despite the controversy, *Some Girls* went on to sell six million copies and remains the Stones' second best-selling record to date. When several Black-owned radio stations boycotted *Some Girls*, Mick replied, "I've always said, if you can't take a fucking joke, it's too fucking bad."

While the Stones released their tribute to an entire decade of cock rock, Marianne was working on an album of her own. Released in the fall of 1979, *Broken English* was Marianne's comeback and a rebel hymn to feminine suffering. Her whiskey-soaked voice was worlds away from the chirping virgin of the past, thick with smoky streetwise experience. A mélange of disco, punk, new wave, and dance, it was far more relevant than anything the Stones were doing. The album went platinum and sold over one million copies worldwide.

Epilogue

Exile on Main Street's release in 1972 marked the end of the Stones' golden age. It was all about the concerts now—not about the albums, which lacked the rambunctious intensity of the earlier years. After that they coasted on their glorified rock image, potent enough to fuel decades of ticket and merchandise revenue. Once positioned as vanguards of the revolution, the Rolling Stones turned into a brand.

The creative women who surrounded them were the real rebels, progressives, and contrarians. After two decades of singing, acting, radio hosting, and deejaying, Marsha turned her attention to writing. For inspiration she looked to her past—not her public persona as "the mother of Mick Jagger's love child" or "the party girl who took her clothes off in *Hair*," but to her Philadelphia childhood and the women who raised her. "I wanted to chart the changes we'd witnessed. I was constantly discovering things about my own racial history—and it blew me away." Eventually she discovered a family secret—a grandmother who'd been locked in a Tennessee mental hospital for over fifty years. In *Repossessing Ernestine* Marsha asks questions about this sinister family history—was her grandmother really insane? Or was she a victim of misogyny and racism? Marsha's other novels include *Joy*—the story of a poor Oakland girl who forms a Motown group with her sisters, and *Like Venus Fading*, inspired by the troubled lives of Josephine Baker and Dorothy Dandridge. Her work—two memoirs, six novels, and a book about Jimi Hendrix—has been compared to that of Maya Angelou and Alice Walker. In 1995 she founded the Saga Prize for Black British novelists.

Marianne produced eighteen albums and collaborates with artists like Damon Albarn, Beck, Nick Cave, and P. J. Harvey. In 2011 she was made a *commandeur* of the Ordre des Arts et des Lettres, one of the highest cultural honors in France. Bianca Jagger, a human rights activist for three decades, serves as chair of the Bianca Jagger Human Rights Foundation, a Council of Europe goodwill ambassador, and a leadership director of Amnesty International. In recent years she has turned her efforts toward women's rights and has campaigned against FGM, forced marriage, and honor-based violence. "The battle is far from over. But I am very encouraged to see more young women speaking out in defense of women's rights today. In those days, women were apprehensive of identifying as feminists. The *f* word was anathema, and most of us tried to avoid it. Today I'm not ashamed to call myself a feminist."

Of all the women involved with the Stones, Anita was the most enmeshed. When Keith distanced himself "for the sake of the band," she struggled to find her own identity. Once worshipped and feared as the sexy "sixth Stone," Anita was now a virtual outcast, ordering heroin packets from black-market doctors and sucking down beer laced with horse tranquilizers. "It was a nightmare," she admitted years later. "I couldn't really make out what was what. I didn't know where my sanity was and where my identity was at that point. I think it was the pain of love. That's what really hurt."

In our society that hails male outlaws but shuns rebel women, Keith was granted a respectable second act. He kicked his heroin habit for good, married model Patti Hansen, and slipped into the cozy realm of bourgeois stability—all while retaining his swashbuckling shimmer. Anita's rock bottom was yet to come.

On the night of July 20, 1979, seventeen-year-old Scott Cantrell shot himself in Anita's home. It was said that he was playing Russian roulette in her bedroom with Keith's .38 Smith & Wesson. There were rumors of "strange singing" and "ritualistic orgies," cops attacked by "hooded, black-caped people," and the bodies of sacrificed cats and dogs scattered throughout the grounds. Anita, the press was quick to report, appeared "strung out on heroin and shockingly bloated," virtually unrecognizable from her late-sixties modeling heyday. She was even compared to a black widow spider. Her house was "dirty, shabby, smelly," her bedroom "grubby and bloodstained." All this was published in lurid detail, along with the least-flattering photos the press could find. She was a middle-aged junkie with a teenage lover, impervious to propriety and living in a pigsty. She was everything the Stones were routinely praised for. In short, she was failing at being a woman.

It would be years before Anita finally got sober, but she rose "like a phoenix from her nest of flames." She threw her energy into her lifelong love of fashion and earned a textile degree at Central Saint Martins. Her graduating show was celebrated as a "triumph of style over substance abuse."

When Anita died at the age of seventy-three, she was hailed worldwide for inventing rock and roll chic. She lives on through her swashbuckling style, routinely referenced by designers and It Girls today. Kate Moss, Alexa Chung, and Courtney Love all cite Anita as their prime style icon, and Hedi Slimane, Bella Freud, and Yves Saint Laurent all paid tribute to her on the runway.

"But what did she really *do*?" ask Anita's many naysayers. Of all the women who inspired the Stones, she's the one who seemed to endow them with superhuman attributes. Considering what percent of being a Rolling Stone is image, her contribution was staggering. Yet for a woman who played so many roles in the lives of famous men, she always remained the star of her own production.

"There is no one role that women played with the Stones," said Robert Greenfield. The band relied on women for elevation, inspiration, and their own crazy versions of stability. The rock royalty lifestyle gave them permission to take, take, take—at the expense of the women they claimed to love—Marianne, Marsha, and Bianca.

And of course Anita—the essential ingredient, the sixth Stone. She was the first to see Brian for who he really was, lending him her own courage at his most vulnerable moments. She pushed the bourgeois Mick far out of his comfort zone, advised him on album covers and remixes of songs. She galvanized the shy, passive Keith Richards and led him to his destiny as rock's craggy patron saint. One of the eulogies after she died: "The woman who out Keithed Keith."

But Anita's real triumph is her survival, her refusal to apologize and pursue some sort of punishing redemptive arc. "When I say she never cared what anyone said, thought, or wrote about her," explained Marianne after the death of her friend, "it wasn't that she talked about it—it was almost as if all that stuff didn't exist." In our world that drills women into self-abasing apologies, Anita Pallenberg is nothing short of a feminist hero.

Shortly after Anita's death in 2017, Marianne Faithfull wrote the song "Born to Live" to honor the friend she missed so much. "I miss calling her up about a lyric, and her always saying something brilliant. I miss her more than I can tell you. Every morning, when I wake up, I read a poem that makes me think about her, Sara Teasdale's 'There Will Be Stars.' It speaks to me so much about her: 'There will be stars over the place forever / There will be stars forever while we sleep.'"

Author's Note

The idea for this book came to me in August 2013. I was driving with a friend down the marshy roads of the Camargue, land of the French cowboys, windows down, listening to the Stones. The day before I'd been reading Keith Richards's memoir on a beach by the Mediterranean. It was easy to imagine the Rolling Stones' infamous summer in Villefranche, or Mick's wedding to Bianca in Saint-Tropez.

I wanted to know more, but not about the Stones (or even their music). I was more interested in learning about two women: Marianne Faithfull and Anita Pallenberg.

As it turned out, it was not at all difficult to keep their narrative at the forefront. These women simply couldn't be outshone—not even by the massive mythos of the Rolling Stones. Even more interesting than their bonds with Mick and Keith was their relationship to each other. As I discovered Anita, I understood Marianne more, and vice versa. Equally compelling was the very different experience of Marsha Hunt, who would become a big part of the narrative in her own right.

The years were 1965–1972—from the release of the Stones album *Out of Our Heads* to the band's double masterpiece *Exile on Main St.* Through hundreds and hundreds of photos, contemporaneous interviews and articles, and memoirs, the story of these women and their involvement with perhaps the most famous band in the world began to reveal itself. Many mysteries and tragedies were untangled. Many questions answered. And the challenges of balancing the men and the women, and writing of their roller-coaster lives, were always softened by anecdotes from the wonderful people who were there.

It was a wild ride, and so is their story.

Acknowledgments

I am grateful to the following people for interviews, for access to documents, and for their correspondence: Chris O'Dell, Robert Greenfield, Victor Bockris, Victoria Balfour, and Amanda Lear.

Marianne Faithfull's *Faithfull: An Autobiography* was a key document in writing this book, as were Marsha Hunt's *Real Life*, A. E. Hotchner's *Blown Away: The Rolling Stones and the Death of the Sixties*, and *Keith Richards: The Biography* by Victor Bockris. Simon Wells's incredible biography of Anita Pallenberg, *She's a Rainbow: The Extraordinary Life of Anita Pallenberg*, was essential to my understanding of Anita's early years and life as a working actress. Paul Trynka's *Brian Jones: The Making of the Rolling Stones* provided insight into Anita's relationship with Brian, band dynamics, and their fateful trip to Tangier in the spring of 1967.

I owe many of the physical details to photographers Gered Mankowitz and Michael Cooper.

It is a pleasure to thank my agent, William Lo Turco. Many thanks to everyone at Hachette Books, especially Ben Schafer and Carrie Napolitano. Fred Francis has my gratitude for his skill and patience in handling edits, and many thanks to Elisa Rivlin for her expert legal read.

I thank my family for their consistent and kind encouragement. I thank Joel and Eli for everything.

Bibliography

Balfour, Victoria. *Rock Wives: The Hard Lives and Good Times of the Wives, Girlfriends, and Groupies of Rock and Roll.* London: Virgin, 1986.

Beaton, Cecil. *Beaton in the Sixties: The Cecil Beaton Diaries as He Wrote Them, 1965–1969.* New York: Knopf, 2004.

Bockris, Victor. *Keith Richards: The Biography.* Cambridge, MA: Da Capo Press, 2003.

Booth, Stanley. *The True Adventures of the Rolling Stones.* Chicago: Chicago Review Press, 2014.

Boyd, Pattie, and Penny Junor. *Wonderful Tonight: George Harrison, Eric Clapton, and Me.* New York: Crown, 2008.

Buck, Paul. *Performance: A Biography of the Sixties Film.* London: Omnibus Press, 2012.

Cohen, Rich. *The Sun & the Moon & the Rolling Stones.* New York: Random House, 2017.

Dalton, David. *The Rolling Stones: The First Twenty Years.* New York: Alfred A. Knopf, 1981.

Des Barres, Pamela. *I'm with the Band.* Chicago: Chicago Review Press, 2005.

Des Barres, Pamela. *Let's Spend the Night Together: Backstage Secrets of Rock Muses and Supergroupies.* Chicago: Chicago Review Press, 2008.

Faithfull, Marianne, and David Dalton. *Faithfull: An Autobiography.* New York: Cooper Square Press, 2000.

Gaignault, A. Essay. In *La Dernière à Alexandre. Critique de M. Lecherbonnier, maire d'Issoudun. Signé: Gaignault.* Issoudun: Impr. de A. Gaignault, 1882.

Greenfield, Robert. *Ain't It Time We Said Goodbye: The Rolling Stones on the Road to Exile.* New York: Da Capo Press, 2014.

Greenfield, Robert. *A Day in the Life: One Family, the Beautiful People, and the End of the Sixties.* Cambridge, MA: Da Capo Press, 2009.

Bibliography

Gysin, Brion, and Jason Weiss. *Back in No Time: The Brion Gysin Reader.* Middletown, CT: Wesleyan University Press, 2002.

Hodkinson, Mark. *Marianne Faithfull: As Tears Go By.* London: Omnibus Press, 1992.

Hotchner, A. E. *Blown Away: A No-Holds-Barred Portrait of the Rolling Stones and the Sixties Told by the Voices of the Generation.* New York: Fireside, 1991.

Howard, Paul. *I Read the News Today, Oh Boy: The Short and Gilded Life of Tara Browne, the Man Who Inspired the Beatles' Greatest Song..* London: Picador, 2016.

Hunt, Marsha. *Real Life.* London: Chatto & Windus, 1986.

Lennon, Cynthia. *John.* London: Hodder and Stoughton, 2005.

Norman, Philip. *Mick Jagger.* New York: Ecco, 2013.

O'Dell, Chris. *Miss O'Dell: Hard Days and Long Nights with the Beatles, the Stones, Bob Dylan, and Eric Clapton.* New York: Atria, 2010.

Richards, Keith, and James Fox. *Life.* New York: Little, Brown and Company, 2011.

Sanchez, Tony. *Up and Down with the Rolling Stones: My Rollercoaster Ride with Keith Richards.* London: John Blake, 2010.

Sandford, Christopher. *The Rolling Stones: Fifty Years.* New York: Simon & Schuster, 2013.

Trynka, Paul. *Brian Jones: The Making of the Rolling Stones.* New York: Viking, 2015.

Wells, Simon. *Butterfly on a Wheel: The Great Rolling Stones Drug Bust.* London: Omnibus Digital Media, 2012.

Wells, Simon. *She's a Rainbow: The Extraordinary Life of Anita Pallenberg.* London: Omnibus Press, 2020.

Wyman, Bill. *Stone Alone.* New York: Viking, 1990.

Index

Index

Index

Index

Index

Index

Index

Index